RELATIONAL DATABASE MANAGEMENT SYSTEM

RELATIONAL DATABASE MANAGEMENT SYSTEM

Riktesh Srivastava
PhD (Computer Science & Engineering)
Assistant Professor (Information Systems)
Skyline University College
Sharjah, UAE

Rajita Srivastava
MSc (Computer Science), MCA and MBA
Associate Editor
Journal of Computer Science and
Information Technology (JCSIT)

NEW AGE MANAGEMENT

An Imprint of

NEW AGE INTERNATIONAL (P) LIMITED, PUBLISHERS

New Delhi • Bangalore • Chennai • Cochin • Guwahati
Hyderabad • Kolkata • Lucknow • Mumbai
Visit us at www.newagepublishers.com

Published by New Age International (P) Ltd., Publishers

First Edition: 2014

BRANCHES

- **Bangalore** 37/10, 8th Cross (Near Hanuman Temple), Azad Nagar, Chamarajpet, Bangalore-560 018
  Tel.: (080) 26756823, Telefax: 26756820, **E-mail: bangalore@newagepublishers.com**
- **Chennai** 26, Damodaran Street, T. Nagar, Chennai-600 017
  Tel.: (044) 24353401, Telefax: 24351463, **E-mail: chennai@newagepublishers.com**
- **Cochin** CC-39/1016, Carrier Station Road, Ernakulam South, Cochin-682 016
  Tel.: (0484) 2377004, Telefax: 4051303, **E-mail: cochin@newagepublishers.com**
- **Guwahati** Hemsen Complex, Mohd. Shah Road, Paltan Bazar, Near Starline Hotel, Guwahati-781 008
  Tel.: (0361) 2513881, Telefax: 2543669, **E-mail: guwahati@newagepublishers.com**
- **Hyderabad** 105, 1st Floor, Madhiray Kaveri Tower, 3-2-19, Azam Jahi Road, Nimboliadda, Hyderabad-500 027
  Tel.: (040) 24652456, Telefax: 24652457, **E-mail: hyderabad@newagepublishers.com**
- **Kolkata** RDB Chambers (Formerly Lotus Cinema) 106A, 1st Floor, S.N. Banerjee Road, Kolkata-700 014
  Tel.: (033) 22273773, Telefax: 22275247, **E-mail: kolkata@newagepublishers.com**
- **Lucknow** 16-A, Jopling Road, Lucknow-226 001
  Tel.: (0522) 2209578, 4045297, Telefax: 2204098, **E-mail: lucknow@newagepublishers.com**
- **Mumbai** 142C, Victor House, Ground Floor, N.M. Joshi Marg, Lower Parel, Mumbai-400 013
  Tel.: (022) 24927869, Telefax: 24915415, **E-mail: mumbai@newagepublishers.com**
- **New Delhi** 22, Golden House, Daryaganj, New Delhi-110 002
  Tel.: (011) 23262368, 23262370, Telefax: 43551305, **E-mail: sales@newagepublishers.com**

ISBN: 978-81-224-3258-9

₹ 175.00

C-13-10-7155

Printed in India at Print-O-Pack , Delhi.

Typeset at In-House, New Delhi.

PUBLISHING FOR ONE WORLD

NEW AGE INTERNATIONAL (P) LIMITED, PUBLISHERS
7/30 A, Daryaganj, New Delhi-110002
Visit us at **www.newagepublishers.com**

Acknowledgements

- Our publishers New Age Publication, their editorial team, and panel reviewers for their valuable contribution towards content enrichment.

- Our technical and editorial consultants for devoting their precious time to improve the quality of the book.

- Management of Skyline University College, with special thanks to Founder President, Mr Kamal Puri, for providing continuous support and guidance. Special Thanks to Mr Nitin Anand, Chairman of Executive Council (COEC) and Dr Amitabh Upadhaya, Dean, for the help and support.

- Thanks to our parents, Maya Srivastava and Ram Ratan Srivastava.

Preface

This book is meant for students of computer science, information technology who need to understand the basics of relational database management system and an introduction to ideas from the discipline of computer science and information technology. The book aims to provide an in-depth knowledge of the most imperative aspects of database systems, especially the relational database systems. The text includes fundamental concepts like database design, languages, and implementation as well as advanced concepts like distributed databases and query processing and optimization. In addition, some emerging technologies like business intelligence using datawarehousing and data mining are also included. The content of the book is designed to suit the requirements of computer science and information technology students at the undergraduate and postgraduate levels as well as for the advanced learners.

Key Features

- Book is written in a clear, concise, and lucid manner, which makes it student-friendly.
- Text is well-structured and demonstrated with examples and block diagrams.
- Inter-chapter dependencies are kept to a minimum.
- Chapter introduction at the beginning of each chapter describe what lies ahead in the chapter for the reader.
- Detailed coverage of the topics makes the book useful to both undergraduate and postgraduate students.

Target Audience

- Primary usage of the book for the students of BE, BTech, BCA, BIT, BIS, BSc, PGDCA, MCA, MIT, and MSc courses offered by computer science, computer engineering, and information technology departments of various universities.
- Professionals working in the areas of software development and database designing and administration.

As a written source in training programmes offered by many computer institutes.

Contents

CHAPTER 1

Introduction to DBMS

In this chapter, you will learn

1.0 INTRODUCTION

Data Base Management System is a **collection of interrelated data** and **set of programs to access to data.**

Consider the figure given below Figure 1.1

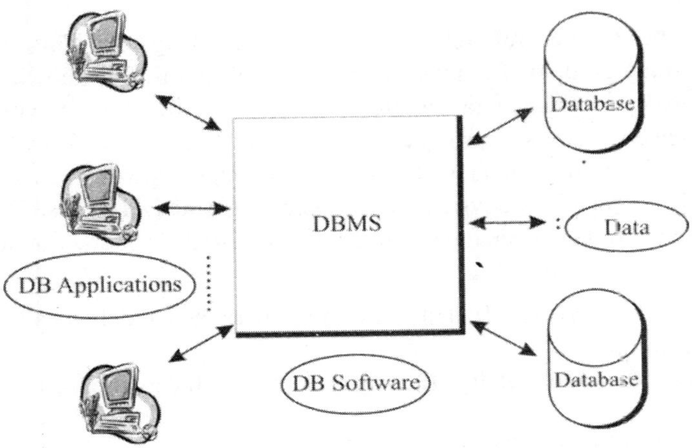

Figure 1.1: *Components of DBMS*

In the above-mentioned figure, we can observe that DBMS acts as an interface between the users and actual storage of Database.

As given in Figure, there are three different components of DBMS:

Data: Data can be considered as stored facts.

Information: Extracted and derived data for a specific purpose.

Knowledge: Knowledge refers to the facts, events and inference rules used by a computer rogram in order to operate intelligently. Knowledge is used in artificial intelligence. Knowledge refers to a person's capability and wisdom as to how much that person knows about one particular subject. Knowledge can be based on learning through information, experience, imagination, guessing or intuition.

DB Software – DBMS: Effectively, efficiently, and reliably manages

- Data storage
- Data retrieval
- Data update for insertion, modification, and deletion

DB Applications: Defines the *Automated tools* — for design, query, and application development

1.1 HISTORY OF DATABASE MANAGEMENT SYSTEM

- Integrated Data Store, first general-purpose DBMS, early 1960s, Charles Bachman, General Electrics
- Information Management System (IMS), late 1960s, IBM
- Relational database model, proposed in 1970, Edgar Codd, IBM's San Jose Laboratory
- Structured Query Language (SQL), standardized in the late 19[illegible]s
- More powerful query languages, complex analysis of data, support for new data types (example: images), late 1980s and 1990s
- Packages which come with powerful customizable application layers
- Nowadays, Internet is powerfully backed by data bases.

1.2 DATABASE ARCHITECTURE

This section describes the general architecture for a database system. This architecture was proposed by ANSI/SPARC study group on Database Management Systems. The knowledge of this architecture is extremely useful in describing general database concept and structure of the individual system. A major purpose of a database system is to provide the users with an abstract view of data. That is, the system hides certain things like how the data is stored and maintained. However, on the other part, data must be retrieved efficiently in order for the system to be usable. Since many data base End Users are not computer trained, the complexity hidden from them in order to simplify their interaction with the system is through three levels of abstraction Figure 1.2.

Physical level (Internal level): This describes where the data physically resides and the specifics of how the data is stored.

Logical level (Conceptual level): This schema of the database, describes the data and its relationships.

External level (View level): This level describes the data that is presented to the user and can present only a portion of a database, or can be a composite from more than one database.

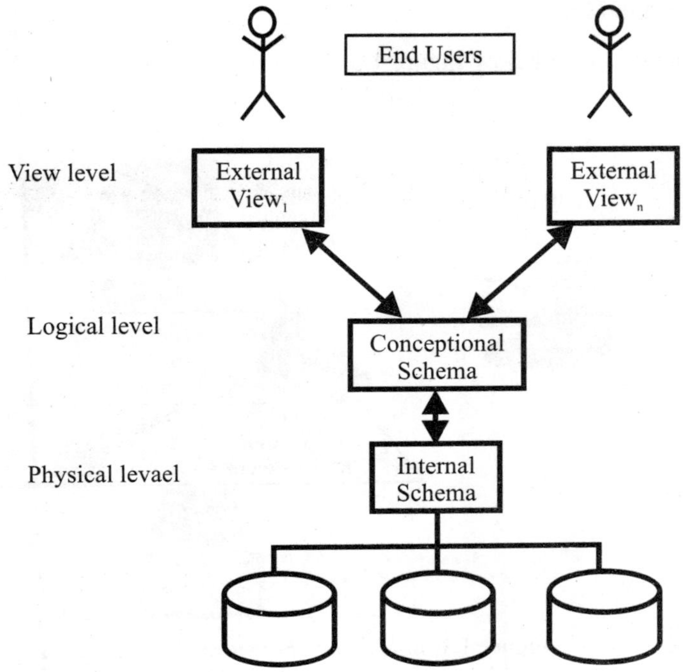

Figure 1.2: *Three-level architecture of DBMS*

1.3 DATABASE MANAGEMENT SYSTEM USERS

As depicted in Figure 1.2, DB Applications has four different types of Data Base Users, which are described as follows:

1. **Application users:** The application programmers interact with the system through DML calls, which are embedded in a program written in a host language.

2. **Specialized users:** The Specialized users are those who write the specialized database applications that are not used for traditional data-processing purposes. Some of the examples are CAD/CAM, Knowledge-base and expert systems, some of the multimedia systems etc.

3. **Sophisticated users:** The Users who write queries for getting the required data in the required format from the database fall in this category.

4. **Teller users:** These users are not sophisticated users and interact with the system by calling or invoking one of the permanent application programs that have been written already.

1.4 ROLE OF DBMS

Consider the structure given below Figure 1.3

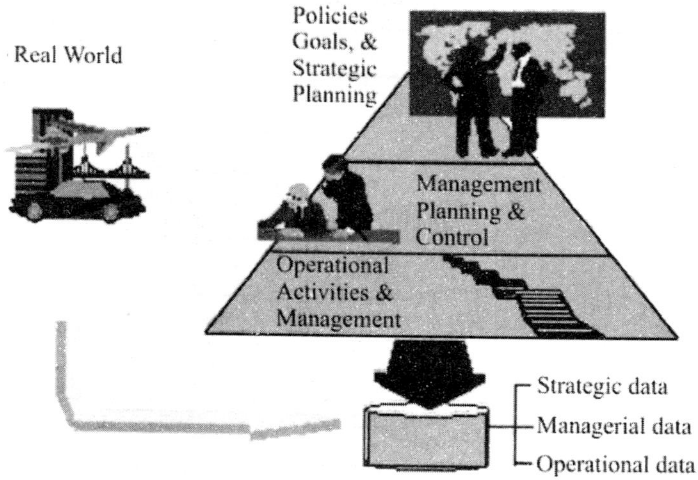

Figure 1.3: *Role of data base management system*

The diagram given above, describes the pyramid structure of the data, which is handled in a corporate environment.

1.5 ADVANTAGES OF DATABASES

- Data sharing
- Privacy (authorization mechanism)
- Decreased redundancy and increased consistency
- Reliable storage of data (backup and recovery mechanisms)

1.6 DATA MODELS

A data model is a description of the organization of a database. Data modeling is used for representing entities and their relationships in a database. Data modeling provides for the conceptualization of the association between different **entities** and their **attributes**.

In a DBMS a group of similar information or data, which is of interest to an organization, is an entity.

Each entity can have a number of characteristics. The characteristics of an entity are called Attribute. For example, an entity, say address, can have characteristics like city and pincode, etc.

A number of models for data representation have been developed. Most data representation models provide mechanisms to structure data for entities being modeled and allow a set of operations to be defined on them. The models can enforce a set of constraints to maintain the integrity of data.

A Data Model is defined as a collection of related object types, operators and integrity rules that form the Database Management System (DBMS).

Data Models can be classifies into following three categories:

(a) File-based data models

(b) Traditional data models

(c) Semantic data models

These models differ in their method of representing associations amongst entities and attributes.

1.6.1 File-based Data Models

The files and the data store in the file must be organized according to user requirements because of the constraints of hardware and Operating System (OS). Some applications are processed daily and can affect each record in the file.

An integrated approach to file design is the data base. The general theme is to handle information as an integrated with minimum of redundancy (data repetition) and improved performance. Software languages are used to manipulate, describe and manage data.

File Structure: There are basic terms used to describe the file hierarchy:

1. ***Byte:*** Byte is the smallest addressable unit in the computer. A byte is a set of eight bits that represent a character.

2. ***Data item or element:*** One or more bytes are combined to form a data item. It describes an attribute of an object. For example, object is employee; attributes may be name, age or address. A data item is also called as a field.

3. ***Record:*** The data items related to an object are combined into a record. For example, is Employee record having as its fields as employee's attributes.

4. ***File:*** A collection or related records make up a file. For example, records of all employees in the organization make a file.

5. ***Data base:*** The highest level in the hierarchy is the data base. It is a set of hierarchical files for processing. It contains the necessary data for problem solving and can be used by several users accessing data concurrently.

File organization: A file is organized to ensure that records are available for processing. A file organization depends upon the nature of storage media. There are four methods of organizing files:

1. Sequential file
2. Direct file organization
3. Indexed sequential file organization
4. Random access files organization

Sequential file: In a sequential file, records are written and stored on a secondary storage device in the same sequence in which they were collected. The records are arranged in order in which they were collected. The records are arranged in order using a unique key as identity number. Consider Figure 1.4, which describes *Sequential file* organization.

First Record
Second Record
Third Record
Fourth Record

Figure 1.4: *Sequential file organization*

Figure 1.4 shows the sequential file in which the records are stored in sequence. In this file, if any record is required then all the records are read and then specific record is selected.

Direct file organization: A sequential file organization is not suitable for on-line enquiry. Suppose a customer at a bank wishes to know the balance amount in his savings account. If the customer file is organized sequentially, the record of this customer has to be obtained by searching sequentially from the beginning. There is no way of picking out the particular record without traversing the file from the beginning and this may take a long time. Hence, in such situations, *direct file organization* provides a means of accessing records speedily.

Actually, in direct file organization, a unique is used to organize files as identity number, which is converted directly to a memory address using hashing algorithm consider Figure 1.5, which gives a better understanding of Direct file Organization:

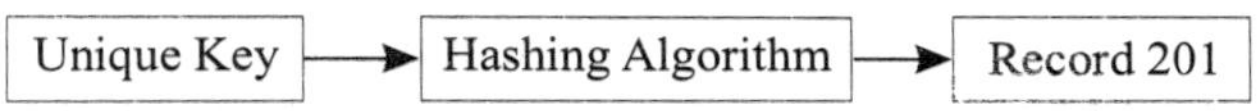

Figure 1.5: *Direct file organization*

Indexed sequential file organization: Some files may be required to support both batch and on-line activities. For example, a stock file may be updated periodically by batch processing and at the same time may have to provide current information about stock availability on-line. They can be thus, organized as indexed sequential files.

In this method, the data is stored in a sequence but an index is created which shows the memory address of each data. A file index shows the memory address or physical location of each data, which makes it easier and quicker to access the data.

Thus, in nutshell, Indexed Sequential file combines the advantages of sequential and direct file organization.

Consider Figure 1.6 for illustration of Indexed Sequential File:

Key	Starting address of block
425	13
563	21
980	35
1178	47
1347	58
1890	69
2690	171

2476	198
3288	561

Figure 1.6: *Indexed sequential file*

Random access file organization: In this file organization, the data is accessed directly and this allows for random access for any record. Every record is allotted fixed number of bytes of memory irrespective of the memory required by the record. The access of record is almost easy because of counting of bytes by the record number. Consider Figure 1.7, for illustration of Random Access File Organization:

200 Bytes	**Record A**
200 Bytes	**Record B**
200 Bytes	**Record C**
200 Bytes	**Record D**
200 Bytes	**Record E**
200 Bytes	**Record F**

Figure 1.7: *Random access file organization*

Limitations of file based systems: The limitations of file based systems are:

1. ***Data availability:*** The problem of "Data availability" arises due to non-uniformity if the design of file structure.

2. ***Data redundancy:*** data may be duplicated and can be present in large number of files, resulting in "Data redundan

3. ***Data integrity:*** The problems are present due to updating of one file while another file containing the same record is not to be updated.

4. ***Management control:*** This problem arises as the date volumes increases; the file structure becomes more complex and unreliable.

The solution of all of these disadvantages is to organize the data in a logical method and there must be logical relationship between the data. Next section follows the same methodology of storing and accessing the data.

1.6.2 Traditional Data Models

Traditional data models consider the characteristics of the data and how the data will be accessed. There are three models in this category:

1. Relational model
2. Network model
3. Hierarchical model

Using these models, database designers can build logical or conceptual views of data that can be physically implemented into virtually any database with any DBMS. Relational DBMS relate data through information contained in the data.

Evolution of data base management system: Consider the Figure 1.8, and the reader can vis ze the evolution of DBMS from File System in 50's to Object Oriented Data Base System in present d[illegible]e.

DBMS EVOLUTION CHART

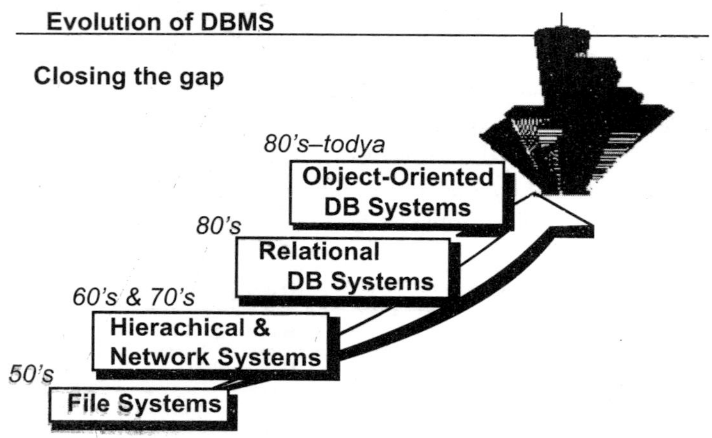

Figure 1.8: *Evolution of data base management system*

Relational data model: In relational data model, the data is stored in terms of tables. In relational data model, the table is mainly referred to as a relation. The relational data model is based on the simple concept of table. Tables allow quick comparisons by row or column and items are easy to retrieve by finding the point of intersection of a particular row or column. In a relational database, the tables on entities are called relations and the model is based on the mathematical theory of sets and relations. The relation is a subset of the Cartesian product of a list of domains. A domain is a set of values. Each table has several columns and each column has a unique name. The row of a table is referred to as a tuple and the values of a single attribute (column) are called a domain. The best suitable example of relational data model is shown in the example given on the next page.

The database consists of two tables;

One shows the student's database and the second shows the student RollNo. Marks_obtained and total_marks relationship.

REL1 (S_Name, S_address, S_city, Qualification, Yearofpassing, RollNo)

S_Name	S_address	S_city	Qualification	Yearofpassing	RollNo
AMIT SINGH	191/2, Vivek Khand, Gomti Nagar	Lucknow	B.Tech(CSE)	1999	100/1999
ROHINI SRIVASTAVA	186/2, Aliganj, Sector-Q	Lucknow	MCA	2001	200/2001
RANJIT	Alka Apartments, Mahanagar	Lucknow	M.Sc(IT)	2002	23/2002

RAJIV KAPUR	K-2, Sector-J Jankipuram	Lucknow	BCA	2001	14/2001

REL2 (RollNo, Marks_obtained, Total_Marks)

RollNo	Marks_obtained	Total_Marks
100/1999	527	600
200/2001	535	600
23/2002	360	500
14/2001	1655	1800

Here the database of different types of students is maintained and from the database it is very easy to know the marks of a particular student or his address or in which year a particular student passed a degree, by simply giving the "RollNo" of the student. In this way, the relational database helped a lot for easy maintenance, updating, sorting and searching of database. Here from the relation1 we can derive different types of relations by having a Cartesian product of domains or by making a join operation of the two relations according to our requirement. Here the relation1 and relation2 each have the degree four, because each table has the four values of domain. In relation, data model the data is stored in relations and the relationship between the records is represented by the values that they contain.

Advantages of this model are as follows:

1. Conceptual simplicity and the ability to link records in a way that is not predefined so it provides great flexibility.
2. Relational model provides more data independence that network and hierarchical data models.
3. The links between data and tables are implicit as they are not necessarily physically linked in a storage device but implicitly linked by the design of the tables into rows and columns.

Network data model: The network model creates relationships among data through a linked list structure in which subordinated records (called members) can be linked to more than one parent (called owner).

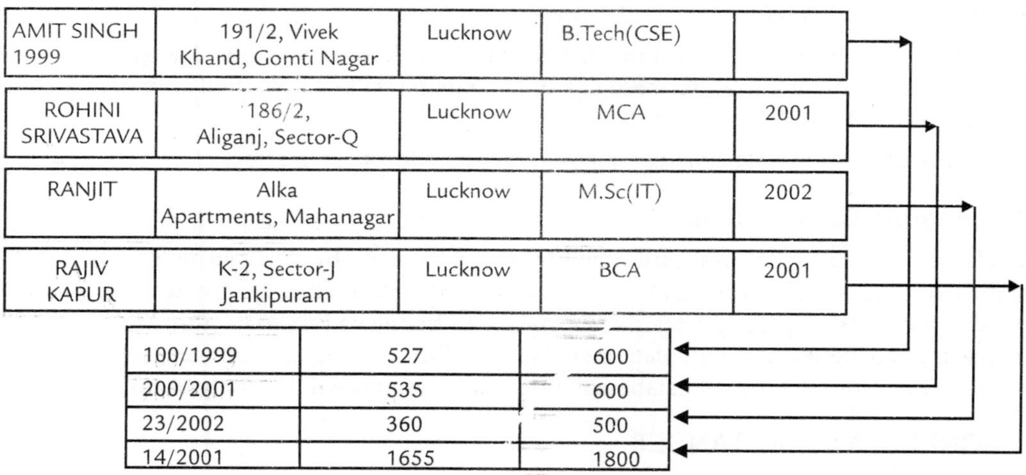

Figure 1.9: *Network data model*

In the network, data model the data is represented as the pointers or links represents a collection of records and the relationships between records. The relationship between records is called a set. In this data model, we can represent the records of the database with the help of arbitrary graph.

Difficulties with this model: The network model becomes complicated to design and implement as the number of sets or relationships increases.

Hierarchical data model: The hierarchical data model is similar to the network data model, because records and pointers or links respectively in both the data models represents the data and the relationship among the data. However, in this data model the records are organized in terms of trees instead of arbitrary graphs. The hierarchical model relates data rigidly by structuring data into an inverted tree in which records contain two elements:

1. A single root (master field) often called a key, which identifies the type, location or ordering of the records.
2. A variable name of subordinate fields that defines the rest of the data within a record.

All fields have only one parent and each parent may have many children. The hierarchical database model is shown in the Figure 1.10 given below:

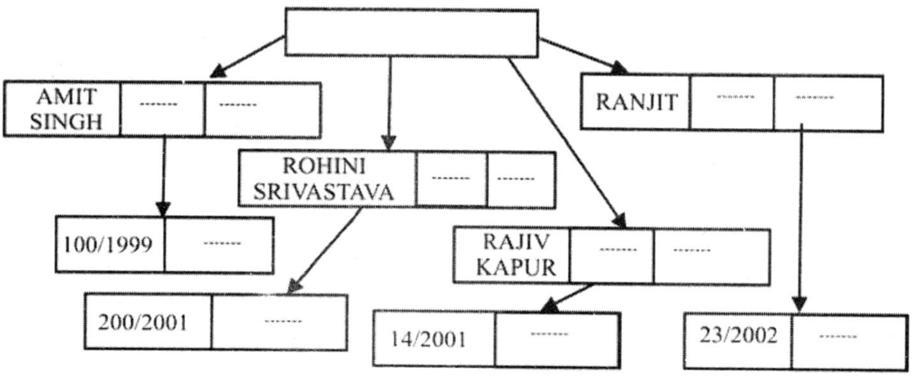

Figure 1.10: *Hierarchical database model*

Difficulties with this model:

1. In this model, each relationship must be explicitly defined when the database is created. Each record in a hierarchical database can only contain one key field, and only one relationship is allowed between any two fields.
2. It is difficult to relate cousins (nodes at the same level) in the tree.

1.6.3 Semantic Data Models

These classes of data models are influenced by the work done by artificial intelligence researchers. Semantic data models are developed to organize and represent not data but knowledge. These types of data models are able to express greater interdependencies among entities of interest. Mainframe databases are increasingly adopting semantic data models. In addition, personal computer database systems are rapidly following suit. In time, all database management systems will be partly or fully "intelligent".

1.7 SCHEMA AND INSTANCES

The overall design of the database is known as schema of the database. In other words, the overall logical database description is referred to as a schema or an overall model of the data. A schema is a complete description of the names of entities and attributes and the relations between data items and types of data that will be stored in the database. A map of the overall logical structure of the database is also known as schema.

Database grows or shrinks over time as the information is added and deleted from the database. The collection of information stored in the database at a particular time (moment) is called an instance of the database.

1.8 DATA INDEPENDENCE

The three level architecture can be used to explain the concept of data independence. Data Independence is defines as the ability to modify a schema definition in one level without affecting or modifying a schema definition in the next higher level. There are two types of Data Independence:

Logical data independence: It is defines as the ability to modify the logical schema without having to transform the external schemas or the application programs. We may change the conceptual schema to expand the database or to reduce the database. Logical Data Independence is complicated to achieve than the physical data independence.

Physical data independence: It is defined as the ability to modify the physical schema without having to transform the conceptual or external schema. Changes to the internal schema may be required because some physical files had to be reorganized. For example, to create an additional access structures to improve the performance of retrieval or updation. If there is no change data in the database, then there will be no need to change the conceptual schema. The modifications in the physical schema are rarely needed to improve the performance.

1.9 DATABASE LANGUAGES

Database languages can be divided into the following parts:

- Physical data description languages
- Schema description languages
- Sub-schema description languages
- Application program in language
- DML (Data Manipulation Language)
- Data Dictionary Languages
- Off-line database report generation facilities
- On-line database DML languages
- Security Control facilities
- Inquiry facilities

Conceptually, a database management system (DBMS) uses two languages. The first one to specify the database schema and the second one to express the database queries and updates.

- Data Definition Languages (DDL)
- Data Manipulation Language (DML)

In other words, we can say that DDL is the link between logical and physical views of the database. A DBMS user defines views or schemas using DDL. There may be many users and application programs utilizing the same database. Therefore, many different views or subschema's can be created or generated from one database.

Data definition language (DDL): Data Definition Language is statements that allow the creation and deletion of database objects. CREATE* and DROP* are the two most frequently used DDL statements. (* indicates SQL statements. SQL is *Structured Query Language* and is defined as The American National Standards Institute (ANSI) industry-standard language to manipulate information stored in relational databases. Oracle (which you will learn in this course) uses ANSI SQL.)

The results of compilation the DDL statements are a set of tables that is stored in special files called a *data dictionary*. The data dictionary contains *metadata* (data about data).

Data manipulation language (DML): Data Manipulation Language is statements that allow the manipulation of data within the database.

- Retrieval of information - SELECT statements
- Insertion of new information - INSERT statements
- Deletion of information - DELETE statements
- Modification of information - UPDATE statements

> **Note:** A *query* is a statement requesting the retrieval of information. The portion of the DML that involves information retrieval is called a *query language.* Although technically incorrect, it is common practice to use the terms *query language* and *data manipulation language* synonymously. To complicate things even more, SQL include both the DDL and the DML.

1.10 DBMS INTERFACES

User-friendly interfaces provided by a DBMS may include the following:

Menu-based interfaces for web clients or browsing: These interfaces present the user with lists of options, called **menus** that lead the user through the formulation of a request. Menus do away with the need to memorize the specific commands and syntax of a query language; rather, the query is composed systematically by picking options from a menu that is displayed by the system. Pull-down menus are a very popular technique in **web-based user interfaces**. They are also often used in **browsing interfaces**, which allow a user to look through the contents of a database in an exploratory and unstructured manner.

Forms-based interfaces: A forms-based interface displays a **form** to each user. Users can fill out all of the form entries to insert new data, or they fill out only certain entries, in which case the DBMS will retrieve matching data for the remaining entries. Forms are usually designed and programmed for native users as interfaces to canned transactions.

Graphical user interfaces: A graphical user interface (GUI) typically displays a schema to the user in diagrammatic form. In many cases, GUI's utilize both menus and forms. Most GUIs use a **pointer** device such as mouse to pick up certain parts of the displayed schema diagram.

Interfaces for the DBA: Most database systems contain privileged commands that can be used only by the DBA's. These include commands for creating accounts, setting system parameters, granting account authorization, changing a schema, and reorganizing the storage structures of a database.

1.11 OVERALL DATABASE STRUCTURE

A DBMS is structured and interfaced with various users including application programmers and DBA's. The major components of a DBMS are as follows:

1. DDL compiler: The DDL statements are sent to DDL compiler, which coverts these statements to a set of tables. These tables contain the metadata concerning the database and are in form that can be used by other components of the DBMS.

2. DML pre-compiler and query processor: It translates the DML statements embedded in an application program to normal procedure calls in the host language. The pre-complier must interact with the DML compiler to generate the appropriate code.

3. Data manager: Data Manager controls the database. It provides the interface between the database and the application programs. Data Manager converts the user's requests coming directly via the query processor or via application programs to a physical file system. The Data Manager is responsible for interactions with the file manager, integrity and security enforcement and concurrency control. If the concurrent users executing the simultaneous operations then data manager synchronizes these operations.

4. File manager: The File Manager manages the allocation of space on disk storage and the data structures used to represent information stored on disk.

5. Data files: These are files, which contains the data.

6. Data dictionary: Data dictionary is used to store the metadata—that is the data about the data.

It keeps track of the definitions of all the data items in the database. It also keeps track of relationships that exist between various data structures. Additionally, it contains the source of each data-field value, the frequency of its use and the information about each modification.

The overall structure of DBMS is depicted in Figure 1.11:

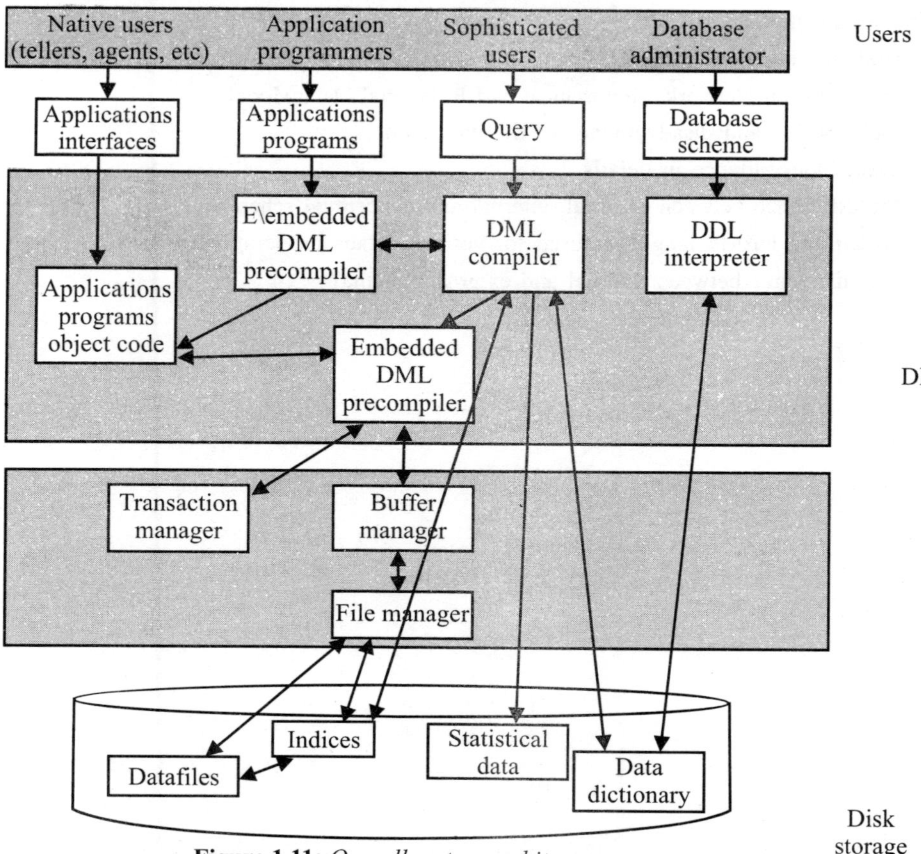

Figure 1.11: *Overall system architecture*

REVIEW QUESTIONS

1. What is data and information? Describe the difference between the two.
2. What is a database? Explain with examples.
3. Discuss the architecture of DBMS.
4. Discuss the difference between the database approaches and file system approach.
5. Explain the following terms:
   (i) File (ii) Database
   (iii) Record (iv) Field
   (v) Schema and Sub-schema (vi) Data Dictionary
   (vii) Data Manager
6. Define the database languages in brief.
7. What are the different types of database end-users? Discuss the main responsibilities of Database Administrator (DBA).
8. Define database concepts in detail.
9. Differentiate between Network, Hierarchical and Relational Data Models.
10. Give the advantages and disadvantages of the data models.
11. Discuss Data Independence in details.
12. Explain the difference between external, internal and conceptual schemas.
13. Briefly explain the DBMS languages used for various database operations.
14. What is the difference between internal and external schema?

CHAPTER 2

Entity-Relationship Model

In this chapter, you will learn

2.0 INTRODUCTION

We have seen different types of traditional databases in Chapter 1. The main disadvantage of Hierarchical data model was that there was no standard defined. This is due to this reason, hierarchical data model lacked a standard data definition language (DDL) component and this created many problems during the database implementation. The lack of a data manipulation language (DML) component made the use of database very difficult. Although the major player in hierarchical data model was IMS, there was much other small hierarchical database system in market. The lack of a common standard made it nearly impossible to move from one hierarchical data model to another.

A meeting of the database professionals was called in 1975, to help in establishing a set of database standards. This meeting was called CODASYL (COnference on DAta SYstem Language). The CODASYL committee formed a DBTG (Data Base Task Group) to create a set of standards for the database systems. DBTG report contained specifications for three database components:

- The network schema, the conceptual organization of the entire database as viewed by the database administrator (DBA). The schema included a definition of the database name, the record type of each record and the components (fields or columns) that make up the records.
- The subschema that defines the portion of the database seen by the application programs that access the database and produce information.
- A data management language to define the data characteristics and data structures and to manipulate the data.

To produce the above-mentioned standardization, the DBTG specified three distinct data management language components – schema DDL, subschema DDL and DML. The schema DDL enabled the DBA to define the schema components. The subschema DDL allowed the application programs to define the database components that will be used by the program and the DML enabled the manipulation of the database contents.

The ANSI/SPARC (ANSI Standard Planning and Requirements Committee) augmented the database standards in 1975. The ANSI/SPARC defined three data models based on their degree of abstraction – external, conceptual and internal or physical. We have already discussed this model in Chapter 1. The visual representation of data definition for this model is called E-R Model.

2.1 E-R MODEL

The overall logical structure of a database can be expressed graphically by an E-R diagram. The entity-relationship (E-R) data model is based on a perception of a real world, which consists of a set of basic objects. The E-R model was introduced by P.P. Chen.

Components of E-R model: The three main components of E-R Model are entities, attributes and relationships. These components are discussed in detail in this section.

Entities: The fundamental item in any data model is the entity. An entity is an object that exists and is distinguishable from other objects. Consider the example:

emp(empno, ename, job, mgr, hiredate, sal, comm., deptno)

Attribute: An attribute is a property of an entity. In the above-mentioned example,

empno, ename, job, mgr, hiredate, sal, comm., deptno

are all attributes. In other words, various kinds of data that describes an entity are known as its attributes.

Each attribute is associated with a set of values called a domain. The domain defines the potential values that an attribute may hold. For example, if the salary is between 1000 and 3000, then we can define a set of values for the "sal" attribute of the "emp" entity as the set of integers between 1000 and 3000.

A fully developed data model includes domains for each attribute in the E-R model. We can classify attributes as following:

- Simple
- Composite
- Single-valued
- Multi-valued
- Derived

Simple attribute: A simple attribute is an attribute composed of a single component with an independent existence. Simple attributes cannot be further subdivided. Examples of simple attributes includes sal, deptno etc. Simple attributes are sometimes called atomic attributes.

Composite attribute: An attribute composed of multiple components, each with an independent existence is called a composite attribute. Some attributes can be further divided to yield smaller components with an independent existence of their own. For example, the "address" attribute can be composed of components like Street number, Area, City, Pincode, etc. The decision to model the "address" attribute as a composite attribute or subdivide the attribute into simple attributes like Street number, Area, City, Pincode is dependent on whether the user view of the model refers to the "address" attribute as a single unit or as individual components.

Single-valued attribute: Most attributes have a single value for a particular entity; such attributes are called single-valued attribute. For example, "hiredate" is a single-valued attribute for an entity "emp".

Multi-valued attribute: A multi-valued attribute is one that holds multiple values for a single entity. For example, we introduce "hobby" attribute in the "emp" entity. Now, the employee can have one hobby or more than more hobbies. A Multi-valued attribute may have lower and upper bounds to constrain the number of values allowed for each individual entity.

Derived attribute: A derived attribute is one that represents a value that is derivable from the value of a related attribute or a set of attributes, not necessarily in the same entity. If we introduce two attributes in "emp" entity, namely "dob" and "age" , then "age" attribute can derive the value from "dob" attribute, hence, "age" attribute is derived attribute.

2.2 NOTATION FOR E-R DIAGRAM

There are conventions for representing the entities and attributes in the E-R Diagram. These conventions are given in Figure 2.1.

Symbol	Meaning
ENTITY NAME	Entity Representation (Entity Name is written in Uppercase Letters)
attribute name	Attribute Representation (Attribute Name is written in Lowercase Letters) (Simple attribute and Single-valued attribute are connected using single line)
<u>attribute name</u>	Key Attribute
derived attribute	If the attribute is derived, a dotted line is used.
multi-valued attribute	If the attribute is multi-valued, then double lines are used.
composite attribute	If the attribute is composite, its composite attributes are shown as ellipses from the composite attribute.

Figure 2.1: *E-R diagram conventions*

Consider the E-R Model given below Figure 2.2:

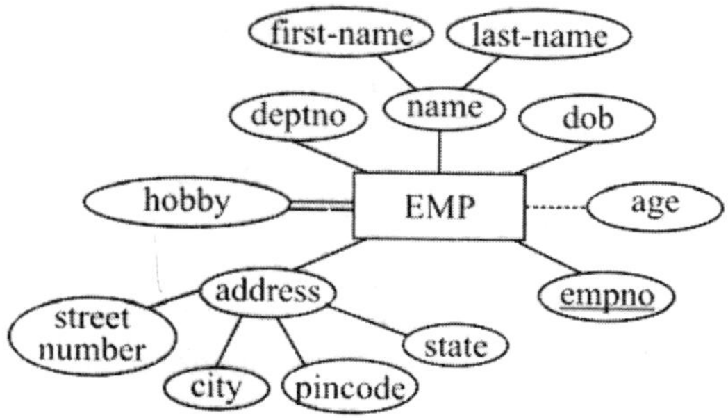

Figure 2.2: *Example of E-R diagram notation*

2.3 MAPPING CONSTRAINTS

An E-R scheme may define certain constraints to which the contents of a database must comply. One important constraint is "Mapping Constraint", which express the number of entities to which another entity can be associated via a relationship set. Mapping Constraints are useful to define the binary relationship sets. Sometimes, even higher degree relationship sets can also be defined using Mapping Constraints.

Relationships are used to model the interactions that exist among entities and constraint that specifies the number of instances of one entity that is associated with other. The types of relationships are:

- One-to-one (1:1)
- One-to-many (1:M)
- Many-to-many (M:M)

as given in Figure 2.3(*a*), Figure 2.3(*b*), Figure 2.3(*c*).

Figure 2.3(*a*)

Figure 2.3(*b*)

Figure 2.3(*c*)

The relationships are explained as follows: A MANAGER in the company manages a single DEPARTMENT (a one-to-one connectivity). A DEPARTMENT can have more than one EMPLOYEE (a one-to-many connectivity). The training department of the company offers many courses to the employees as a part of the employee development program. Each EMPLOYEE can join for more than one COURSE (a many-to-many connectivity).

2.4 KEYS

A key is the data item that exclusively identifies a record. For example, *empno* in ***EMP*** is used as a key field because it is used to identify a record stored in a database.

Super Key: A super key is a set of one or more attributes which; taken collectively, allow us to identify uniquely an entity in the entity set. Consider a subset S of one or more attributes in relation R. If for two rows r1 and r2

$$\mathbf{r1(S) \neq r2(S)}$$

i.e., corresponding to any two rows if values of S are unique, then, S is said to be the super key. Every relation has at least one default super key – the set of all its relation.

For example, in an entity set EMP, *empno+ename+deptno*, forms a super key. Also, empno+deptno are a super key. It must be noted that ename alone cannot be a super key, as two employees can have the same name.

Candidate key: A super key may contain inappropriate attributes, and we are often interested in the smallest super key because if ***A*** is a super key then any superset of ***A*** will be a super key.

A super key for which no subset is a super key, is called a candidate keys or in other words, Candidate keys are which such minimal keys whose subset is not a super key.

In EMP, it is possible to have numerous combinations that can serve as super keys. For example, *empno, empno+ename, empno+ename+job* etc. are super keys. But out of the first three empno is, sufficient to distinguish a row uniquely. So, we can take *empno, ename+job* as candidate keys.

Primary key: A primary key is a candidate key (out of many candidate keys) that is preferred by database designer to identify entities in an entity set.

For example, as we discussed above there may be two (or more) candidate keys:

- *ename+job*
- *empno*

Out of these two candidate keys, any one could be primary key; it all depends upon the database designer to which he selects as a primary key.

2.5 STRONG AND WEAK ENTITY SETS

There are two types of entities, namely, dependent entities (also called weak entities) and independent entities (called strong entities).

In other words, an entity set that does not possess sufficient attributes to form a primary key is called a weak entity set. One that does have a primary key is called a strong entity set. A weak entity set does not have a primary key, but we need a means of distinctive among the entities. The discriminator of a weak entity set is a set of attributes that allows this characteristic to be made.

Consider the example given below,

- The entity set DEPENDENT has attributes *name, age, gender* and *relationship*.
- There can be more than one dependents of an employee. Also, we can assume that some dependencies may be having the same values for all attributes.

For example, there may be two dependents having same *name, age, gender* and *relationship* but the relationship will be for different employees.

- Thus, this entity set does not have sufficient attribute to form a primary key, which can uniquely identify a dependent. So we can call *dependent* as a weak entity set.

The primary key of a weak entity set is formed by taking the primary key of the strong entity set on which its existence depends plus discriminator of the weak entity set.

- *DEPENDENT* is a weak entity. Its existence depends on *EMP*.
- The primary key of *EMP* is *empno*.
- We can consider *name* as the discriminator of *DEPENDENT* (weak entity set).
- The primary key of *DEPENDENT* will be *empno* and *name*.

Remember, the primary key of a weak entity is found by taking the primary key of the strong entity on which its existence depends, plus, the discriminator of the weak entity set.

name	age	gender	relationship
Roxy	12	F	Daughter
Michael	9	M	Son
Sunny	8	M	Son
Mist	3	M	Son
Smith	5	M	Son
Scott	13	M	Son
Roxy	12	F	Daughter

Figure 2.4: *Improper representation of dependent relation*

Figure 2.4 describes the improper representation of *DEPENDENT* relation, where 1st and 7th row contains the same values for all the four attributes. This relation does not have sufficient attributes so that a primary key can be formed. As we stated above, we can consider *name* as discriminator for this relation.

We represent the weak entity by including a column for the primary key of the strong entity (*empno* in this case) with its own attributes *name, age, gender* and *relationships* as shown in Figure 2.5.

empno	name	age	gender	relationship
7788	Roxy	12	F	Daughter
7788	Michael	9	M	Son
7932	Sunny	8	M	Son
7932	Mist	3	M	Son
7896	Smith	5	M	Son
7654	Scott	13	M	Son
7654	Roxy	12	F	Daughter

Figure 2.5: *Proper representation of dependent relation*

From the above Figure 2.5, it is clear that *empno* 7788 has two dependents, namely, Roxy and Michael. Similarly, we can define the number of dependents of other employees also. Here one dependent of *empno* 7788, Roxy, has the same characteristics as one dependent of *empno* 7654. But in this case if we look at primary key (*empno, name*) then both the keys are unique, i.e., 7788+Roxy and 7654+Roxy, which fulfills the condition of primary key.

So we can now have E-R Diagram of *EMP-DEPT* relationship.

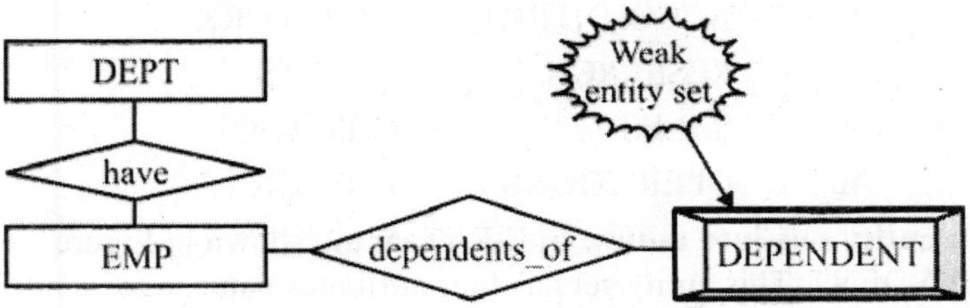

Figure 2.6: *E-R diagram showing weak entity set*

2.6 REDUCING E-R DIAGRAM TO TABLES

As we have discussed earlier in this chapter that a database can be represented with the help of E-R notations. Now, we shall discuss that any E-R diagrams can be reduces to collection of tables. For every entity set, relationship set in a database can be represented in tabular form. The name of the table is the name of corresponding entity set or relationship set.

Each table would have columns, the number of columns would be equal to the number of attributes each entity set or relationship set have.

We shall convert E-R Diagram of Figure 2.6 into tables:

We can divide this E-R Diagram into three sections:

1. Strong Entity Sets (DEPT, EMP)
2. Weak Entity Sets (DEPENDENT)
3. Relationship Sets (have, dependents_of)

Reducing strong entity sets into tables: As mentioned above, DEPT and EMP are two Strong Entity Sets. Reducing this into tabular format is given below:

EMP relation

EMPNO	ENAME	JOB	MGR	HIREDATE	SAL	COMM	DEPTNO
7369	SMITH	CLERK	7902	17-DEC-80	800		20
7499	ALLEN	SALESMAN	7698	20-FEB-81	1600	300	30
7521	WARD	SALESMAN	7698	22-FEB-81	1250	500	30
7566	JONES	MANAGER	7839	02-APR-81	2975		20
7654	MARTIN	SALESMAN	7698	28-SEP-81	1250	1400	30
7698	BLAKE	MANAGER	7839	01-MAY-81	2850		30
7782	CLARK	MANAGER	7839	09-JUN-81	2450		10
7788	SCOTT	ANALYST	7566	19-APR-87	3000		20
7839	KING	PRESIDENT		17-NOV-81	5000		10
7844	TURNER	SALESMAN	7698	08-SEP-81	1500	0	30
7876	ADAMS	CLERK	7788	23-MAY-87	1100		20
7900	JAMES	CLERK	7698	03-DEC-81	950		30
7902	FORD	ANALYST	7566	03-DEC-81	3000		20
7934	MILLER	CLERK	7782	23-JAN-82	1300		10

DEPT relation

DEPTNO	DNAME	LOC
....	....	....
10	ACCOUNTING	NEW YORK
20	RESEARCH	DALLAS
30	SALES	CHICAGO
40	OPERATIONS	BOSTON

Reducing weak entity sets into tables: In E-R Diagram, shown in Figure 2.6, we have only one weak entity set, DEPENDENT. This entity set has four attributes name, age, gender and relationship.

The DEPENDENT is dependent on the primary key *empno* of entity type EMP. Thus, DEPENDENT is represented by a table with five attributes, *empno, name, age, gender* and *relationship* as shown in Figure 2.5.

Reducing relationship sets into tables: In E-R diagram shown in Figure 2.6, we have two relationship sets, have and dependents_of, have relationship set involves two entity sets DEPT with primary key deptno and EMP with primary key empno, which is depicted in Figure 2.7.

DEPTNO	EMPNO
------------	------------
10	7782
10	7839
10	7934
20	7369
20	7876
20	7902
20	7788
20	7566
30	7499
30	7698
30	7654
30	7900
30	7844
30	7521

Figure 2.7: *Have relation*

Now, we shall deal with the case of relationship set, *dependents_of*, linking a weak entity set (DEPENDENT) to its corresponding strong entity set (EMP).

These relationships are many-to-one and have no descriptive attributes. We also recognize that the primary key of a weak entity set is formed by the combination of primary key of a strong entity set and discriminator of weak entity set.

The weak entity set, DEPENDENT, is dependent on strong entity set, EMP, through the relationship *dependents_of*. The primary key of EMP is *empno* and the primary key of DEPENDENT is *empno+name*. Since, the relationship *dependents_of* does not have any descriptive attributes, so that the table for *dependents_of* would have only two columns *empno* and *name*. The table for entity set DEPENDENT, which has columns *empno, name, age, gender* and *relationship.* So we can say that *dependents_of* table is redundant.

Usually, the table for the relationships, which links weak entity sets to its strong entity sets, is redundant and these tables need not to be shown independently.

2.7 GENERALIZATION

Generalization is used to emphasize the similarities among lower-level entity sets and to hide the differences. It also permits an economy of representation so that shared attributes are not repeated.

In other words, Generalization is a relationship that exists between a higher-level entity set and the lower level entity set.

Generalization is the result of taking the union of several lower level entity sets to produce higher-level entity sets Figure 2.8.

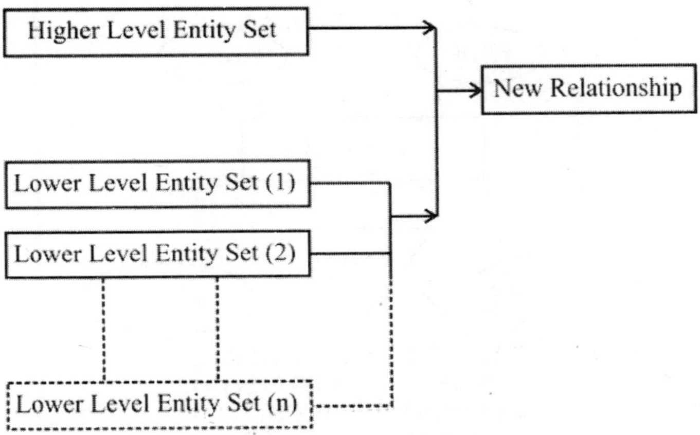

Figure 2.8: *Concept of generalization*

For describing Generalization, consider an example of entity set ACCOUNT with *acc_no* and *balance*.

We will extend our example by classifying each ACCOUNT as being one of the following:

1. Saving account
2. Current account

To describe these we require a set of attributes, which are common to all of entity set ACCOUNT, plus some additional attributes.

For example, Saving Account entity is described further by attribute *interest_rate* whereas Current Account entity is described further by attribute *overdraft_amt*.

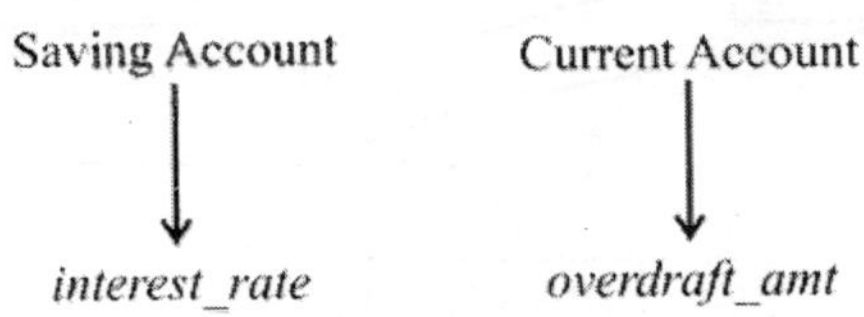

There are similarities between Saving Account entity set and Current Account entity set, in the view that have several attributes in common. Thus, this relationship can be expressed by Generalization.

In this example, ACCOUNT is a higher-level entity set and SAVING ACCOUNT and CURRENT ACCOUNT are lower level entity sets. Generalization can be expressed in terms of E-R diagram, which is denoted by a triangle component with a label "ISA" on it. The label "ISA" stands for "is a".

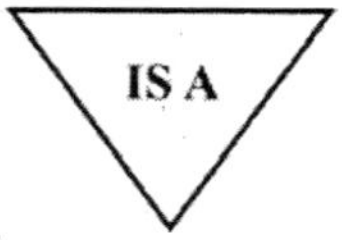

Figure 2.9: *Generalization notation*

In Figure 2.10, ACCOUNT is the higher-level entity set and SAVING ACCOUNT and CURRENT ACCOUNT are the lower-level entity sets. Higher – and Lower-level entity sets also may be designated by the term superclass and subclass respectively. The ACCOUNT entity set is the superclass of SAVING ACCOUNT and CURRENT ACCOUNT.

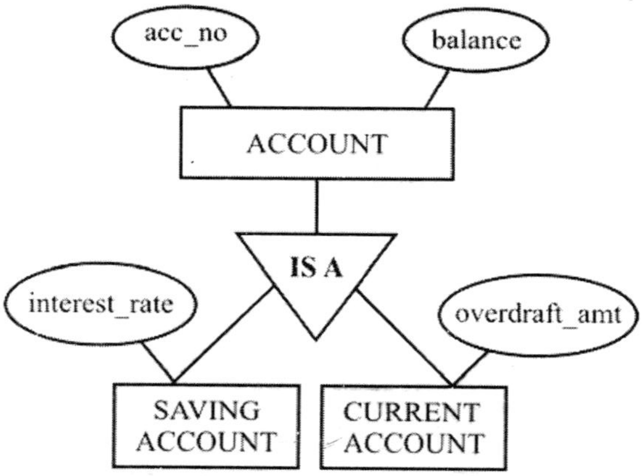

Figure 2.10: *Example of generalization*

2.8 AGGREGATION

Aggregation is a new feature of the E-R Modeling. *It is the process of compiling information on an object, thereby abstracting a higher-level object.*

Aggregation technique expresses "relationship among relationships".

We shall take an example with which we shall illustrate the need of aggregation.

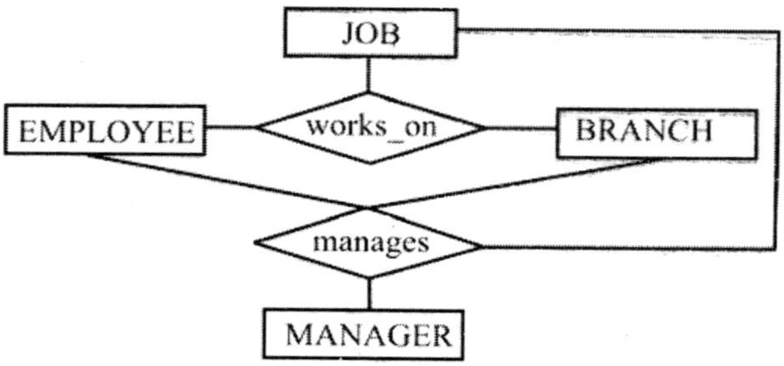

Figure 2.11: *E-R diagram with redundant relationships*

To illustrate the need for aggregation, consider the relation *works_on*, which creates the relationships between EMPLOYEE, BRANCH and JOB. Now, suppose we want to record managers for tasks performed by an employee at a branch.

2.9 RELATIONSHIPS AMONG DATA

A relationship is defined as "an association among entities". For example, there is some relationship between entities "INSTRUCTOR" and "STUDENT".

This relationship represents the fact that an instructor teaches several students and a student is taught by several instructors.

Degree of relationship: The degree of a relationship indicates the number of associated entities. Degree of relationship is classified as:

- Unary relationship
- Binary relationship
- Ternary relationship
- Quaternary relationship

A unary relationship exists when an association is maintained within single entity. Consider Figure 2.12

Figure 2.12: *Unary relationship*

Consider the case when to take a particular subject, student have to take another subject. For example, to take "Compiler Design", student has to take "Automata Theory" as another subject. This kind of relationship is called Unary relationship.

A binary relationship exists when two entities are associated. Consider Figure 2.13

Figure 2.13: *Binary relationship*

This relationship represents the fact that an instructor teaches several students and a student is taught by several instructors.

A ternary relationship exists when there are three entities associated. For example, the entities INSTRUCTOR, SUBJECT and STUDENT are related using ternary relationship. This is illustrated in Figure 2.14.

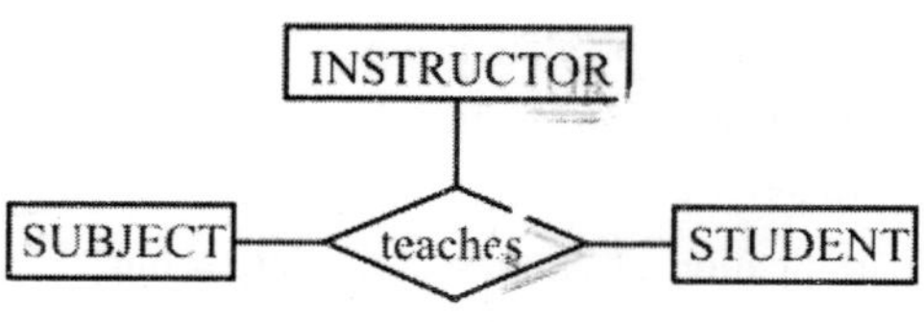

Figure 2.14: *Ternary relationship*

A quaternary relationship exists when there are four entities associated. An example, quaternary relationship is "studies" where four entities are involved – STUDENT, INSTRUCTOR, SUBJECT and STUDY_MATERIAL. This relationship (shown in Figure 2.15) represents a situation where a STUDENT taught by an INSTRUCTOR with the help of the STUDY_MATERIAL studies a SUBJECT.

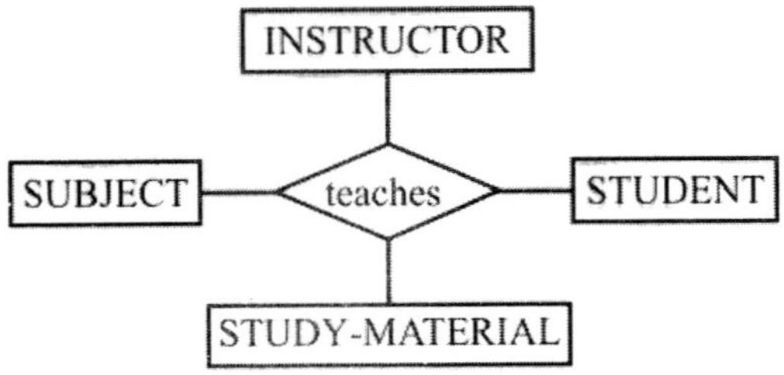

Figure 2.15: *Quaternary relationship*

REVIEW QUESTIONS

1. What are the different database models and what are their advantages and disadvantages?
2. What were the main problems of the earlier database models?
3. What were the major problems faced by database community due to lack of standardization?
4. What is the purpose of creating a high-level data model?
5. What is E-R modeling?
6. What are the components of an E-R model?
7. What are entities?
8. What are attributes?
9. What is a domain?
10. What are the different types of attributes?
11. What are the conventions for representing entities and attributes in the E-R diagram?
12. What are relationships?
13. What do you mean by the degree of a relationship?
14. What are unary relationships?
15. What are binary relationships?
16. What are ternary relationships?
17. What are quaternary relationships?
18. What do you mean by the connectivity of a relationship?
19. What do you mean by the cardinality of a relationship?
20. What do you mean by the dependency of a relationship?
21. What are strong and weak entities?
22. What do you mean by the participation of entities in a relationship?
23. What is the difference between total and partial participation?

24. What are composite entities?
25. What are E-R diagrams?
26. What are E-R modeling symbols?
27. Draw an E-R Diagram for Library Management System?

CHAPTER 3

Enhanced Entity-Relationship (EER) Model

In this chapter, you will learn

3.0 INTRODUCTION

The original E-R model was developed by Chen in the 1970s. This fundamental model was able to handle the data modeling of the common business problems and was quite sufficient for the representation of the majority of the business problems that existed in the 1970s and in the early 1980s.

In the 1980s, there was a rapid boost in the development of many new database applications like computer aided design (CAD), computer aided manufacturing (CAM), and computer aided software engineering (CASE), geographical information systems (GIS), and multimedia applications and so on. These applications are more challenging when it comes to database requirements than the traditional applications that were modeled by the E-R model. The basic E-R modeling concepts were no longer sufficient to represent the requirements of these newer and complex applications. This necessitated the database designers and practitioners to explore for and develop additional semantic modeling concepts. Many semantic data models were projected and developed during this period, but the most popular was the one that incorporated this semantic concepts into the existing E-R model.

The E-R model that is supported with the additional semantic concepts iş called the **Enhanced Entity-Relationship model or the EER model.** The EER model includes all the concepts of the original E-R model together with the following additional concepts:

- Specialization
- Generalization
- Categorization.

We will perceive each of these concepts in detail in the following sections. Before discussing the concepts of specialization, generalization and categorization we must make ourselves familiar with the entity types called superclasses (supertype) and subclasses (subtype) and moreover with the process of attribute inheritance.

3.1 SUPERCLASS AND SUBCLASS ENTITY TYPES

One of the most important new modeling constructs that were incorporated into the EER model was the superclass and subclass entity types (also known as supertype/subtype entities). This characteristic allows us to model a general entity (superclass or supertype) and then subdivide it into several specialized entity types (subclass or subtypes). EER diagrams are used to capture business rules such as constraints in the supertype/subtype relationships. Thus, a superclass is an entity type that includes distinct subclasses that require to be represented in a data model. A subclass is an entity type that has a distinct role and is also a member of a superclass.

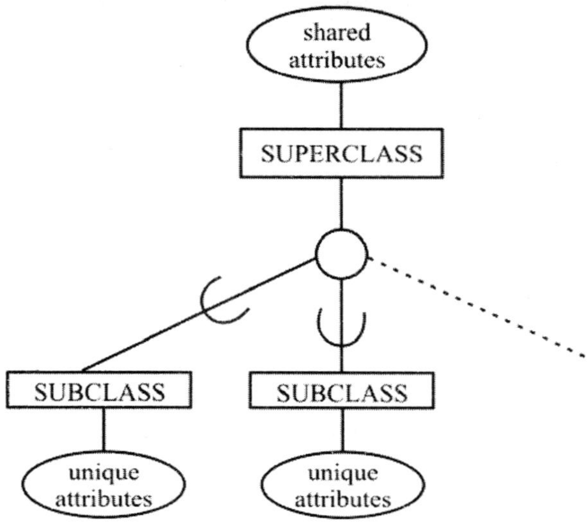

Figure 3.1: *Basic notation of the superclass/subclass relationship*

In some cases, an entity type may have many distinct subclasses. For example, the EMPLOYEE entity can have subclasses such as FULL_TIME, PART_TIME and CONSULTANT. Alternatively, the EMPLOYEE entity can have subclasses such as MANAGER, SUPERVISOR, MARKETING_PERSONNEL SECRETARY, PEON and so on. In the above examples, we call the EMPLOYEE entity as the superclass or supertype and the other entities as the subclass or subtypes. The relationship between a superclass and one of its subclasses is called a superclass/subclass (or supertype/ subtype) relationship. For example, EMPLOYEE/CONSULTANT is a supertype/subtype relationship.

Each member of the subclass or subtype is also a member of the superclass or supertype. In other words, the subclass member (for example, fulltime employee) is the same as the entity in the superclass (employee), however, has a distinct role. The relationship between a superclass and a subclass is a one-to-one (1:1) relationship. In some cases, a superclass can have overlapping subclasses. For example, if an employee is the manager of the marketing department, then he will be a member of the MANAGER and MARKETING_PERSONNEL subclasses. However, it is not necessary that all the members of the superclass are members of anyone of the subclasses. For example, there can be employees in the company who are not in any of the subclasses.

The superclass/subclass relationship is represented as shown in Figure 3.1. The superclass is connected to a circle with a line. The subclasses are also connected to the circle by lines. The U-shaped symbols indicate that the subclass is a subset of the superclass. The attributes shared by all the entities of the superclass (or shared by the all the subclasses) are associated with the superclass entity. The attributes that are unique to each subclass are associated with the respective subclass.

Now we will explain the superclass/subclass relationship with an example. As we have seen earlier, the EMPLOYEE entity has three subclasses FULL_TIME, PART_TIME and CONSULTANT. Now, if we make up the entity lists of these subclasses it will be as follows:

- FULL_TIME_EMPLOYEE (employee_no, name, address, date_of_birth, date_of_joining, salary, allowances)
- PART_TIME_EMPLOYEE (employee_no, name, address, date_of_birth, date_of_joining, hourly_rate)
- CONSULTANT (employee_no, name, address, date_of_birth, date_of_joining, contract_no, billing_rate)

Notice that all the three categories have some attributes in common—employee_no., name, address, date_of_birth and date_of_joining. In addition to these common attributes, each category has one or more attribute that is unique to that category. For example, salary and allowances are unique to a fulltime employee, where as the hourly rate is unique to the part time employee and so on. When faced with such a business situation the database designer can either treat these entities as three separate ones or as a single entity, which contains a superset of all the attributes. In the first case—where the entities are treated as three separate ones—the model fails to exploit the common attributes of *all* the employees and thus creating an inefficient model. In the second case—where all the three entities are combined into a single master entity—the model requires the use of nulls (for the attributes for which the different entities have no value) thus making the design more complex.

This is an ideal situation for the use of a superclass/subclass representation. The EMPLOYEE entity can be defined as a superclass entity and the FULL_TIME_EMPLOYEE, PART_TIME_EMPLOYEE and CONSULTANT as the subclass entities. The attributes that are common to all the three subclasses can be associated with the superclass. This representation is shown in Figure 3.2.

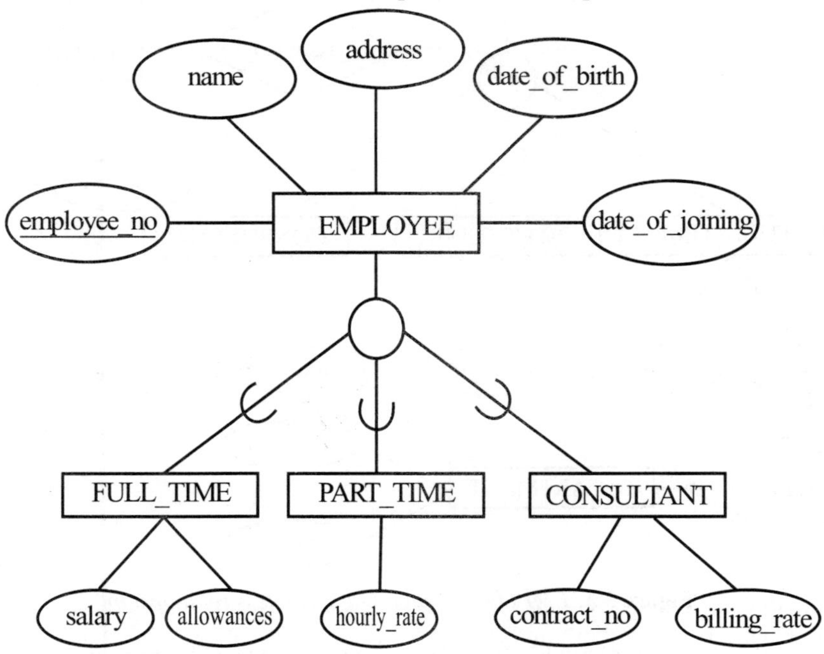

Figure 3.2: *EMPLOYEE superclass with three subclasses*

There are two important reasons for introducing the concepts of superclasses and subclasses into an E-R model. First, it avoids the need to describe similar concepts more than once, thus saving time for the person doing the data modeling and also results in more *readable* and better-looking E-R diagrams. The second reason is, that the superclass/subclass relationships add more semantic content and information to the design. For example, when you create a superclass/subclass relationship between the EMPLOYEE and CONSULTANT entities, you are communicating the fact that consultant is a special type of employee in a precise and concise form.

3.2 ATTRIBUTE INHERITANCE

We have seen that a subclass is an entity on its own right. For example, the FULL_TIME employee is an EMPLOYEE and an entity instance of the subclass represents the same entity instance of the superclass. As a consequence, an entity in a subclass must possess not only the values for its own attributes, but also values for its attributes as a member of the superclass. Attribute inheritance is the property by which subclass entities inherit values of all the attributes of the superclass entity. This feature makes it unnecessary to associate the superclass attributes with the subclass entities thus avoiding redundancy.

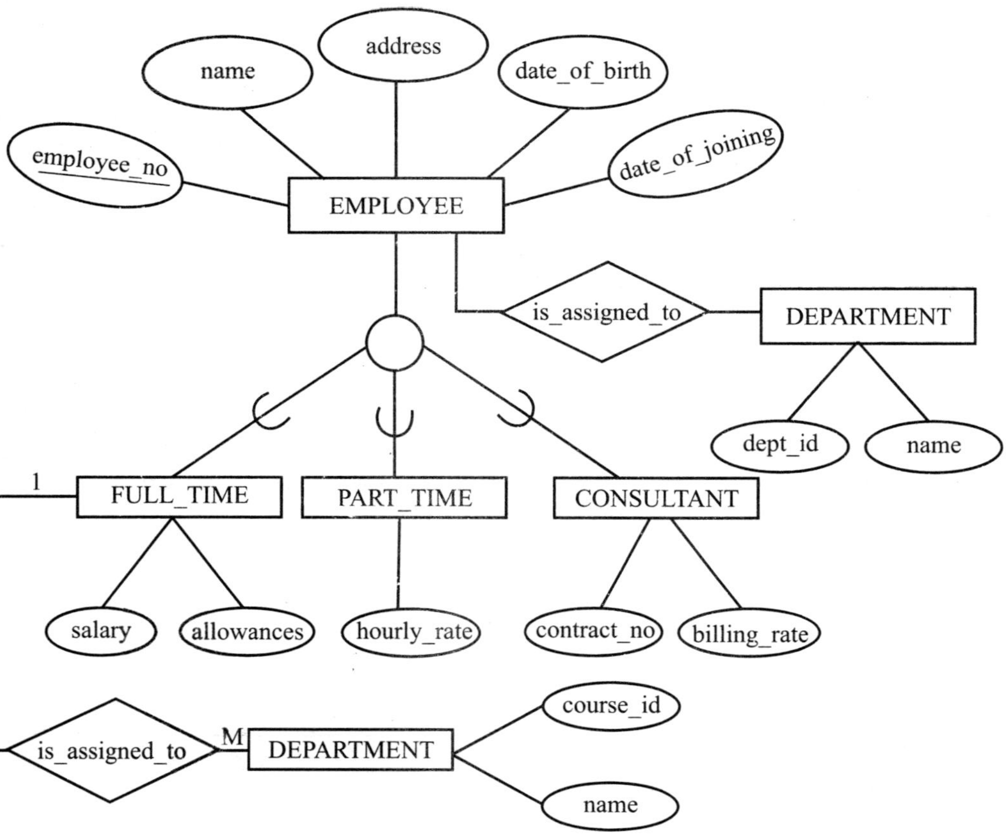

Figure 3.3: *EMPLOYEE superclass/subclass relationship*

For example, the attributes of the EMPLOYEE superclass entity like employee_no., name, address, etc., are inherited to the subclass entities. As we have seen, a subclass is a member of its superclass.

However, the converse is not always true. That is a superclass need not be consisted entirely of entities from the subclasses alone. For example, there can be employees in the company who are not fulltime, part time or consultants (an example, can be a temporary worker). The superclass/subclass relationships should be used when either or both of the following condition are satisfied:

- There are many attributes that are common to some (but not all) of the instances of an entity.
- The instances of a subclass participate in a relationship unique to that subclass.

Consider the EMPLOYEE example shown in Figure 3.3, where the EMPLOYEE superclass has three subclasses—FULL_TIME_EMPLOYEE, PART_TIME_EMPLOYEE and CONSULTANT. All employees have attributes like employee_no, name, and address and so on. Each subclass has attributes unique to that subclass. Fulltime employees have salary and allowances, part time employees have hourly rate and consultants have contract_no and billing_rate. The fulltime employees have a unique relationship with the COURSE entity. Only fulltime employees can enroll in the executive improvement courses conducted by the company. Thus, this is a case where you have to use a superclass/subclass relationship as there *exists* an instance of a subclass that participate in a relationship that is unique to that subclass.

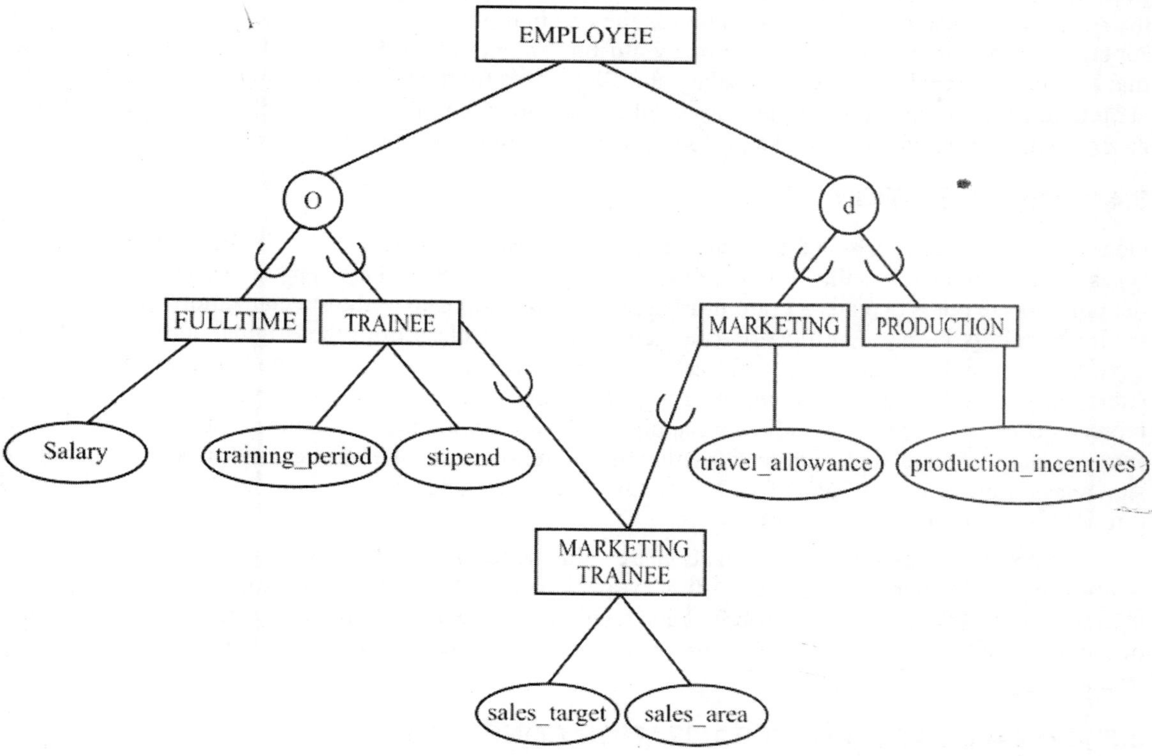

Figure 3.4: *Share subclass and multiple inheritance*

We have mentioned earlier that the subclasses inherit all the attributes of the superclass entity. The Figure 3.3 also shows the principle of **relationship inheritance**—the subclasses inherit the relationships of the superclass. For example, all the employee subclasses—full/time, part time and consultants-inherit the relationship **"EMPLOYEE is assigned to DEPARTMENT."**

We have seen that a subclass is an entity on its own right. Therefore, a subclass can have its own subclasses. An entity and its subclasses and their subclasses and so on are called a type hierarchy. Type hierarchies can be classified into specialization hierarchy, generalization hierarchy, and so on. A subclass with more than one superclass is called a shared subclass. For example, the MARKETING_TRAINEE in the Figure 3.4 is an example of a share subclass as it is a member of the TRAINEE subclass and the MARKETING subclass. Since the shared subclass has two parents, the attributes of both the superclasses—TRAINEE and MARKETING—is inherited by the MARKETING_TRAINEE subclass. This process is referred to as multiple inheritances. We will discuss these topics in detail in the following sections.

3.3 SPECIALIZATION

Specialization is the process of maximizing the differences between members of an entity by identifying the distinguishing and unique characteristics (or attributes) of each member. Specialization is a top-down process. Suppose that we have defined an entity with its attributes. Specialization is the process of defining one or more subclasses for the superclass and forming superclass/subclass relationships. Each subclass is formed based on the some unique or distinguishing attribute or relationship specific to the subclass. An example of specialization is the creation of the three subclasses for the EMPLOYEE superclass. The three subclasses have many attributes in common. However, there are also attributes that are unique to each subclass (like salary and allowances for the fulltime employee). In addition, there are relationships unique to some subclasses (like the relationship of fulltime employee to course). In this case, specialization has permitted a preferred representation of the problem domain.

3.4 GENERALIZATION

Generalization is the process of defining a more general entity type from a *set* of more specialized entity types. In other words, it is the process of minimizing the differences between the entities by identifying the common features. This is a bottom-up approach, just opposite to the specialization approach. This approach results in the identification of a generalized superclass from the original subclasses. As we have said before the process of generalization can be seen as a reverse of the specialization process. For example, consider a model where, the full_time employee, part_time employee and consultant are represented as distinct entities. When we apply the generalization process to these entities, we will try to find out the attributes and relationships that are common to all the entities and make a generalized superclass-in this case EMPLOYEE. The distinct entities will be subclasses of the superclass identified through the generalization process.

Both specialization and generalization are valuable techniques for developing superclass/subclass relationships. Whether to use generalization or specialization at a particular time depends on factors like nature of the problem, nature of the entities and relationships and more importantly the personal preference of the person doing the modeling. The best way is to try both the methods and then make a decision by trial and error.

3.5 SPECIALIZATION/GENERALIZATION CONSTRAINTS

Constraints in specialization and generalization allow us to capture some of the important business rules that apply to the relationships. The constraints that are applicable to specialization and generalization are disjoint constraint and participation constraint.

Disjoint constraint: The disjoint constraint specifies that if the subclasses of a specialization/ generalization are disjoint then an entity can be a member of only one of the subclasses of that specialization/generalization. The disjoint constraint is represented by placing a 'd' in the circle that connects the subclasses to the superclass. For example, the subclasses of the EMPLOYEE superclass—FULL_TIME, PART_TIME and CONSULTANT are connected as shown in Figure 3.5. This means that an employee has to be one of the three subclasses—fulltime employee, part time employee or consultant.

If the subclasses of a specialization/generalization are not disjoint then an entity may be a member of more than one subclass of the specialization/generalization. To represent an **overlapping or non-disjoint** specialization/generalization an "o" is placed inside the circle that connects the subclasses to the superclass.

For example, the subclasses of the EMPLOYEE superclass—WORKER, UNION_MEMBER and CLUB_MEMBER are connected as shown in Figure 3.6. This means that an employee can be a member of one, two or three of the subclasses. That is, an employee can be a worker as well as a union member as well as a club member. In addition, it means that there can be employees (for example, a manager) who are club members.

Participation constraint: The participation constraint can be total or partial. A specialization/generalization with total participation means that every entity in the superclass must be a member of a subclass in the specialization/generalization. To represent total participation double line~ are used to connect the superclass and the specialization/generalization circle.

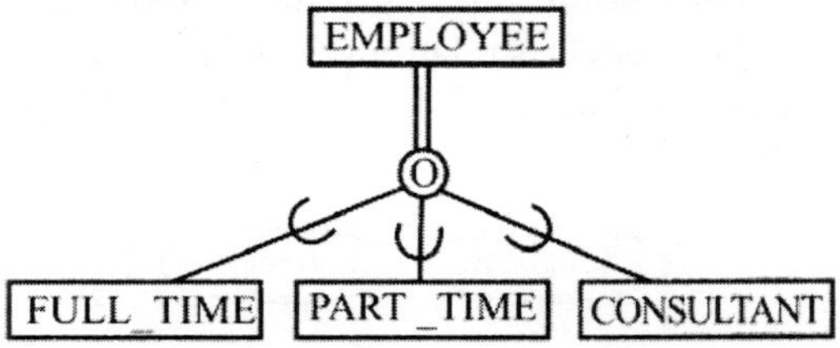

Figure 3.5: *Disjoint and participation constraints (disjoints, total)*

For example, the EMPLOYEE superclass is connected to the circle using double lines as shown in Figure 3.5. This means that every employee in the company has to be one of the three subclasses—fulltime employee, part time employee or consultant. In other words, there can be no other type of employees in the company.

A specialization/generalization with a partial participation specifies that an entity need not *belong* to any of the subclasses of a specialization/generalization. A partial participation is represented using a single line between the superclass and the specialization/generalization circle.

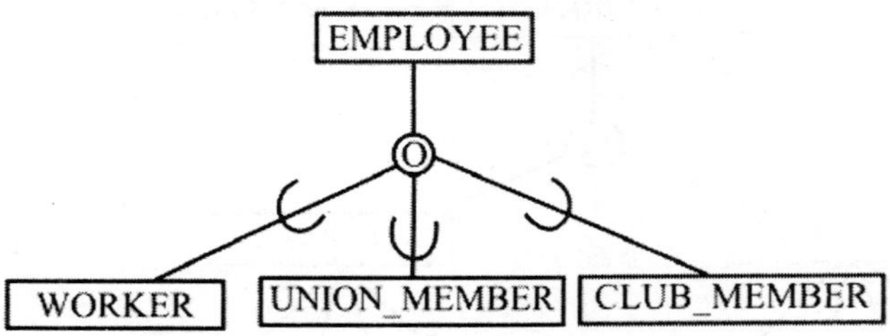

Figure 3.6: *Overlapping and participation constraints (overlapping, partial)*

For example, the Figure 3.6 shows the superclass connected to the circle using a single line. This means that a member of the employee entity type need not have an additional role as a worker, union member or club member. In other words, there can be employees who are not workers, union members or club members.

Here one point that should be remembered is that the disjoint and participation constraints are independent. Hence, we have the following four possible constraints on specialization/ generalization:

- Disjoint, total
- Disjoint, partial
- Overlapping, total
- Overlapping, partial

The correct constraint is determined from the real-world meaning that applies to each specialization/ generalization. However, a superclass that was identified through the generalization process is usually total because the superclass is derived from the subclasses and hence contains only the entities that are in the subclasses.

3.6 CATEGORIZATION

The modeling of a single subclass with a relationship that involves more than one distinct superclass is called categorization. Every superclass/subclass relationship in a specialization/generalization hierarchy has a single distinct superclass.

For example, the shared subclass MARKETING_TRAINEE in Figure 3.4 has two distinct superclass/ subclass relationships, where each relationship has a single superclass. However, certain situations require the modeling of a superclass/subclass relationship with more than one distinct superclass. This subclass—a subclass having more than one superclass—is called a category and the process of defining a category is called categorization.

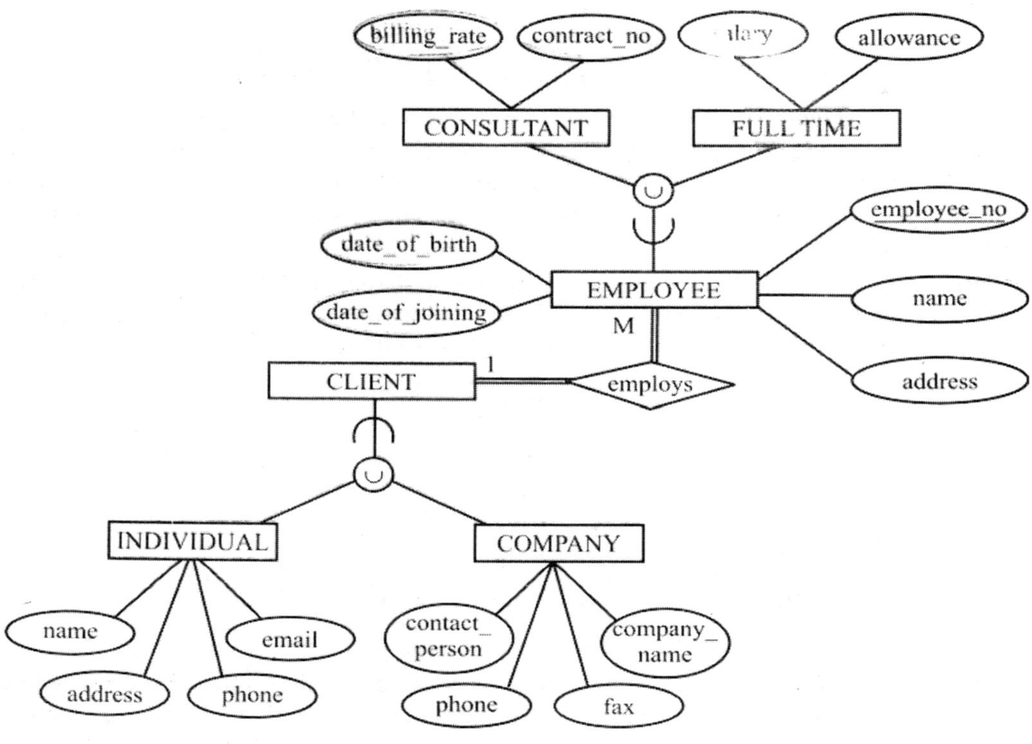

Figure 3.7: *Client and employee categories*

For example, consider the two categories called CLIENT and EMPLOYEE shown in Figure 3.7. The CLIENT category is associated with two distinct superclass entity types—INDIVIDUAL and COMPANY. The EMPLOYEE category is associated with two superclass entity types, namely CONSULTANT and FULL TIME employee.

The line connecting the category subclass to the categorization circle has the subset symbol ($\subset$) and the circle itself contains the union symbol ($\cup$).

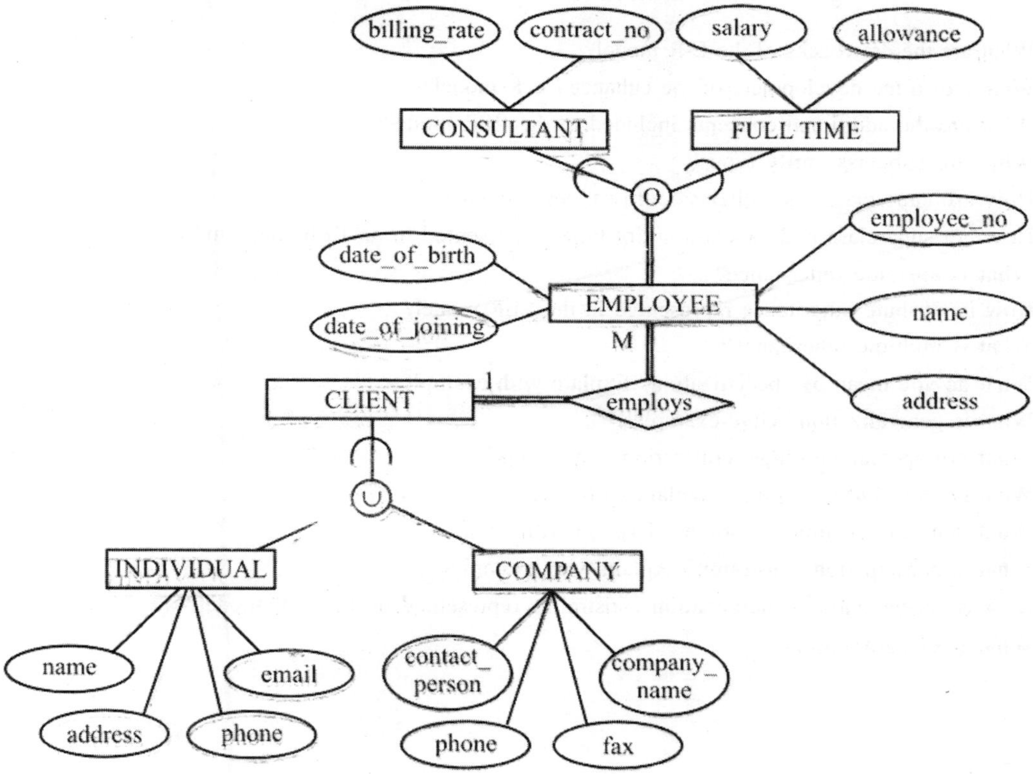

Figure 3.8: *Specialization / generalization of EMPLOYEE*

A category subclass has **selective inheritance.** This means that the category will inherit only the attributes of one of the superclasses at a time. For example, CLIENT entity will inherit only the attributes of either the INDIVIDUAL superclass or the COMPANY superclass at a time. A category can be subdivided based on total or partial participation. For **total participation,** every occurrence of all the superclasses must appear in the category (represented by a double line connecting the category and the categorization circle). For **partial participation,** the constraint is removed so that not every occurrence of all the superclasses need appear in the category. A single line connecting the category and the categorization circle represents this. For example, the CLIENT category has partial participation as every occurrence of the INDIVIDUAL and COMPANY superclasses need not be represented by the category CLIENT. However, the EMPLOYEE category exhibits total participation, as every member of the CONSULTANT and FULL TIME employee superclasses is a member of the EMPLOYEE category. When a category has total participation, as in the case of the EMPLOYEE category, the entities can be represented as a specialization/generalization. Although the use of specialization/generalization is a decision of the person doing the modeling. It is better to use them when the superclass entities represent the same type of entities and share most of the attributes. This is implemented for the above example and is shown in Figure 3.8.

REVIEW QUESTIONS

1. What are the drawbacks of the E-R model?
2. What led to the development of the enhanced E-R model?
3. What are the additional concepts included in the EER model?
4. What are subclass entity types?
5. How are superclass and subclass entity types related?
6. How are superclass and subclass entity types represented in an EER diagram?
7. What is attribute inheritance?
8. How is attribute inheritance represented in the EER model?
9. What is multiple inheritance?
10. What do you mean by specialization? Explain with examples.
11. What is generalization? Give examples.
12. What are specialization/generalization constraints?
13. What is a disjoint constraint? Explain with examples.
14. What is an overlapping constraint? Explain with examples.
15. What is participation constraint? Explain with examples.
16. How is specialization/generalization constraints represented in the EER model?
17. What is categorization?

CHAPTER 4

Relational Data Model

In this chapter, you will learn

4.0 INTRODUCTION

An accepted way to represent data to a user is with a two-dimension table. A table must be set up in a way that no information about the relations among the data elements is missing. A table should contain the following properties:

(a) Each entry in a table only represents one data item and no two fields with the same name.
(b) In each column, the data items are of the same type, i.e., the column should be homogeneous.
(c) Each column is assigned with a distinctive heading.
(d) All rows are distinct; duplicate rows are not allowed.
(e) Both the rows and the columns can be viewed in any sequence at any time without affecting the information.

4.1 DEFINITION OF RELATION

All data and relationships are represented in a two-dimensional table called a *relation*. For example, the table shown in Figure 4.1 is referred to as a relation. A database constructed by means of relations is referred to as a *relational database.*

Attributes

EMPNO	ENAME	JOB	MGR	HIREDATE	SAL	COMM	REPTNO
7369	SMITH	CLERK	7902	17-DEC-80	800		20
7499	ALLEN	SALESMAN	7698	20-FEB-81	1600	300	30
7521	WARD	SALESMAN	7698	22-FEB-81	1250	500	30
7566	JONES	MANAGER	7839	02-APR-81	2975		20
7654	MARTIN	SALESMAN	7698	28-SEP-81	1250	1400	30
7698	BLAKE	MANAGER	7839	01-MAY-81	2850		30
7782	CLARK	MANAGER	7839	09-JUN-81	2450		10
7788	SCOTT	ANALYST	7566	19-APR-87	3000		20
7839	KING	PRESIDENT		17-NOV-81	5000		10
7844	TURNER	SALESMAN	7698	08-SEP-81	1500	0	30
7876	ADAMS	CLERK	7788	23-MAY-87	1100		20
7900	JAMES	CLERK	7698	03-DEC-81	950		30
7902	FORD	ANALYST	7566	03-DEC-81	3000		20
7934	MILLER	CLERK	7782	23-JAN-82	1300		10

Tuples

Entity Set **Domain**

Figure 4.1: *EMP relation*

Each attribute of a relation has a distinct name. Each tuple or row has a set of permitted values for the attribute called the Domain. For example, the domain of attribute *ename* is the set of all alphabetic strings of finite length. The domain of attribute *deptno* is the set of whole numbers.

Attribute of an entity: Two-dimensional tables in a relational database are much like the traditional file system with its records, fields and files. Rows of the relation are referred to as *Tuples* of the relation and columns are referred to as *Attributes*.

An entity usually has an attribute whose values are distinct for each individual entity in the collection. Such an attribute is called a *key attribute* and its values can be used to identify each entity uniquely. For example, *empno* attribute is a key of the EMP entity in Figure 4.1, because no two employees will have the same *empno*.

All the relations have three components:

(a) Name

(b) Degree

(c) Cardinality

Name

Name is represented by the *title* or the *entity-identifier* EMP relation as in Figure 4.1.

Degree

The number of columns associated with the table or relations is called as the *Degree*. In the table EMP, degree is 8, i.e., there are 8 attributes or fields associated with the table.

Cardinality

The number of rows in the table is called as *Cardinality*. In the table EMP, cardinality is 14, i.e., there are 14 rows or records (tuples) associated with the table.

Types of relations: There are two types of relations. These are:

(a) Base relation

(b) Derived relation

Base Relation

The *base relations* are those relations, which are created prior to use. They are also called as "tables" and they exist as physical file.

Derived Relation

The *derived relations* are those relations, which are derived from a base relation. They do not exist as physical files. The derived relations are also called as *views*.

Entities, entity sets and instance: An entity is an object that exists and is distinguishable from other objects. In other words, an entity is a real-world person, place or thing, or a conceptual (logical) person, place or thing, of significant interest to the organization and about which the organization must collect and maintain data. Each entity has particular properties called attributes that describe it. For example, an EMP entity may be described by *empno, ename* and *deptno*. Figure 4.2 shows entity and the values of their attributes.

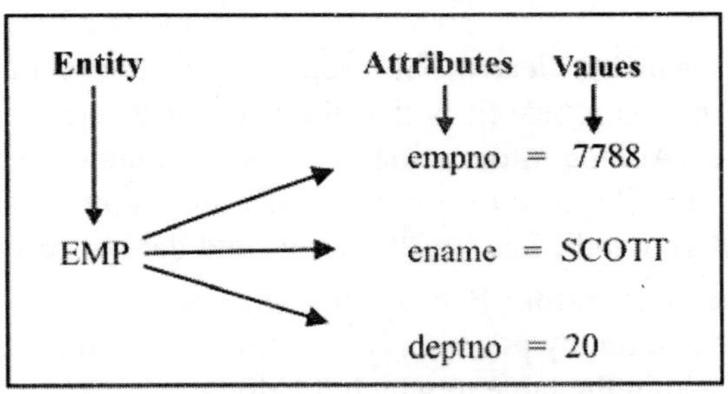

Figure 4.2: *Entity and the values of its attributes*

The EMP entity has three attributes *empno, ename* and *deptno* with their values "7788", "SCOTT", and "20" respectively.

An entity set is a set of entities of the same type i.e., which share common properties or attributes. The set of all employees of an organization can be defined as the entity set (Figure 4.1). An entity set is represented by a set of attributes.

The collection of information stored in a database at a particular moment is called instance or occurrence.

4.2 PROPERTIES OF RELATIONAL TABLES

Relational tables have the following properties:

Values are atomic: This property implies that columns in a relational table are not repeating group or arrays. Hence, composite and multi-valued attributes are not permissible. Multivalued attributes have got to be represented by a separate tables, and composite attributes are represented only be their simple component attributes. The atomic value property of relational tables is significant because it is one of the cornerstones of the relational model. The key benefit of the one value property is that it simplifies data manipulation logic.

Column values are of the same kind: In relational terms, this means that all values in a column come from the same domain. A domain is a set of values, which a column may have. For example, an *ename* column contains only name of the employees. It never contains other information such as *empno, deptno* etc.

This property simplifies data access because developers and users can be certain of the type of data contained in a given column. It also simplifies data validation. Because all values are from the same domain, the domain can be defined and enforced with the Data Definition (DDL) of the database software.

Each row is unique: This property ensures that no rows in a relational table are identical; there is at least one column, or a set of columns, the values of which uniquely identify each row in the table. Such columns are called primary keys. This property guarantees that every row in a relational table is meaningful and that a specific row can be identified by specifying the primary key value.

The sequence of columns is insignificant: This property states that the ordering of the columns in the relational table has no meaning. Columns can be retrieved in any order and in various sequences. The benefit of this property is that it enables many users to share the same table without concern of how the table is organized. It also permits the physical structure of the database to change without affecting the relational tables.

The sequence of rows is insignificant: This property is analogous of the one above but applies to rows instead of columns. The main benefit is that the rows of a relational table can be retrieved in different order and sequences. Adding information to a relational table is simplifies and does not affect existing queries. However, in a file, records are physically stored on disk so there always is an order among the records. This ordering indicates 1st, 2nd ......n^{th} and the last record.

Each column has a unique name: Because the sequence of columns is insignificant, columns must be referenced by name and not by position. In general, a column name need not be unique within an entire database but only within the table to which it belongs.

4.3 CODD'S RULE

Codd's rule forms the base of relational database management system. The detailed description of the E.F. Codd's rule is given below:

Rule zero: For any system that is advertised as, or claimed to be, a relational database management system, that system must be able to manage databases entirely through its relational capabilities.

Rule 1: The information rule: All information in a relational database is represented explicitly at the logical level and in exactly one way - by values in a table.

Rule 2: Guaranteed access rule: Each and every datum (atomic value) in a relational database is guaranteed to be logically accessible by resorting to a combination of table name, primary key value and column name.

Rule 3: Systematic treatment of null values: Null values (distinct from the empty character string or a string of blank characters and distinct from zero or any other number) are supported in a fully relational DBMS for representing missing information and inapplicable information in a systematic way, independent of data type.

Rule 4: Dynamic online catalogue based on the relational model: The database description is represented at the logical level in the same way as ordinary data, so that users can apply the same relational language to its interrogation as they apply to the regular data.

Rule 5: Comprehensive data sub-language rule: A relational system may support several languages and various modes of terminal use (for example, the fill-in-the-blanks mode). However, there must be at least one language whose statements are expressible, per some well-defined syntax, as character strings and that is comprehensive in supporting all of the following items:

- Data definition
- View definition
- Data manipulation (interactive and by program)
- Integrity constraints
- Transaction boundaries (begin, commit, rollback)
- Authorization

Rule 6: View updating rule: All views that are theoretically updatable are also updatable by the system.

Rule 7: High-level insert, update, delete: The capability of handling a base relation or a derived relation as a single operand applies not only to the retrieval of data but also to the insertion, update and deletion of data.

Rule 8: Physical data independence: Application programs and terminal activities remain logically unimpaired whenever any changes are made in either storage representations or access methods.

Rule 9: Logical data independence: Application programs and terminal activities remain logically unimpaired when information preserving changes of any kind that theoretically permit unimpairment are made to the base tables.

Rule 10: Integrity independence: Integrity constraints specific to a particular relational database must be definable in the relational data sublanguage and storable in the catalogue, not in the application programs.

Rule 11: Distribution independence: A relational DBMS has distribution independence.

Rule 12: Non-subversion rule: If a relational system has a low-level (single-record-at-a-time) language, that low-level cannot be used to subvert or bypass the integrity rules and constraints expressed in the higher-level relational languages (multiple-records-at-a-time).

4.4 CONCEPT OF KEYS

Keys are nothing, but attributes, which are used to uniquely identify the rows in a relation. In Figure 4.1, the attribute *empno* has this property. This can be used to distinguish a row or tuples from other rows or tuples. Relationships are expressed in the data values of the primary and foreign keys.

Super key: A super key is a set of one or more attributes which; taken collectively, allow us to identify uniquely an entity in the entity set. Consider a subset S of one or more attributes in relation R. If for two rows r1 and r2

$$\mathbf{r1(S) \neq r2(S)}$$

i.e., corresponding to any two rows if values of S are unique, then, S is said to be the super key. Every relation has at least one default super key—the set of all its relation.

For example, in an entity set EMP, *empno+ename+deptno*, forms a super key. In addition, *empno+deptno* are a super key. It must be noted that *ename* alone cannot be a super key, as two employees could have the same name.

Candidate key: A super key may contain inappropriate attributes, and we are often interested in the smallest super key because if A is a super key then any superset of A will be a super key.

A super key for which no subset is a super key, is called a candidate keys or in other words, Candidate keys are which such minimal keys whose subset is not a super key.

In EMP, it is possible to have numerous combinations that can serve as super keys. For example, *empno, empno+ename, empno+ename+job* etc., are super keys. However, out of the first three empno is sufficient to distinguish a row uniquely. Therefore, we can take *empno, ename+job* as candidate keys.

Primary key: A primary key is a candidate key (out of many candidate keys) that is preferred by Database designer to identify entities in an entity set.

For example, as we discussed above there may be two (or more) candidate keys:

- *ename+job*
- *empno*

Out of these two candidate keys, any one could be primary key; it all depends upon the database designer to which he selects as a primary key.

Composite key: In many cases, as we design a database, we will have tables that will use more than one column as part of the primary key. These are called *Composite Keys* or (concatenated keys). In other words, when a record cannot be uniquely identified by a single field, in such cases a composite key is used. A composite key is a group of fields that uniquely identify a record.

Secondary key: A *Secondary Key* is an attribute or combination of attributes that may not be a candidate key but classifies the entity set on a particular characteristic. For example, the entity set EMP having attribute *deptno,* which identifies by its value, which means all instances of EMP who belong to a given department.

More than one employee may belong to a department, so that *deptno* attribute is not a candidate key for the entity set EMP, since it cannot uniquely identify an individual employee. However, the *deptno* attribute does identify all employees belonging to a particular *deptno*.

Foreign key: A *Foreign Key* is a column or columns whose values are same as the primary key of another table. We can think of a Foreign Key as a copy of primary key from another relational table. The relationship is made between two relational tables by matching the values of the Foreign Key in one table with the values of the primary key in another.

Consider Figure 4.3, which explains the concept of foreign key.

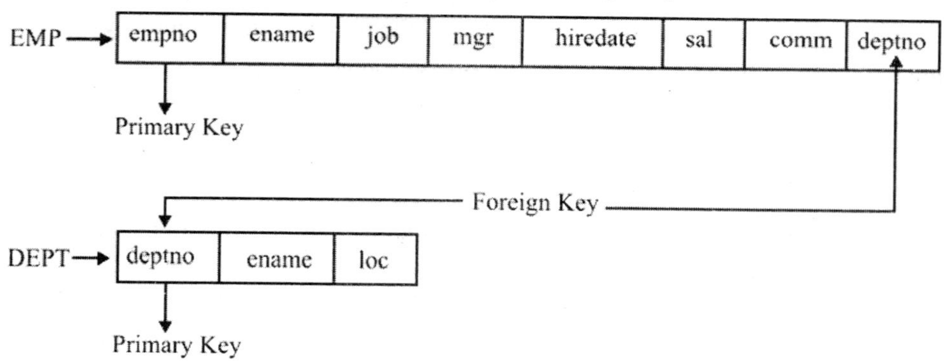

Figure 4.3: *Concept of foreign key*

4.5 INTEGRITY CONSTRAINTS

In viable applications, we may need several business rules in the database. For example, in EMP relation our requirement is that all employees should get the salary in between 3500 and 7000 or only possible jobs in the organization are either manager or salesman.

Therefore, it is the integrity constraints through which we can employ these types of rules on our database.

An integrity constraint is the provision that can be applied on a database schema to confine the data according to the need. If the condition is fulfilled then only it can be stored in the database. These integrity constraints can be applied on the database when the DBA or end users define the database schema.

There are many such constraints, which are desired to authenticate the soundness of the data in a database.

There are two general integrity rules in relational model, which define the sets of consistent database states or change of state or both besides specifying integrity constraints.

Integrity rules formatted by Codd are as follows:

1. Integrity rule 1 (entity integrity): This rule states that:

"If an attribute of a table is prime attribute, then it cannot accept null values, or, in other words, no component of primary key values may be null."

2. Integrity rule 2 (referential integrity): This rule is concerned with the concept of the foreign keys. Foreign keys are used to relate the rows in one relation to rows in other relations. For example, DEPT relation is used with EMP relation to give the information of the departments of all employees. Therefore, it is extremely significant that the values of department numbers in any row in EMP relation communicate to an actual department in DEPT relation. Otherwise, the employee department number would point nowhere.

A database in which all non-null foreign keys reference actual key values in other relations, give the idea of referential integrity rule, which is as follows:

"Let A & B be two relations where A relation is having an attribute(s) with primary key. Let B be having a foreign key, which refers to relation A via the same set of attributes. Then the value of the foreign key in a tuple in B relation must either be equal to primary key of a tuple in A relation or be entirely null."

More simply, we can write it as foreign key must either be null or it must be having the same value of a primary key attribute in another relation.

A valid relationship between a tuple in EMP to one in DEPT requires that the values of the attributes in the foreign key of EMP correspond to the primary key of a tuple in DEPT. This ensures that the reference from a tuple of a relation EMP is made an unambiguously to an existing tuple in DEPT relation.

4.6 DOMAIN CONSTRAINTS

A domain is a collection of data that can appear in each column and the data type of every column, or to be more precise, we can call as the data type of every domain is already defined. We specify the data type for data values that form a domain. The name of the domain be specified in such a way that it may interpret the data type of its domain.

For example:

- *ename* → the set of names of employees that may be a set of character string of user defined length.
- *sal* → is a possible salary of employees that in no case may be less than 800 or more than 5000. Therefore, it can be number between 800 and 5000.

In above example, we have seen that a data type or we can call it as data format is specified for each domain. As it is shown, in the above illustration, that each domain name gives little idea about its data types and the type of values that has to be inserted in the particular domain.

The SQL supports only restricted domain types, which are as follows:

- Integer
- Small integer
- Fixed point numbers (with user defined precision)
- Fixed character string (with user defined length)
- Floating point numbers (with user defined precision)
- Floating point and double floating point numbers (with machine dependent precision)

4.7 ASSERTIONS

An assertion is a method of expressing a situation that we want database to satisfy, always. We have a variety of other methods to define such constraints, example domain constraints, referential integrity and functional dependencies. These constraints can also be tested incredibly easily. However, these three constraints can be called as "special forms of assertions".

The general form of assertion is:

assert < assertion-name > : < condition >
Where condition is any valid SQL clause.

When we define any assertion, the system tests it for its validity. If system found that assertion is valid, then only it allows any modification to the database. This testing may cause a considerable amount of overhead if complex assertions have been made.

Due to the high overhead of testing arbitrary assertions, the assert statement has been vanished from more recent version of SQL. In place of assertion, there are other constraints, domain constraints, referential integrity and functional dependencies. These constraints are easily tested constraints.

4.8 TRIGGERS

Triggers are used to define code that is executed/fired when certain actions or event occurs. At the data base level, triggers can be defined for events such as inserting a record into a table, deleting a record, and updating a record.

The trigger definition consists of following basic parts.

- The events that fires the trigger
- The database table on which event must occur
- An optional condition controlling when the trigger is executed
- A PL/SQL block containing the code to be executed when the trigger is fired.

A trigger is a database object, like a table or an index. When you define a trigger, it becomes a part of the database and it is always is executed when the event for which it is defined occurs.

Syntax for creating a database trigger is shown below.

```
CREATE   [ or REPLACE ] TRIGGER  trigger-name
{ BEFORE | AFTER }  verb-list  ON  table-name
[ FOR EACH ROW [ WHEN condition ] ]
DECLARE
    declarations
BEGIN
    PL/SQL code
END;
```

In the above syntax:

REPLACE	Is used to recreate if trigger already exists.
trigger-name	Is the name of the trigger to be created.
verb-list	The SQL verbs that fire the Create, i.e., it may be INSERT, UPDATE or DELETE.
table-name	The table on which the trigger is defined.
condition	An optional condition placed on the execution of the triggers.
declarations	Consists of any variable, record or cursor declarations needed by this PL/SQL blocks.
PL/SQL code	PL/SQL code that gets executed when the trigger fires.

4.9 QUERY LANGUAGES

A query language is a language through which we correspond with database. When we read or write something into or from existing database, we apply query language. Query languages are of a higher level than typical programming language. We can categorize these query languages as either "procedural query language" or "non-procedural query language". Relational Algebra and Relational Calculus are two formal query languages.

In this segment, we will discuss these two formal query languages of relational data model, which forms the basis for commercial languages used with relational database.

- Relational algebra
- Relational calculus

"Relational Algebra" is a procedural language whereas "Relational Calculus" is a non-procedural language.

In a non-procedural language we specify, what the job has to be done to computer. We do not specify each step to be executed in order to complete the task, whereas in a procedural language we specify each step to be executed for getting the job done. Nevertheless, in both the cases the end consequence is identical.

We will now consider example to exemplify the variation between procedural and non-procedural language.

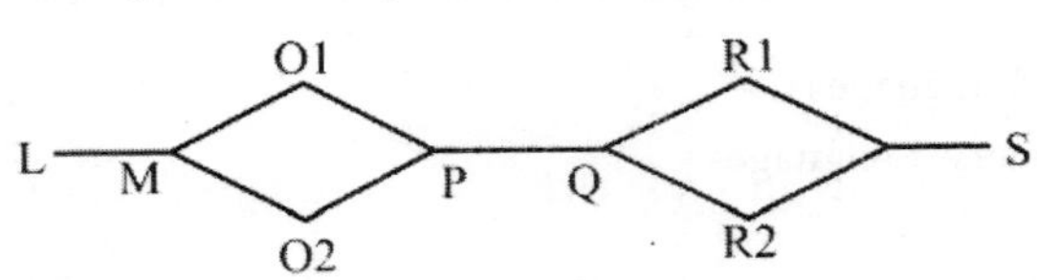

Figure 4.4: *Example for query language*

As given in Figure 4.4, our task is to start from L and reach to point S.

There are four possible paths to move from point L to point S.

Path 1:

L→M→O1→P→Q→R1→S

Path 2:

L→M→O1→P→Q→R2→S

Path 3:

L→M→O2→P→Q→R1→S

Path 4:

L→M→O2→P→Q→R2→S

As explained above,

In case of procedural language, we have to give only desired output as input. We have not mentioned how each step is to be executed in order to obtain End-result.

In case of non-procedural language, we have to give the steps to obtain the result.

Conclusion,

End-result in both the cases is same.

From the above design we can conclude that in non-procedural language we get desire results without stating *"how to get it"* whereas in procedural language we do get the *"desire result"* , but we have to identify each step to *"how to get it"*.

It appears that non-procedural language is better to procedural language. However, we cannot model all relational language using relational calculus (non-procedural query language) because relational algebra (procedural query language) does have some distinct advantage. To fully recognize the relational model and the languages, it is imperative to understand both approaches.

REVIEW QUESTIONS

1. What is the role of Integrity Constraints in Relational Model? Define various Integrity Constraints of Relational Model.
2. Discuss the various features of relational data model.
3. Define Triggers. How triggers can be used to enforce integrity constraints in a database?
4. Write short notes on:
   - Entity Integrity
   - Referential Integrity
   - Domain Constraints
   - Assertions
   - Procedural Query Languages
   - Non-procedural Query Languages.

CHAPTER 5

Relational Algebra

In this chapter, you will learn

5.0 INTRODUCTION

Relational algebra uses a procedural query language which is a collection of operations to manipulate relations. It consists of a set of operations that take one or more relations as input and produce a new relation as their result.

Relational algebra operations can be divided into basic set-oriented operations like union, difference, intersection, Cartesian-product and relational-oriented operations like joins, selection, projections, division etc. We shall understand various operations of relational algebra one by one.

5.1 OPERATIONS IN RELATIONAL ALGEBRA

Select *(σ)*: The select operation extracts specific tuples from a relation. We can use the lower Greek letter sigma *(σ)* to denote selection. One can consider the Select operation to be a filter that keeps only those tuples that satisfy a qualifying condition.

Suppose you want to see tuples which have *empno = 7788* from EMP table. In such case, we can specify this condition with a select operation.

The conditions are specified as mentioned below:

EMP(*empno, ename, job, mgr, hiredate, sal, comm, deptno)*

$$\sigma_{empno=7788}(EMP)$$

In general select operations is denoted by

$$\sigma_{<Selection\_Condition>}(< \text{RELATION NAME} >)$$

where the symbol **σ** (sigma) is used to denote the "select operator", and the selection condition is a boolean expression specified on the attributes of relation.

We can also find tuples of employees whose salary is more than Rs. 2000/- by writing the following:

$$\sigma_{sal > 2000}(EMP)$$

In general, we allow comparisons using relational operators (=, ≠, <, ≤, >, ≥) in such selection predicate. Furthermore, we can combine several predicates into a larger predicate by using the logical connection namely AND (Λ), OR (V) and NOT (¬) operators.

Consider another example. Suppose we want the tuples of an employee whose salary is more than Rs. 1500 and who works for deptno 10.

$$\sigma_{sal > 1500 \wedge deptno = 10}(EMP)$$

The following table gives the brief overview of each comparison operator:

	EMPNO	ENAME	JOB	MGR	HIREDATE	SAL	COMM	DEPTNO
> $\sigma_{sal > 3000}$ (EMP)	7839	KING	PRESIDENT		17-NOV-81	5000		10

	EMPNO	ENAME	JOB	MGR	HIREDATE	SAL	COMM	DEPTNO
≥ $\sigma_{sal \geq 1500}$ (EMP)	7788	SCOTT	ANALYST	7566	19-APR-87	3000		20
	7839	KING	PRESIDENT		17-NOV-81	5000		10
	7902	FORD	ANALYST	7566	03-DEC-81	3000		20

	EMPNO	ENAME	JOB	MGR	HIREDATE	SAL	COMM	DEPTNO
= $\sigma_{sal = 1500}$ (EMP)	7844	TURNER	SALESMAN	7698	08-SEP-81	1500	0	30

	EMPNO	ENAME	JOB	MGR	HIREDATE	SAL	COMM	DEPTNO
< $\sigma_{sal < 1500}$ (EMP)	7369	SMITH	CLERK	7902	17-DEC-80	800		20
	7521	WARD	SALESMAN	7698	22-FEB-81	1250	500	30
	7654	MARTIN	SALESMAN	7698	28-SEP-81	1250	1400	30
	7876	ADAMS	CLERK	7788	23-MAY-87	1100		20
	7900	JAMES	CLERK	7698	03-DEC-81	950		30
	7934	MILLER	CLERK	7782	23-JAN-82	1300		10

	EMPNO	ENAME	JOB	MGR	HIREDATE	SAL	COMM	DEPTNO
≤ $\sigma_{sal \leq 1500}$ (EMP)	7369	SMITH	CLERK	7902	17-DEC-80	800		20
	7521	WARD	SALESMAN	7698	22-FEB-81	1250	500	30
	7654	MARTIN	SALESMAN	7698	28-SEP-81	1250	1400	30
	7844	TURNER	SALESMAN	7698	08-SEP-81	1500	0	30
	7876	ADAMS	CLERK	7788	23-MAY-87	1100		20
	7900	JAMES	CLERK	7698	03-DEC-81	950		30
	7934	MILLER	CLERK	7782	23-JAN-82	1300		10

Figure 5.1: *Comparison operators in relational algebra*

Project(Π): The project operation is a unary operation which extracts attributes (Columns) from a relation. If we are interested in only certain specific attributes of a relation, we use the project operation to project the relation over these attributes only. Projection is denoted by Greek letter pi (Π).

The Select operation selects some of the rows from a table while discarding other rows. The Project operation, on the other hand, selects certain columns from the table and discards the other columns.

Suppose we want to know the Employee Names(*ename*) and their salary*(sal)* from EMP relation, then we may write the query:

$$\Pi_{ename,\ sal}(EMP)$$

The general form of the project operation is:

$$\Pi_{<\ attribute\_List\ >}(R)$$

where **Π**(*pi*) is the symbol used to represent the project operation and <attribute list> is a list of attributes of relation.

Composition of relational operations: The fact that the result of a relational operation is itself a relation is important. Let us consider more complicated query ***"Find name of those employees who works in deptno. 10"*** we write

$$\Pi_{ename}(\sigma_{deptno=10}(EMP))$$

Notice that, instead of giving the name of a relation as the argument of the projection operation, we give an expression that evaluates to a relation. In general, since the result of a relational algebra operation is of the same type (relation) as its inputs, relational algebra can be composed together into a relational algebra expression. Composing relational algebra operations into relational algebra expression is just like composing arithmetic operational into arithmetic expressions.

5.2 SET OPERATIONS

There are four other relational algebraic operations. These are:

(a) set-union

(b) set-intersection

(c) set-difference

(d) Cartesian (cross) product.

Set union: The result of union operation is denoted by the symbol ∪. For example, $X \cup Y$ (where X and are two compatible relations) which is a relation that includes all tuples that are either in X in Y or in both X and Y. Duplicate tuples would be eliminated, by using set union.

For example, if X and Y are two relations as shown below:

X
a b c
d c a
b f e

Y
b c a
c d f
b f e

then,

X ∪ Y =

a b c
d c a
b f e
b c a
c d f

Let us consider a query

Find all employees names whose salary is more than 1500 or belongs to deptno. 10.

To answer the above query we shall split it into two parts.

Find all employee names who belongs to department no. 10.

$$\Pi_{ename}\ (\sigma_{deptno=10}\ (EMP))$$

Find all employee names whose salary is more than 1500.

$$\Pi_{ename}\ (\sigma_{sal>1500}\ (EMP))$$

If we look at the query then we shall find that both queries are joined using "OR" operator. So we can now write query for above:

$$\Pi_{ename}\ (\sigma_{deptno=10}\ (EMP)) \cup \Pi_{ename}\ (\sigma_{sal>1500}\ (EMP))$$

We are taking union of two relations, that is, all employees appearing in either or both of two relations.

$\Pi_{ename}(\sigma_{deptno=10}(EMP))$	$\Pi_{ename}(\sigma_{sal>1500}(EMP))$	$\Pi_{ename}(\sigma_{deptno=10}(EMP)) \cup \Pi_{ename}(\sigma_{sal>1500}(EMP))$
ENAME	**ENAME**	**ENAME**
CLARK	**ALLEN**	**ALLEN**
KING	**JONES**	**JONES**
MILLER	**BLAKE**	**BLAKE**
	CLARK	**CLARK**
	SCOTT	**SCOTT**
	KING	**KING**
	FORD	**FORD**
		MILLER

Observe that, we took union of two sets, both of which consists ename values. In general must ensure that unions should be taken between compatible relations. For example, it would not make sense to take the unions of EMP relation and DEPT relation.

The former is a relation of 14 attributes and the latter is of 4 attributes.

Furthermore, consider a union of a set of *ename* and *sal*. Such union would not make sense in most of the situation.

So for valid union operator, we require following conditions must hold:

Rule 1: Both relations must have same number of attributes.

For example, if we have two relations **r** and **s** then for valid **r** $\cup$ **s** operation we must check that number of attributes in **r** relation and number of attributes in **s** relation should be same.

Rule 2: The *n*th attribute of **r** relation must be same as *n*th attribute of **s** relation.

Let us consider two relations as follows:

EMPNO	ENAME	JOB
7782	CLARK	MANAGER
7839	KING	PRESIDENT
7934	MILLER	CLERK

relation **r**

EMPNO	ENAME	JOB
7369	SMITH	CLERK
7566	JONES	MANAGER
7788	SCOTT	ANALYST
7876	ADAMS	CLERK
7902	FORD	ANALYST

relation **s**

Figure 5.2: *Example for union operation*

Now we shall confirm these two relations for valid union.

We shall first apply rule no. 1, which says the both relation must have same number of attributes.

In Figure 5.2 both relation (r & s) have equal number of attributes, both relation have three attributes. So first condition for valid union satisfies.

Now we shall confirm for rule no. 2, which says that *nth* attribute of **r** relation must be same as *nth* attribute of **s** relation.

Let's check this condition step by step. In this case we have *n=3*, as there are three attributes.

1st attribute of relation **r** = *empno*
1st attribute of relation **s** = *empno*

2nd attribute of relation **r** = *ename*
2nd attribute of relation **s** = *ename*

3rd attribute of relation **r** = *job*
3rd attribute of relation **s** = *job*

Here we observe 1st attribute of **r** relation is similar as 1st attribute of **s** relation and also 2nd and 3rd attributes of **r** relation are similar as 2nd and 3rd attributes of **s** relation.

So for relation **r** and **s** both conditions satisfy, as we have seen above. So the union of relation **r** and relation **s** **(r∪s)** is a valid union.

EMPNO	ENAME	JOB
7369	SMITH	CLERK
7566	JONES	MANAGER
7782	CLARK	MANAGER
7788	SCOTT	ANALYST
7839	KING	PRESIDENT
7876	ADAMS	CLERK
7902	FORD	ANALYST
7934	MILLER	CLERK

Figure 5.3: *Relation $r \cup s$*

Set Difference

The set-difference operation, denoted by ***X -Y*** allows us to locate tuples that are in one relation but are not in another relation.

For example, taking values of X and Y from the earlier example. We shall perform set difference operation as given underneath:

X-Y =

a b c
d c a

In this case, only two tuples are such that they are in one relation.

Consider the following query:

Query: Find all employee names who have salary more than 2000 but not in deptno. 20.

To answer above query we can divide above query into two parts:

First step: We know how to find out "Employee name that have salary more than 2000"

$r = \Pi_{ename}(\sigma_{sal>2000}(EMP))$

ENAME
JONES
BLAKE
CLARK
SCOTT
KING
FORD

Second step: Now find out the employees in deptno 20

$s = \Pi_{ename}(\sigma_{deptno=20}(EMP))$

ENAME
JONES
BLAKE
CLARK
SCOTT
KING
FORD

Final step: In this step we shall take the difference of these two relations which will give the correct answer to the above query.

To answer the above query **r-s** =

ENAME
ADAMS
SMITH

Set intersection: The result of Intersection operation denoted by $X \cap Y$ is an operation that includes all tuples that are in both X and Y.

For example, taking values of X and Y from the earlier example, if we do $X \cap Y$

$X \cap Y$ = b f e

Let us consider a query

Find all employees names whose salary is more than 1500 and belongs to deptno. 10.

To answer the above query, we shall divide it into two parts.

Find all employee names who belongs to department no. 10.

$$\Pi_{ename}\,(\sigma_{deptno=10}\,(EMP))$$

Find all employee names whose salary is more than 1500.

$$\Pi_{ename}\,(\sigma_{sal>1500}\,(EMP))$$

So we can now write query for above:

$$\Pi_{ename}\,(\sigma_{deptno=10}\,(EMP)) \cap \Pi_{ename}\,(\sigma_{sal>1500}\,(EMP))$$

The result is given below:

$$\Pi_{ename}\,(\sigma_{deptno=10}\,(EMP)) \quad \Pi_{ename}\,(\sigma_{sal>1500}\,(EMP)) \quad \Pi_{ename}\,(\sigma_{deptno=10}\,(EMP))\text{"}\ \Pi_{ename}\,(\sigma_{sal>1500}\,(EMP))$$

$$\Pi_{ename}\,(\sigma_{deptno=10}\,(EMP)) \quad \Pi_{ename}\,(\sigma_{sal>1500}\,(EMP))\Pi_{ename}\,(\sigma_{deptno=10}\,(EMP)) \cap \Pi_{ename}\,(\sigma_{sal>1500}\,(EMP))$$

ENAME	ENAME	ENAME
CLARK	ALLEN	CLARK
KING	JONES	KING
MILLER	BLAKE	
	CLARK	
	SCOTT	
	KING	
	FORD	

Figure 5.4: *Relation r ∩ s*

Any relation algebra expression using set intersection can be rewritten by replacing the intersection with a pair of set of difference operation as follows:

$$R1 \cap R2 = R1 - (R1 - R2)$$

Cartesian-product operation: This operator is indicated by * or ×. It is identical to mathematical operation which creates cartesian product of two sets.

relation r = DEPT × EMP

The relation scheme for **r** is

(DEPT.*deptno*, DEPT.*dname*, DEPT.*loc*, EMP.*empno*, EMP.*ename*, EMP.*job*, EMP.*sal*, EMP.*deptno*)

DEPT. deptno	*DEPT. dname*	*DEPT. loc*	*EMP. empno*	*EMP. ename*	*EMP. job*	*EMP. sal*	*EMP. deptno*
30	SALES	CHICAGO	7499	ALLEN	SALESMAN	1600	30
30	SALES	CHICAGO	7521	WARD	SALESMAN	1250	30
30	SALES	CHICAGO	7654	MARTIN	SALESMAN	1250	30
30	SALES	CHICAGO	7900	JAMES	CLERK	950	30
30	SALES	CHICAGO	7844	TURNER	SALESMAN	1500	30
30	SALES	CHICAGO	7698	BLAKE	MANAGER	2850	30
20	RESEARCH	DALLAS	7369	SMITH	CLERK	800	20
20	RESEARCH	DALLAS	7902	FORD	ANALYST	3000	20
20	RESEARCH	DALLAS	7876	ADAMS	CLERK	1100	20
20	RESEARCH	DALLAS	7566	JONES	MANAGER	2975	20
20	RESEARCH	DALLAS	7788	SCOTT	ANALYST	3000	20
10	ACCOUNTING	NEW YORK	7782	CLARK	MANAGER	2450	10
10	ACCOUNTING	NEW YORK	7839	KING	PRESIDENT	5000	10
10	ACCOUNTING	NEW YORK	7934	MILLER	CLERK	1300	10

Figure 5.5: *Result of DEPT × EMP*

To get the product of two relations (in this case two relations are EMP relation and DEPT relation) we follow the following steps:

1. We identify heading of every column as attributes.
2. We basically list all the attributes of both relations, and attach the name of the relation from which the attribute originally came.
3. We need to attach relation name to distinguish DEPT.*deptno* from EMP.*deptno*.
4. We attach relation-name with every attribute.
5. Alternatively we drop the relation-name prefix for the attributes that appear only one in the two scheme.

In the above Figure 5.5 we can see that except one attribute (*deptno*) all attributes are appearing only once.

So according to final point, we can drop relation name prefix for all attribute (those appearing only once) except one attribute *deptno*, which is appearing twice. So to avoid ambiguity, we add relation name prefix with the attribute DEPT.*deptno* and EMP.*deptno*.

We can re-write the header of Figure 5.6 as given below:

DEPT.*deptno*	*dname*	*loc*	*empno*	*ename*	*job*	*sal*	EMP.*deptno*

Figure 5.6: *Header representation*

Similarly, we can also simplify relation scheme r without leading to any ambiguity. For the point of simplification we may re-write relation schema as

(DEPT.deptno, dname, loc, empno, ename, job, sal, EMP.deptno)

Now we will discuss how to write queries using the concept of cartesian product.

Query: Find Details of all Employees for Accounting Department with their Salary.

For above query, consider relation EMP, and we have *ename, sal* but we do not have department name, instead we have *deptno*. The corresponding names of department are given in relation DEPT.

To find out the names of corresponding department numbers, we shall locate out a product of EMP X DEPT. So if we write

$$\sigma_{dname = \text{"ACCOUNTING"}}(DEPT \times EMP)$$

The result is given in Figure 5.7

DEPT.deptno	*dname*	*loc*	*empno*	*ename*	*job*	*sal*	*EMP.deptno*
10	ACCOUNTING	NEW YORK	7782	CLARK	MANAGER	2450	10
10	ACCOUNTING	NEW YORK	7839	KING	PRESIDENT	5000	10
10	ACCOUNTING	NEW YORK	7934	MILLER	CLERK	1300	10

Figure 5.7: *Details of all employees for accounting department*

However, the EMP.*deptno* may contain employees of other departments also. Since the Cartesian product operation associates every tuple of DEPT relation with every tuple of EMP relation.

Now to get the correct answer to above query we shall apply following condition:

DEPT.*deptno* = EMP.*deptno*

We can now write query with the above condition

$$\sigma_{DEPT.deptno = EMP.deptno}(\sigma_{dname = \text{"ACCOUNTING"}}(DEPT \times EMP))$$

Since we want only employees name and salary, so finally we can write

$$\Pi_{ename,salary}(\sigma_{DEPT.deptno = EMP.deptno}(\sigma_{dname = \text{"ACCOUNTING"}}(DEPT \times EMP)))$$

So the result of this expression, which is shown in Figure 5.8, is the correct answer to the above query.

ENAME	SAL
CLARK	2450
KING	5000
MILLER	1300

Figure 5.8: $\Pi_{ename,salary}(\sigma_{DEPT.deptno = EMP.deptno}(\sigma_{dname = \text{"ACCOUNTING"}}(DEPT \times EMP)))$

5.3 OTHER SET OPERATORS

(a) Assignment operator
(b) Join operator
(c) Divide operator

The Assignment operation: This operator is also identified as "*Rename operator*".

In order to eradicate all possible ambiguities we used naming conventions, as we discussed in cartesian product operation, we used naming convention. For example, DEPT.*deptno* or EMP.*empno* in which prefix is table name *(relation name)* which is followed by column name *(attribute name)*.

So, we can write naming convention as *relation-name.attribute-name*.

Another form of probable ambiguity may happen when the similar relation appears more than once in a query.

The symbol used for this operation is Greek letter *Rho*(ρ).

$$\rho_z(E)$$

Here the result of expression *E* is evaluated and it is assigned a name Z. If we want to rename a relation along with their attributes then we can write the expression as

$$\rho_z(a_1, a_2, a_3, ..., a_n)\ (E)$$

The above expression returns the result of expression *E* under the name Z and with the attributes renamed as $a_1, a_2, a_3, ..., a_n$.

To illustrate, consider following query:

Query: Find the Names of all Employees Who are in the Same *deptno* as '*SMITH*'.

Step 1: To find the deptno of SMITH

We can find the deptno of SMITH by writing

$$\Pi_{deptno}(\sigma_{ename=\text{"SMITH"}}\ (EMP))$$

However, to find other employees with same *deptno*, we shall reference the EMP relation for second time.

Therefore, we can write the above expression as:

$$r1 = \rho_d(\Pi_{deptno}(\sigma_{ename=\text{"SMITH"}}\ (EMP)))$$

Step 2: To find the name of other employees of the same department as 'SMITH'

$$\Pi_{ename}(\sigma_{EMP.deptno=d.deptno}(d*EMP))$$

ENAME
SMITH
JONES
SCOTT
ADAMS
FORD

Join operation: The Join operator, indicated by *"X"*, is used to connect data across relations.

There are three types of Join operation:

1. Natural join
2. Theta join
3. Outer join

The join is most vital function in any database language and out of its three version natural join is most useful and important function.

It is often desirable or sometimes it becomes necessary to take Cartesian product of two relations when are to be joined.

Natural-join operation: It is binary operation. It combines certain selections and a cartesian product into one operation. It is denoted by join symbol. The natural join operation forms a cartesian product of its two arguments, performs a selection forcing equality on those attributes that appear in both relation schemes, and remove duplicate attributes.

Theta (θ) join: A general join condition is of the form:

<Condition> AND <Condition> AND. ...AND <Condition>

where each condition is of the form $A_i \theta B_j$, A_i is an attribute of relation X. B_j is an attribute of relation Y. Here A_i and B_j have the same domain. The Greek letter θ (theta) is one of the comparison operators ($=, <, \leq, >, \geq, \neq$). A join operation with such a general join condition is called a *Theta join.* By theta join, tuples whose join attributes are null do not appear in the result.

Outer join: An outer join is a type of equi join that is used to show all data from one table, even if corresponding data is not found in a second table. Outer joins are most commonly used with tables having one-to-many relationship.

Query: Find Employee Name along the Department name of Every Employee

The expression is:

$$\Pi_{emp.ename,dept.dname}\ (\sigma_{EMP.deptno=DEPT.deptno}(DEPT\ *\ EMP))$$

Using Natural Join, the same expression can be written as:

$$\Pi_{emp.ename,dept.dname}\ (DEPT \times EMP)$$

Divide operator: The *Divide* operation, denoted by "/", creates a new relation by selecting the rows in one relation that match every row in another relation. Consider a query to illustrate this operator.

Query: Find all Employees of Department located at 'CHICAGO'.

Again we shall execute this query in two steps:

Step 1: In first step we shall find out *deptno* located at 'CHICAGO'

DEPTNO
30

Figure 5.9: *Deptno for department in 'CHICAGO'*

$$r1 = \Pi_{deptno}(\sigma_{loc=\text{"CHICAGO"}}(DEPT))$$

Step 2: Now find *ename, deptno* pairs

$$r2 = \Pi_{ename,deptno}(EMP)$$

ENAME	DEPTNO
CLARK	10
KING	10
MILLER	10
SMITH	20
ADAMS	20
FORD	20
SCOTT	20
JONES	20
ALLEN	30
BLAKE	30

MARTIN	30
JAMES	30
TURNER	30
WARD	30

Figure 5.10: *ename and deptno of every employee*

To give correct answer to above query we shall divide relation answer rl by r2.

Or we can also write rl/r2 =

ENAME	DEPTNO
ALLEN	30
WARD	30
MARTIN	30
BLAKE	30
TURNER	30
JAMES	30

Figure 5.11: *result of r1/r2*

5.4 SOLVED QUERY EXAMPLES

Considering the database given under, give the relational algebra expression queries for the following problems:

Employee(employee-name, street, city)
Works(employee-name, company-name, salary)
Company(company-name, city)
Managers(employee-name, manager-name)

1. Find the names of all employees who work for "xyz" company.

$$\Pi_{\text{employee-name}}(\sigma_{\text{company-name=“xyz”}}(WORKS))$$

2. Find the names and cities of residence of all employees who work for "xyz" company.

$$\Pi_{\text{employee-name,city}}(\sigma_{\text{company-name= “xyz”}}(EMPLOYEE*WORKS))$$

3. Find the names, street address and cities of residence of all employees who work for "xyz" company and earn more than Rs. 100000 per annum.

$$\Pi_{\text{employee-name,street,city}}(\sigma_{\text{company-name= “xyz”}\wedge\text{salary>100000}}(EMPLOYEE*WORKS))$$

4. Find the names of all employees in the database who live in the same city as the company for which they work.

$$\Pi_{\text{employee-name}}(\sigma_{\text{EMPLOYEE.city=COMPANY.city}}(EMPLOYEE*COMPANY))$$

OR

$$\Pi_{\text{employee-name}}(EMPLOYEE*COMPANY)$$

5. Find the names of all employees who live in the same city and on the same street as do their managers.

$$\Pi_{\text{employee-name}}(EMPLOYEE*MANAGER)$$

6. Find the names of all employees in the database who do not work for "xyz" company.

$$\Pi_{\text{employee-name}}(\sigma_{\text{company-name= "xyz"}}(EMPLOYEE*COMPANY))$$

By using set difference

$$\Pi_{\text{employee-name}}(EMPLOYEE*COMPANY)$$
$$-$$
$$\Pi_{\text{employee-name}}(\sigma_{\text{company-name= "xyz"}}(EMPLOYEE*COMPANY))$$

7. Find the names of all employees who earn more than every employee of "abc" company.

$$r1= \rho_d(\sigma_{\text{company-name="abc"}}(WORKS)$$
$$r2=WORKS-r1$$
$$\Pi_{\text{employee-name}}(\sigma_{\text{r2.salary>d.salary}}(r2*d))$$

8. Find the companies located in every city in which "abc" company is located. Assuming the companies may be located in several cities.

$$\Pi_{\text{employee-name}}(\sigma_{\text{d.city=company.city}\wedge\text{d.company-name="abc"}}(COMPANY*\rho_d(COMPANY))$$

REVIEW QUESTIONS

1. Consider the following relation:

   DEPT (#deptno, dname, loc)

   EMP (#empno, ename, address, job, hiredate, deptno)

   SALARY (#empno, basic, hra, ta, da, t_sal)

   Write the queries in terms of relational algebra:

   (a) Get the name of all the employees.

   (b) Get the name of all those employees, who are Managers.

   (c) Get all the Managers who are in department number 10.

   (d) Get all the employees from SALES department.

   (e) Give the complete break up salary of employee 'SCOTT'.

   (f) Display the name of the employee, his department name along with his total salary.

   (g) Find the employees from SALES department who are getting the more salary than the salary of SMITH from RESEARCH department.

CHAPTER 6

Relational Calculus

In this chapter, you will learn

6.0 INTRODUCTION

Relational calculus is the combined term for **tuple calculus** and **domain calculus.** The queries in the relational algebra are procedural. The relational database management system frees the user from the details of how to acquire information from the database. The users need only to specify what information they need and the RDBMS will make a decision how to get it.

In relational calculus, a query is expressed as a formula consisting of a number of variables and an expression involving these variables. The formula describes the properties of the relation to be obtained. There is no mechanism to specify how the formula should be evaluated. It is up to the RDBMS to transform these non-procedural queries into equivalent, efficient procedure queries. In relational tuple calculus, the variables represent the tuples from specified domains. In domain calculus the variables represent the values drawn from specified domains.

Relational calculus is a formal query language where the queries are expressed as variables and formulas on these variables. Such formulas specify the properties of the required result relation without specifying the method of evaluating it. Thus a relational calculus expression specifies what is to be retrieved rather than how to retrieve it. Therefore relational calculus is considered to be a non-procedural language. This is where relational calculus differs from relational algebra, which is a procedural language, where we must write a sequence of operations to specify a retrieval requests.

It is possible to state in relational calculus any retrieval that can be specified in the relational algebra and vice versa. In other words the expressive powers of both the languages are identical. This has led to the development of the concept of a relationally complete language. A relational query language is considered relationally complete, if we can express any query that can be expressed in relational calculus in that query language.

Relational completeness is an important basis for comparing the expressive power of query languages. However, some of the most common data manipulation operations that are needed in commercial query language cannot be performed with the basic relational algebraic operations of relational calculus formulas. These include aggregate functions (like SUM, COUNT, AVERAGE, MIN, MAX etc.), recursive relations, etc. Thus most commercial relational query languages are relationally complete but have more expressive power than relational algebra or relational calculus because they include additional operations such as aggregate functions, grouping and ordering.

6.1 TUPLE RELATIONAL CALCULUS

The tuple relational calculus is based on specifying a number of **tuple variables.** Each such tuple variable in general ranges over a particular database relation. This means that the variable may take any individual tuple from that relation as its value. A simple tuple relational calculus expression of the form {t | COND(t)}, where 't' is a tuple variable and COND(t) is a conditional expression involving 't'. The result of such a query is a relation that contains all the tuples (rows) that satisfy COND(t).

For example, the relational calculus query {t | BOOK(t) **and** t.PRICE>150} will get you all the books whose price is greater than 150. In the above example, the condition 'BOOK(t)' specifies that the range relation of the tuple variable 't' is BOOK. Each BOOK tuple 't' that satisfies the condition 't.PRICE>150' will be retrieved. Note that 't.PRICE' references the attribute PRICE of the tuple variable 't'.

The query {t | BOOK(t) **and** t.PRICE>150} retrieves all attribute values for each selected BOOK tuple. To retrieve only some of the attributes (say TITLE, AUTHOR and PRICE) we can modify the query as follows;

{t.TITLE, t.AUTHOR, t.PRICE | BOOK(t) **and** t.PRICE>150)

Thus in a tuple calculus expression we need to specify the following information:

- **For each tuple variable 't', the range relation 'R' of 't':** This value is specified a condition of the form R(t).
- **A condition to select the required tuples from the relation:** Tuple variables range over their respective range relations and the condition is evaluated for every possible combination of tuples to identify the selected combinations for which the condition evaluates to TRUE.
- **A set of attributes to be retrieved. This set is called the requested attributes:** The values of these attributes are retrieved for each selected combination of tuples. If the requested attribute list is not specified, then all the attributes of the selected tuples are retrieved.

Thus to retrieve the particulars of all books (Title and Author name) which were published 'CyberTech' and whose price is greater than 150 we will write the query as follows:

{t.TITLE, t.AUTHOR | BOOK(t) **and** t.PUBLISHER='CyberTech' **and** t.PRICE>150}

Expressions and formulas: A general expression of the tuple relational calculus is of the following form:

$$\{t_1.A_1, t_2.A_2, \ldots t_n.A_n \mid COND(t_1, t_2 \ldots. t_n, t_{n+1}, t_{n+2}, \ldots t_{n+m})\}$$

where $t_1, t_2, \ldots t_n, t_{n+1}, t_{n+2}, \ldots t_{n+m}$ are tuple variables, each A_i is an attribute of the relation on which t_i ranges and COND is a condition or formula of the tuple relational calculus. A formula is made up of predicate calculus atoms that can be one of the following:

1. An atom of the form $R(t_i)$, where R is a relation and t_i is a tuple variable. This atom identifies the range of the tuple variable t_i as the relation whose name is R.
2. An atom of the form t_i.A <comparison operator>t_j.B, where t_i and t_j are tuple variables and the <comparison operator> is any one of the following: $=, \neq, <, \leq, >$ or $\geq$; A is an attribute of the relation on which t_i ranges and B is an attribute of the relation on which t_j ranges.

3. An atom of the form t_i.A <comparison operator> c or c <comparison operator> t_j. B, where t_i and t_j are tuple variables and the <comparison operator> is any one of the following: $=, \neq, <, \leq, >$ or $\geq$; A is an attribute of the relation on which t_i ranges, B is an attribute of the relation on which t_j ranges and 'c' is a constant value.

Each of the preceding atoms evaluates to either TRUE or FALSE for a specific combination of tuples and this is called the **truth-value** of an atom. In general, a tuple variable ranges over all possible tuples in the 'universe'. For atoms of *type 1*, if the tuple variable is assigned to a tuple that is a member of the specified relation R, the atom is TRUE; otherwise, it is FALSE. In atoms of *types 2* and *3*, if the tuple variables are assigned to tuples such that the values of the specified attributes of the tuples satisfy the condition, then the atom is TRUE.

A **formula or condition** consists of one or more atoms connected via the logical operators **and, or** and **not.** A formula is defined as follows:

1. Every atom is a formula.
2. If F_1 and F_2 are formulas, so are (F_1 **and** F_2), (F_1 **or** F_2), **not**(F_1) and **not**(F_2).
   - (F_1 **and** F_2) is TRUE if both F_1 and F_2 are TRUE otherwise it is FALSE.
   - (F_1 **or** F_2) is FALSE if both F_1 and F_2 are FALSE, otherwise it is TRUE.
   - **not**(F_1) is TRUE if F_1 is FALSE and it is FALSE if F_1 is TRUE.
   - **not**(F_2) is TRUE if F_2 is FALSE and it is FALSE if F_2 is TRUE.

Existential and universal quantifiers: Two special symbols called quantifiers can appear in formulas—Universal quantifier($\forall$) and existential quantifier ($\exists$). Truth-values for formulas with quantifiers are described below:

- If F is a formula, so is ($\exists$ t)(F), where 't' is a tuple variable. The formula ($\exists$ t)(F) is TRUE if the formula F evaluates to TRUE for some (at least one) tuples assigned to free occurrences of 't' in F; otherwise ($\exists$ t)(F) is FALSE.
- If F is a formula, so is ($\forall$t)(F), where 't' is a tuple variable. The formula ($\forall$t)(F) is TRUE if the formula F evaluates to TRUE for every tuple assigned to free occurrences of 't' in F; otherwise, ($\forall$t)(F) is FALSE.

The ($\exists$) quantifier is called an *existential quantifier* because a formula ($\exists$ t)(F) is true if there exists some tuple that makes 'F' TRUE. For the universal quantifier ($\forall$t)(F) is TRUE if every possible tuple that can be assigned to free occurrences of 't' in F is substituted for 't' and F is TRUE in every such substitution. It is called the *universal* or *'for all'* quantifier because every tuple in the *'universe'* of tuples must make F TRUE to make the quantified formula TRUE.

6.2 SOLVED TUPLE RELATIONAL CALCULUS EXAMPLES

Considering the database given under, give the tuple relational calculus expression queries for the following problems:

Employee(employee-name, street, city)
Works(employee-name, company-name, salary)
Company(company-name, city)
Managers(employee-name, manager-name)

1. **Find the names of all employees who work for "xyz" company.**

   {t | ∃ S ε Works (t [company-name] = s[company-name] = "xyz")}

2. **Find the names and cities of residence of all employees who work for "xyz" company.**

   {t | ∃ U ε Employee (U [employee-name] = t [employee-name] Λ ∃ S ε Works (S[employee-name] = U [employee-name] Λ S[company-name]= "xyz")}

3. **Find the names, street address and cities of residence of all employees who work for "xyz" company and earn more than Rs. 100000 per annum.**

   {t | Λ ∃ U ε Employee Λ ∃ S ε Works (S[company-name] = "xyz" Λ S[salary]=100000)}

4. **Find the names of all employees in the database who live in the same city as the company for which they work.**

   {t | ∃ Uε Employee (U [employee-name] = t [employee-name] Λ ∃ S ε Company [city]=U[city])}

5. **Find the names of all employees who live in the same city and on the same street as do their managers.**

   {t | ∃ Uε Employee (U [street] = t[street] Λ U[city]=t[city]) Λ ∃ S ε Managers (S[manager-name] = U [employee-name])}

6. **Find the names of all employees in the database who do not work for "xyz" company.**

   {t | ∃ Uε Employee Λ ∃ S ε Works (S[company] ≠ "xyz")}

7. **Find the names of all employees who earn more than every employee of "abc" company.**

   {t | ∃ Uε Employee (U [employee-name] = t [employee-name]) Λ ∃ S ε Works (t[salary] > S[salary] ΛS[company-name]= "abc")}

8. **Find the companies located in every city in which "abc" company is located. Assuming the companies may be located in several cities.**

   {t | ∃ Uε Company (U [city] = t[city] Λ U [company-name]= "abc")}

6.3 DOMAIN RELATIONAL CALCULUS

There is another type of relational calculus called domain relational calculus or domain calculus. QBE or Query-by-Example is a query language related to domain relational calculus. QBE was developed almost concurrently with SQL by M. M. Zloof IBM Research Laboratory, Yorktown Heights. The formal specification of the domain calculus was proposed after the development of the QBE system. The domain calculus differs from the tuple calculus in the type of variables used in formulas. In domain calculus the variables range over single values from domains of attributes rather than ranging over tuples. To form a relation of degree '*n*' for a query result, we must have '*n*' of these domain variables—one for each attribute. An expression of the domain calculus is of the following form:

$$\{x_1, x_2, \ldots\ldots\ldots x_n \mid \text{COND}(x_1, x_2 \ldots x_n, x_{n+1}, x_{n+2} \ldots x_{n+m})\}$$

In the above expression $x_1, x_2, \ldots, x_n, x_{n+1}, x_{n+2}, \ldots, x_{n+m}$ are domain variables that range over domains of attributes and COND is a condition or formula of the domain relational calculus, a formula is made up of atoms. The atoms of a formula can be one of the following:

1. An atom of the form $R(x_1, x_2, \ldots, x_j)$, where R is the name of the relation of degree 'j' and each x_i, where $1 \leq i \leq j$, is a domain variable. This atom states that a list of values of $<x_1, x_{-2}, \ldots, x_j>$ must be a tuple in the relation named R, where x_i, is the value of the ith attribute value of the tuple. To make the domain calculus expression more readable we omit the commas and write $R(x_1\ x_2\ x_3)$ instead of writing $R(x_1,x_2,x_3)$.
2. An atom of the form **x_i<comparison operator>x_j**, where x_i and x_j are domain variables and < comparison operator > is any one of the following: $=, \neq, <, \leq, >$ or $\geq$.
3. An atom of the form **x_i<comparison operator>c** or **c <comparison operator > x_j**, where x_i and x_j are domain variables, c is a constant value and < comparison operator > is any one of the following: $=, \neq, <, \leq, >$ or $\geq$.

Atoms evaluate to either TRUE or FALSE for a specific set of values called the **truth-values** of the atoms. In case 1, if the domain variables are assigned values corresponding to a tuple of the specified relation R, then the atom is TRUE. In cases 2 and 3, if the domain variables are assigned values that satisfy the condition, then the atom is TRUE.

6.4 SOLVED DOMAIN RELATIONAL CALCULUS EXAMPLES

Considering the database given under, give the domain relational calculus expression queries for the following problems:

Employee(employee-name, street, city)
Works(employee-name, company-name, salary)
Company(company-name, city)
Managers(employee-name, manager-name)

1. **Find the names of all employees who work for "xyz" company.**

   {<e>|∀ e(<e,s,c> ε Employee)Λ∃ e,cn(<e,cn,sal> ε Works Λ cn="xyz")}

2. **Find the names and cities of residence of all employees who work for "xyz" company.**

   {<e,c>|∀ e(<e,s,c> ε Employee)Λ∃ e,cn(<e,cn,sal> ε Works Λ cn= "xyz")}

3. **Find the names, street address and cities of residence of all employees who work for "xyz" company and earn more than Rs. 100000 per annum.**

   {<e,s,c>|∀ e(<e,s,c> ε Employee)Λ∃ e,cn(<e,cn,sal> ε Works Λ cn="xyz" Λ sal>1000000)}

4. **Find the names of all employees in the database who live in the same city as the company for which they work.**

   {<e>|∀ e(<e,s,c>ε Employee)Λ∃ e,cn(<e,cn,sal>ε Works Λ∃ b1(<cn,b1> ε Company Λ (b1=c))}

5. **Find the names of all employees who live in the same city and on the same street as do their managers.**

   {<e>|∀ e(<e,s,c>ε Employee)Λ∃ e,cn(<e,cn,sal>ε Works Λ∃ b1(<cn,b1> ε Company Λ (b1=c))}

6. Find the names of all employees in the database who do not work for "xyz" company.

{<e>|∀ e(<e,s,c> ε Employee)Λ∃ b1,b2(<b1,b2> ε Managers Λ (b1=b2))}

7. Find the names of all employees who earn more than every employee of "abc" company.

{<e>|∀ e(<e,s,c> ε Employee) Λ∃ b1,b2(<e,cn,b1> ε Works Λ e,cn,b1ε Works Λ b1>b2 (<e,cn,b2> ε Works Λ (cn1="abc"))}

8. Find the companies located in every city in which "abc" company is located. Assuming the companies may be located in several cities.

{<cn>| cn(<cn,c> ª Employee) Λb1,b2(<b1,c> ª Company Λ cn,b2 (<cn,b2> ª Company Λ (cn="abc") Λ(b2=c))}

REVIEW QUESTIONS

1. Consider the following relations:

   DEPT (#deptno, dname, loc)

   EMP (#empno, ename, address, job, hiredate, deptno)

   SALARY (#empno, basic, hra, ta, da, t_sal)

   Write the queries in terms of tuple calculus and domain calculus:

   (a) Get the name of all the employees.

   (b) Get the name of all those employees, who are Managers.

   (c) Get all the Managers who are in department number 10.

   (d) Get all the employees from SALES department.

   (e) Give the complete break up salary of employee 'SCOTT'.

   (f) Display the name of the employee, his department name along with his total salary.

   (g) Find the employees from SALES department who are getting the more salary than the salary of SMITH from RESEARCH department.

CHAPTER 7

Structured Query Language

In this chapter, you will learn

7.0 INTRODUCTION

- Conceived in the mid-1970s as a database language for the then new relational model, SQL was first standardized in 1986 (SQL-86) and was modestly enhanced in 1989 (SQL-89). In 1992, work was completed on a significantly revised version of the SQL standard (SQL-92).
- SQL is a *data sub-language* with respect to the primary programming languages, or host language.
- SQL is heavily oriented toward a nonprocedural model, whereas C, COBOL, ADA, and most languages with which you are familiar tend to be procedural in nature.
- The original version of SQL was developed at IBM's San Jose Research Laboratory (now the Almaden Research Center). This language, originally called Sequel, was implemented as part of the System R project in the early 1970s. The Sequel language has evolved since then, and its name has changed to SQL (Structured Query Language).
- In 1986, the American National Standards Institute (ANSI) published an SQL standard. IBM has published its own corporate SQL standard, the Systems Application Architecture Database Interface (SAA-SQL).
- SQL has clearly established itself as *the* standard relational database language.
- SQL is based on the relational model, but it is not a perfect implementation of that model.
- SQL's basic data object is the table and not the relation. A table is equivalent to a *multi-set*, which is defined to be set-like, but with duplicates permitted.

7.1 PARTS OF SQL LANGUAGE

SQL language has several parts, which are explained as follows:

1. Data definition language (DDL): The SQL DDL provides commands for defining relation schemes, deleting relations, creating indices, and modifying relation schemes.

2. Interactive data manipulation language (DML): The SQL DML includes a query language based on both the relational algebra and the tuple relational calculus. It includes also commands to insert, delete, and modify tuples in the database.

3. Embedded data manipulation language: The embedded form of SQL is designed for use within general-purpose programming languages such as PL/1, Cobol, Pascal, Fortran, and C.

4. View definition: The SQL DDL includes commands for defining views.

5. Authorization: The SQL DDL includes commands for specifying access rights to relations and views.

6. Integrity: The original System R Sequel language includes commands for specifying complex integrity constraints. Newer versions of SQL, including the ANSI standard, provide only a limited form of integrity checking. Future products and standards are likely to include enhanced features for integrity checking.

7. Transaction control: SQL includes commands for specifying the beginning and ending of transactions.

7.2 HOW TO START ORACLE SQL

Step 1:

tiger

scott

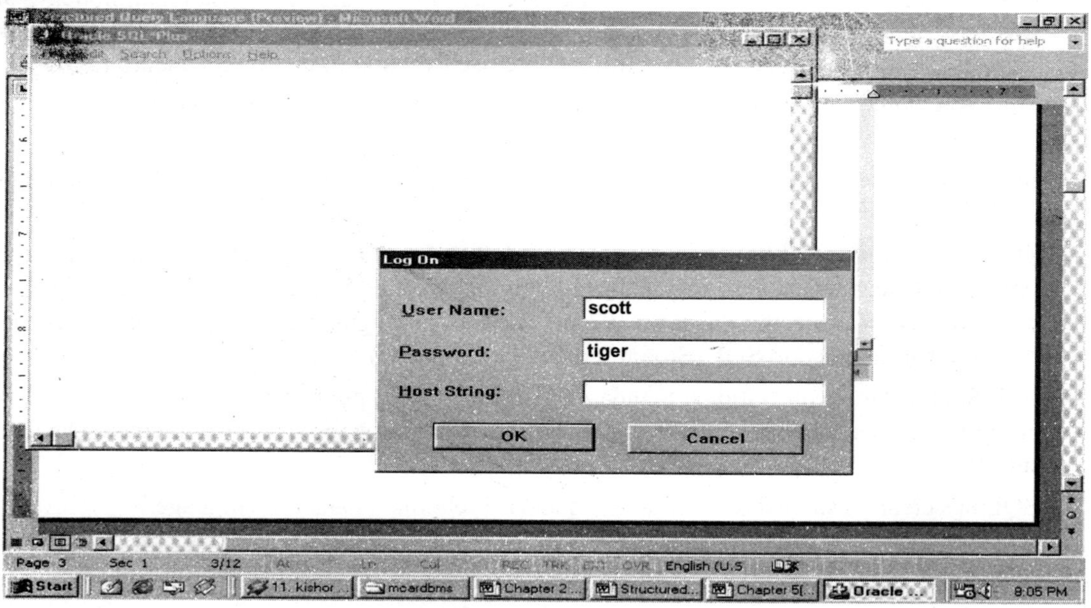

Then press OK Button on Log on Window

Step 2:

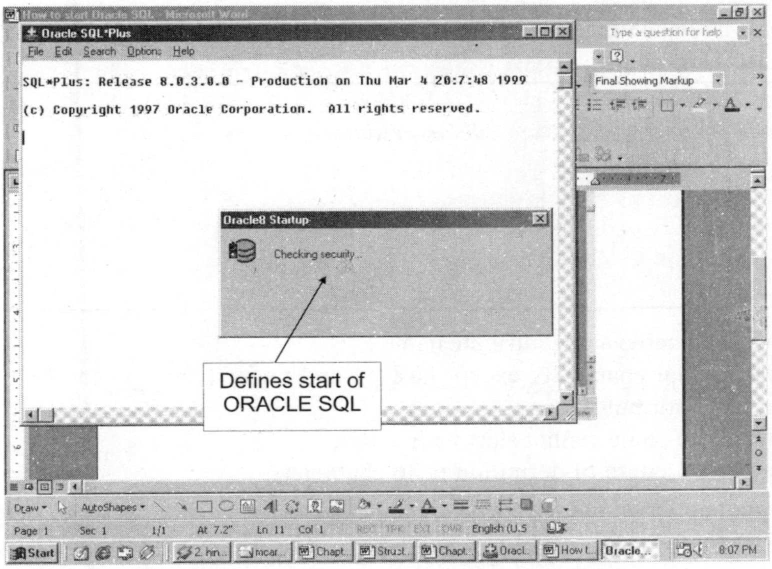

Setp 3:

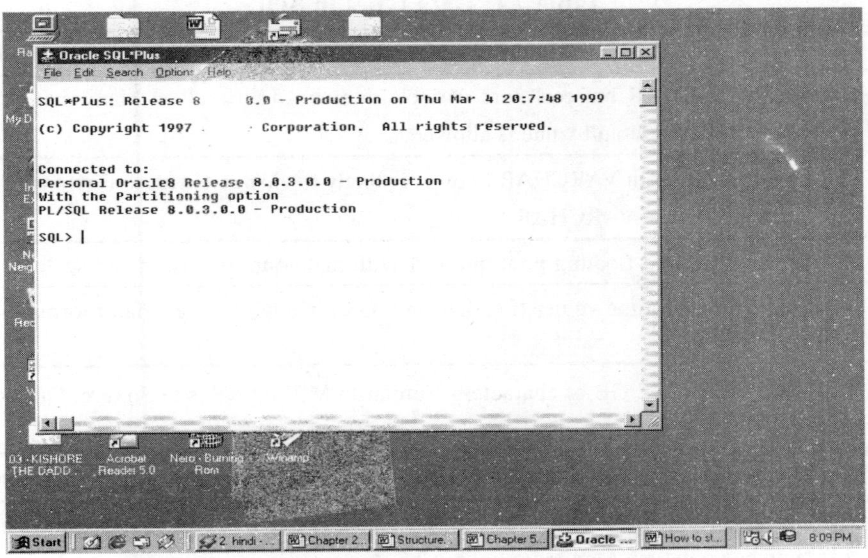

7.3 DATA DEFINITION LANGUAGE

The Data Definition Language is used to create object, alter the structure of an object and also to drop the object created. The Data Definition Language can be classified into four categories:

- Create table command
- Alter table command

- Drop table command
- Truncate table command

Syntax for Create Command:

```
create table <table_name>(
<attribute_name>                datatype(datasize),
:
:
:
:
);
```

Rules to define the table name/attribute name:

(1) No other special characters except hash(#) and underscore(_) can be used to define the name of table/attribute.

(2) Table/Attribute name cannot start with a digit.

(3) The maximum length of definition is 36 characters.

The data types supported by SQL depend on the particular DBMS package. Here we will take the example of ORACLE. The main data types available in Oracle are NUMBER, CHAR, VARCHAR2, DATE, and RAW etc. The brief overview of each data type is given in the following table (Table 7.1):

Table 7.1: Data types in SQL

Char	To store string type of data of fixed length. Maximum up to 2000 characters. Default is 1.
Varchar2	Similar to CHAR but can store variable number of characters. Maximum length is 4000 characters. No default value is allowed.
Varchar	Synonymous with VARCHAR2 however likely to change in future versions of Oracle. It is suggested to use VARCHAR2.
Number	Stores fixed and floating point number with maximum precision and scale in 38 digits.
Date	Stores point-in-time values (i.e. data and time) in a table. The default format is DD-MON-YY.
Long	Can store up to 2 GB of characters. Similar to MEMO fields in FoxPro. Only one long per table is allowed.
Raw	Used to store binary data such as graphics sound etc. Maximum width is 2000 bytes.
Long Raw	Contains raw binary data otherwise the same as LONG column. The values entered must be in hex notation. Maximum limit is 2 GB.
CLOB	Character Large Objects. Max. Limit in 4 GB.
NCLOB	National Language Support character Large Objects
BFILE	External Binary File, Maximum Limit is 4 GB.

An example of CREATE TABLE command is given below, which creates the EMP table.

```
CREATE TABLE emp
(empno NUMBER(4), ename VARCHAR2 (25), sal NUMBER (7,2),
hiredate DATE, job VARCHAR2 (15), deptno NUMBER(2));
```

The table name is "emp" and it has six attributes, fields, or columns. Every field has a data type and a width specified along with data type. Data type restricts the column to accept only specified type of data. For example, in empno column, we can store only number type of data, it will not accept any string or date type data. Width specifies the maximum limit of the individual data. For example, *ename* has the width 25, which means that any name cannot be longer than 25 characters (including blank spaces).

DATA constraints

Besides the column name, data type and column width, there are other parameters i.e. data constraints that can be specified at the table creation time. These constraints can associate to any column by the DBA as flags. Whenever a user attempts to load a column with data, the data will be checked automatically against these data constraints. If the data being loaded fails any of the data constraint, the data will not be loaded into the column and the entire record is rejected with an error message. The major data constraints available in most of the RDBMS packages are given below (Table 7.2):

Table 7.2: Data Constraints in SQL

Constraint	Description
NOT NULL	If a column is defined as NOT NULL, then it becomes a mandatory column i.e. the user has to enter the data into it. It can take duplicate values if it is not a unique column but cannot take NULLs.
UNIQUE	The purpose of unique key is to ensure that the information in that column for each record is unique as with the students Roll number or employee identification number.
CHECK	The CHECK constraint is used to enforce integrity rules that can be evaluated based on a logical expression. For example, we want that no employee should be entered in our database that is older than 60 years or the minimum salary in our organization is Rs. 3000, these types of business rules can be imposed through CHECK constraint.
PRIMARY KEY	A primary key is a one or more column used to uniquely identify each row in the table. These values should never be changed and should never be NULL. Through this key. rows in the table are individually identified. NULLs are not allowed in the primary key column. The important point about primary key is that only one primary key per table is allowed. The reason may be that only function a primary key performs is to uniquely identify the row and thus identifier as good as another primary key has no other inherent meaning.
FOREIGN KEY	Foreign key represents the relationships between tables. Foreign key ensures the Referential Integrity rule. A foreign key is a column or a group of columns whose values are derived from the primary key of the same or some other table. It can also be used elsewhere e.g. to prevent deletion of a department in DEPT table if employee exist it is with the same department in EMP table. A foreign key must have a corresponding primary key value in the primary key table to have a meaning. A foreign key value can be left null. It rejects an INSERT or UPDATE of a value,

	if a corresponding value does not currently exist in the primary key table. It also rejects DELETE from the primary table if corresponding records exist in foreign key table.
DEFAULT	We can assign a default value to the columns. Now when a row is inserted in the table then all the corresponding columns will take their values as specified. If some column is not having a value then in place of NULL it will store the default value.

Now the syntax for these constraints is given in the examples given below:

```
CREATE TABLE dept(
        (deptno NUMBER(2) PRIMARY KEY,
         dname VARCHAR2(10) NOT NULL,
         loc VARCHAR2(25) CHECK (loc in ('Dehradun', 'Lucknow', 'Allahabad')));
```

In the above example, 'DEPT' table has three fields namely *deptno, dname,* and *loc*. The column *deptno* will accept the number type of data with maximum width of 2. It has a constraint PRIMARY KEY, means that we have to enter the unique *deptno* for every valid department which is to be stored in the database. The *dname* column is not null means that every new department will be having a valid name. We cannot leave this column as NULL. The last column, *loc* is of string type with having a CHECK constraint, which allows only three locations namely 'Dehradun', 'Lucknow', and 'Allahabad'. Any value other than these three will not be accepted.

Example for the foreign key constraint is given as:

```
CREATE TABLE tmp
(empno NUMBER (4) PRIMARYKEY
ename VARCHAR2 (20)
sal NUMBER (7,2),
hiredate DATE,
job VARCHAR2 (15)
deptno NUMBER (2) REFERENCES dept(deptno)):
```

In this case, only new thing is the foreign key constraint on the *deptno* column. For this constraint, the master table (DEPT) must be created first and in that attribute, *deptno* should be a primary key column.

To see the structure of the already created table, we use the DESC command in ORACLE.

DESC emp;

Drop command

The DROP command is used to drop an object permanently.

```
DROP TABLE <object_name>;
```

For example, to drop emp table, the syntax is

```
DROP TABLE emp;
```

Alter command

To change the definition of a table, we have to use the ALTER TABLE command. It has three clauses ADD, MODIFY and DROP, which are used to

- Add a new column
- Add a new constraint
- Modify a column
- Modify a constraint
- Drop a column
- Drop a constraint.

The general syntax for ALTER command is as follows:

```
ALTER TABLE <table_name> {ADD | MODIFY | DROP}(column specifications);
```

The ADD clause: The ADD clause is used to add a column and/or constraints to an existing table. To add a column say commission to emp table, the syntax will be as follows

```
ALTER TABLE emp ADD( commission NUMBER (7,2));
```

This will add a column, commission to the emp table, which will accept NUMBER type of data and the maximum width for that data is (7,2). If this table is having some existing data corresponding to other columns then it will take NULL for commission column corresponding to those records. If we are adding a NOT NULL or PRIMARY KEY constraint along with the column description and the table is having some data then command will not be executed successfully and will give an error message. The following syntax will be executed only in that case if table is empty.

```
ALTER TABLE emp ADD (commission NUMBER(7, 2) NOT NULL);
```

For this situation, first of all add the column without specifying NOT NULL or Primary Key clause. Then fill the column with values corresponding to existing records by using UPDATE command and then modify the column to NOT NULL or Primary Key constraint.

Now suppose we want to add a constraint, say commission should not be greater than the salary column then syntax will be:

```
ALTER TABLE emp ADD CONSTRAINT c1 CHECK(conmission<sal);
```

Here it will check the already existing data in commission and sal column. If for any record, the above said rule violates then this constraint will not be applicable and the above syntax will give an error. Similarly, if we want to add a primary key constraint to a column then that column must not have any NULL value corresponding to existing records.

MODIFY clause: This clause is used to modify the column specifications and the constraints. In case of constraints, only possibilities are to modify a NULL to NOT NULL and NOT NULL to NULL. Other constraints, which are to be modified, should be first deleted and then recreating with the modification.

Suppose we want to increase the width of a column, syntax is

```
ALTER TABLE emp MODIFY (commission NUMBER (8,2))
```

It will increase the width of commission column from NUMBER(7,2) to NUMBER(8,2).

However, there is one restriction for decreasing the width of a column or changing the data type of the column and that is, the column must not contain any data. If the column is having some data corresponding to existing records then we cannot decrease the size or change the data type. But we can increase or decrease the number of decimal places in a NUMBER column at any time.

For modification in the constraint, the syntax is

```
ALTER TABLE emp MODIFY (commission NUMBER (8,2) NOT NULL);
```

Now commission column will become NOT NULL column (again it must not contain any NULL value).

DROP clause: In Oracle 8i, we can remove a column from table directly by using the DROP clause. For example:

```
ALTER TABLE emp DROP COLUMN commission;
```

This will drop the commission column from the table along with the data. But in Oracle8 or prior versions, the dropping of column is not so easy. In that case, we use some indirect way. First a new table has to be created with the help of old one, having the same column and data except that column which we want to drop.

Then we drop the old table and rename the new table with same name as the old one was having. Lastly we impose all the constraints to the new table again.

For example, suppose we want to drop the column commission from emp table. Then the sequence of steps will be

```
CREATE TABLE emp1 AS SELECT empno, ename, sal, hiredate, deptno FROM emp;
```

It will create a new table with name emp1, having all the fields of emp table, except commission.

```
DROP TABLE emp;
```

It will drop the emp table permanently.

```
RENAME emp1 TO emp;
```

It will rename the emp1 table to emp again. Now we can impose all the constraints again which emp table was having by using the ALTER TABLE commands.

To drop a constraint, the different syntaxes are

```
ALTER TABLE emp DROP CONSTRAINT c1;
ALTER TABLE emp DROP PRIMARY KEY;
ALTER TABLE emp DROP PRIMARY KEY CASCADE;
```

The last command will drop all the dependencies of the Primary Key (i.e. the Foreign Key constraints in different table, which are based on this Primary Key) and then will drop this Primary key in a single step.

Truncate command

Using truncate command, structure of table remains, but, the data stored in the table is lost. Consider the example given below

```
TRUNCATE TABLE emp;
```

7.4 DATA MANIPULATION COMMANDS

Data Manipulation Commands are the most frequently used SQL commands, and they are as follows.

(i) Insert (ii) Select (iii) Update (iv) Delete

Let us discuss about these commands in detail.

(i) Insert command: The Insert command is used to add one or more rows to a table. While using this command the values are separated by commas and the data types char and date are enclosed in apostrophes. The values must be entered in the same order as they are defined in the table.

Syntax:

```
insert into <table_name> values (a list of data values);
```

The following example illustrates the insert command.

Example:

SQL>insert into emp values (7800, 'RIKTESH', 'MANAGER', 7788, '01-JAN-01, 10000, 5000, 10);

1 row created.

The following example illustrates the concept of inserting more than one record using a single insert command.

Example:

SQL> insert into emp values (&empno, '&ename', '&job', &mgr, '&hiredate', &sal, &comm, &deptno);

Enter value for empno : 7890

Enter value for ename : rajiv

Enter value for job : manager

Enter value for mgr : 7788

Enter value for hiredate : 01-jan-89

Enter value for sal : 10000

Enter value for comm : 0

Enter value for deptno : 10

Old 1 : insert into emp values (&empno, '&ename', '&job', '&mgr,' &hiredate', &sal, &comm, &deptno)

New 2 : insert into emp values (7890, 'rajiv', 'manager', 7788, '01-jan-89', 10000, 0, 10)
1 row created.

If a user wants to skip any one of the fields then he can enter Null against that column's value.

Note:

- To insert Null values in the field, instead of entering Null we can list only the columns and values that we want to enter. The syntax follows:

Syntax:

```
insert into table_name(col_names) values (list of values );
```

Inserting date values

The following example introduces a new function called ***to_date*** function to insert date values other than the standard format for date.

Example:

```
SQL >  Insert into emp values (7812, 'RAJIV)
  2    'MANAGER', 7788, to_date ('14/02/88 09:30', 'dd/mm/yy hh:mi'),
  3    10000, 500,10);
```

1. Row Created

We know that the standard format for the date datatype is "DD-MON-YY". In the table EMP, for column *hiredate*, when the user enters a date with a format say "MM/DD/YY" then it can be converted to the standard data format with the help of the to_date function.

Date formatting function to_date consists of two arguments, the first argument specifies the char value that contains the date and time, and the second one specifies the format according to which date and time has to be displayed. SQL*Plus interprets char value according to the format, converts it to the standard date value and then inserts it into the table.

(ii) Select command: To perform a query we use the select command. The query is a request for infor- mation. It is the most common database operation used. The syntax for select command is given below:

```
Select column_name ......from table_name... ;
```

The following example selects all the columns from the table EMP.

Example:

EMP NO	ENAME	JOB	MGR	HIREDATE	SAL	COMM	DEPTNO
7369	SMITH	CLERK	7902	17-DEC-80	800		20
7499	ALLEN	SALESMAN	7698	20-FEB-81	1600	300	30
7521	WARD	SALESMAN	7698	22-FEB-81	1250	500	30
7566	JONES	MANAGER	7839	02-APR-81	2975		20
7654	MARTIN	SALESMAN	7698	28-SEP-81	1250	1400	30
7698	BLAKE	MANAGER	7839	01-MAY-81	2850		30
7782	CLARK	MANAGER	7839	09-JUN-81	2450		10
7788	SCOTT	ANALYST	7566	19-APR-87	3000		20
7839	KING	PRESIDENT		17-NOV-81	5000	0	10
7844	TURNER	SALESMAN	7698	08-SEP-81	1500		30
7876	ADAMS	CLERK	7788	23-MAY-87	1100		20

7900	JAMES	CLERK	7698	03-DEC-81	950		30
7902	FORD	ANALYST	7566	03-DEC-81	3000		20
7934	MILLER	CLERK	7782	23-JAN-82	1300		10
7800	RIKTESH	MANAGER	7788	01-JAN-01	10000	5000	10
7890	rajiv	manager	7788	01-JAN-89	10000	0	10
7812	RAJIV	MANAGER	7788	14-FEB-88	10000	500	10

17 rows seelcted.

We can display either all the columns in a table or only specific columns from the table. For example, if we want only columns *empno, ename* and *job* from order table, then, we include only those columns in the select statement. The order of column names in the select command specifies the order in which they should be displayed.

Example:

```
SQL > select empno, ename, job from emp;
```

EMPNO	ENAME	JOB
7369	SMITH	CLERK
7499	ALLEN	SALESMAN
7521	WARD	SALESMAN
7566	JONES	MANAGER
7654	MARTIN	SALESMAN
7698	BLAKE	MANAGER
7782	CLARK	MANAGER
7788	SCOTT	ANALYST
7839	KING	PRESIDENT
7844	TURNER	SALESMAN
7876	ADAMS	CLERK
7900	JAMES	CLERK
7902	FORD	ANALYST
7934	MILLER	CLERK
7800	RIKTESH	MANAGER
7890	rajiv	manager
7812	RAJIV	MANAGER

17 rows selected.

The above example displays *empno* first, followed by *ename* and *job.*

Selecting distinct rows

As we know how to select rows or specific columns from a table, let us go about discussing how to prevent the selection of duplicate rows. To prevent the selection of duplicate rows, we include "distinct clause" in the select command. The following example would eliminate duplicate values present in *"job"* column of the EMP table.

Example

```
SQL> select distinct (job) from emp;
JOB
---------
ANALYST
CLERK
MANAGER
PRESIDENT
SALESMAN
manager
```

Select command with "where" clause

To select specific rows from a table we include a "where" clause in the select command. It can appear only after the "from" clause. We can retrieve only the rows which satisfy the "where" condition. To arrange the displayed rows according to some pre-defined order we can use the "order by" clause. It is also used to arrange rows in descending or ascending order. The "order by" clause can also be used to arrange multiple columns. The syntax for the select command along with the "where" clause is given below:

select columns.. from table where conditions [order by];

Example:

SQL > select * from emp order by deptno;

EMPNO	ENAME	JOB	MGR	HIREDATE	SAL	COMM	DEPTNO
7782	CLARK	MANAGER	7839	09-JUN-81	2450		10
7839	KING	PRESIDENT		17-NOV-81	5000		10
7800	RIKTESH	MANAGER	7788	01-JAN-01	10000	5000	10
7934	MILLER	CLERK	7782	23-JAN-82	1300		10
7890	rajiv	manager	7788	01-JAN-89	10000	0	10
7812	RAJIV	MANAGER	7788	14 FEB-88	10000	500	10
7369	SMITH	CLERK	7902	17-DEC-80	800		20
7876	ADAMS	CLERK	7788	23-MAY-87	1100		20
7902	FORD	ANALYST	7566	03-DEC-81	3000		20
7788	SCOTT	ANALYST	7566	19-APR-87	3000		20
7566	JONES	MANAGER	7839	02-APR-81	2975		20
7499	ALLEN	SALESMAN	7698	20-FEB-81	1600	300	30
7698	BLAKE	MANAGER	7839	01-MAY-81	2850		30
7654	MARTIN	SALESMAN	7698	28-SEP-81	1250	1400	30
7900	JAMES	CLERK	7698	03-DEC-81	950		30
7844	TURNER	SALESMAN	7698	08-SEP-81	1500	0	30
7521	WARD	SALESMAN	7698	22-FEB-81	1250	0	30

17 rows selected.

The above "where" clause can also use a *character* or *date* value. In such a case, they should be enclosed within parenthesis.

Notes:

- The "order by" clause should be the last clause in a select command.
- The "where" clause in a select command which retrieves specific rows from a table is also applicable to delete and update commands. In these cases it will delete or update row or rows from a table according to the conditions specified by the "where" clause.

(iii) Update command: Update command is used to alter the column values in a table. The update command consists of a "set" clause and an optional "where" clause. The syntax for the update command is given below:

```
update table_name set field = value, ... where condition:
```

In the above syntax, the "where" clause and the "set" clause can also include queries. Update sets each field with the value that we supply, provided it satisfies the 'where' condition. In the following example a query has been included in the 'where' clause to select the rows which are to be updated.

In the following example the *sal* of *empno 7788* is Rs. 3000 in the EMP table, which is now incremented to Rs. 4000

Example:

SQL>update emp set sal=4000 where empno = 7788;

1 row updated.

SQL> select * from emp;

EMPNO	ENAME	JOB	MGR	HIREDATE	SAL	COMM	DEPTNO
7369	SMITH	CLERK	7902	17-DEC-80	800		20
7499	ALLEN	SALESMAN	7698	20-FEB-81	1600	300	30
7521	WARD	SALESMAN	7698	22-FEB-81	1250	500	30
7566	JONES	MANAGER	7839	02-APR-81	2975		20
7654	MARTIN	SALESMAN	7698	28-SEP-81	1250	1400	30
7698	BLAKE	MANAGER	7839	01-MAY-81	2850		30
7782	CLARK	MANAGER	7839	09-JUN-81	2450		10
7788	SCOTT	ANALYST	7566	19-APR-87	4000	changed	20
7839	KING	PRESIDENT		17-NOV-81	5000		10
7844	TURNER	SALESMAN	7698	08-SEP-81	1500	0	30
7876	ADAMS	CLERK	7788	23-MAY-87	1100		20
7900	JAMES	CLERK	7698	03-DEC-81	950		30
7902	FORD	ANALYST	7566	03-DEC-81	3000		20
7934	MILLER	CLERK	7782	23-JAN-82	1300		10
7800	RIKTESH	MANAGER	7788	01-JAN-01	10000	5000	10
7890	rajiv	manager	7788	01-JAN-89	10000	0	10
7812	RAJIV	MANAGER	7888	14-FEB-88	10000	500	10

17 rows selected.

(iv) Delete command: After inserting rows in a table we can also delete them if required. The delete command consists of a "from clause" followed by an optional "where clause"

delet from <table_name> where conditions;

To delete several rows from a table, select the rows with appropriate conditions in a "where" clause. The "where" clause can also include a query. The following example will delete the details of the employee whose name is 'RAJIV'.

SQL> delete from emp where ename = 'RAJIV';

1 row updated.

SQL> select*from emp;

EMPNO	ENAME	JOB	MGR	HIREDATE	SAL	COMM	DEPTNO
7369	SMITH	CLERK	7902	17-DEC-80	800		20
7499	ALLEN	SALESMAN	7698	20-FEB-81	1600	300	30
7521	WARD	SALESMAN	7698	22-FEB-81	1250	500	30
7566	JONES	MANAGER	7839	02-APR-81	2975		20
7654	MARTIN	SALESMAN	7698	28-SEP-81	1250	1400	30
7698	BLAKE	MANAGER	7839	01-MAY-81	2850		30
7782	CLARK	MANAGER	7839	09-JUN-81	2450		10
7788	SCOTT	ANALYST	7566	19-APR-87	4000		20
7839	KING	PRESIDENT		17-NOV-81	5000		10
7844	TURNER	SALESMAN	7698	08-SEP-81	1500	0	30
7876	ADAMS	CLERK	7788	23-MAY-87	1100		20
7900	JAMES	CLERK	7698	03-DEC-81	950		30
7902	FORD	ANALYST	7566	03-DEC-81	3000		20
7934	MILLER	CLERK	7782	23-JAN-82	1300		10
7800	RIKTESH	MANAGER	7788	01-JAN-01	10000	5000	10
7890	rajiv	manager	7788	01-JAN-89	10000	0	10

The delete command allows deletion of rows from a table. A single row or many rows could be deleted. Alternatively, all rows of a table could also be deleted while the structure is maintained. To delete specific rows from a table the 'where' clause is used in combination with the delete command.

7.5 OPERATORS IN SQL*PLUS

The following are the operators supported by SQL*Plus:

(i) Arithmetic operators

(ii) Comparison operators

(iii) Logical operators

Let us discuss them in detail.

(i) Arithmetic operators: To perform calculations based on number values, we include arithmetic expressions in SQL command. An arithmetic expression consists of column names with number datatype and an arithmetic operator connecting them. The arithmetic operators are + (addition), - (subtraction), * (multiplication) and / (division). Consider the following example:

Example:

```
SQL > select sal + 1000 from emp;

SAL + 1000
----------
      1800
      2600
      2250
      3975
      2250
      3850
      3450
      5000
      6000
      2500
      2100
      1950
      4000
      2300
     11000
     11000
16 rows selected.
```

We know that sal+100 is not a column in the table EMP, yet SQL*Plus would display it as a separate column. Arithmetic operations can also be performed in a "where clause".

If there are several operators in an arithmetic expression then the precedence of each operator must be known. ∗ and / have equal higher precedence whereas + and – have equal lower precedence.

An example given below illustrates the precedence of operators.

Example:

```
SQL> select sal, 10*(sal+100) from emp;
  ----     ----------
   SAL     10*(SAL + 100)

   800          9000
  1600         17000
  1250         13500
  2975         30750
  1250         13500
  2850         29500
```

```
 2450      25500
 4000      41000
 5000      51000
 1500      16000
 1100      12000
  950      10500
 3000      31000
 1300      14000
10000     101000
10000     101000
```

16 row selected.

In the above example, only after adding Rs. 100 to *sal* it is multiplied by 10. If parenthesis is omitted then multiplication will be performed first followed by addition. Thus we can control the order of evaluation by with parenthesis.

We now move on to study about comparison operators.

(ii) Comparison operators: Comparison operators are used in conditions to compare one expression with another. The comparison operators are =,!=, <, >, <=, >=, between (to check between any two values), in (to match with any of the values in the list), like (to match a character pattern) and is Null (to check whether it is Null).

The last four operators mentioned above can also be used for checking the NOT conditions like NOT BETWEEN, NOT LIKE and NOT IN. The following example illustrates the comparison operator "greater than"

Example:

```
SQL> select ename,sal from emp where sal>1500;
ENAME          SAL
ALLEN         1600
JONES         2975
BLAKE         2850
CLARK         2450
SCOTT         4000
KING          5000
FORD          3000
RIKTESH      10000
rajiv        10000
9 rows selected
```

The above example displays the rows for which the *sal* is greater than 1500. An example discussed below is used to check for negations (i.e., check for NOT conditions)

Example:

SQL> select * from emp where not (deptno = 10 or deptno = 30);

EMPNO	ENAME	JOB	MGR	HIREDATE	SAL	COMM	DEPTNO
7369	SMITH	CLERK	7902	17-DEC-80	800		20
7566	JONES	MANAGER	7839	02-APR-81	2975		20
7788	SCOTT	ANALYST	7566	19-APR-87	4000		20
7876	ADAMS	CLERK	7788	23-MAY-87	1100		20
7902	FORD	ANALYST	7566	03-DEC-81	3000		20

The above command will display all columns where *deptno* is neither 10 nor 30. The IN operator can be used to select rows that match one of the values in a list.

Example:

SQL> select ename, sal from emp where sal in (1000, 2000, 3000, 4000, 5000);

ENAME	SAL
SCOTT	4000
KING	5000
FORD	3000

The above example lists all the columns in a table for which *sal* lies in the given list. When we search for character values using IN operator, the column name must exactly match with the values present in the list. In the case of LIKE operator, which is used to search a character pattern, we need not know the exact character value. The LIKE operator recognizes special characters like % and _ . The former can match zero or more characters, while the latter matches exactly one character.

Example:

SQL> select ename from emp where ename like 'S%';

ENAME
SMITH
SCOTT

The above-mentioned statement gives the name of all employees which the first letter as 'S'. Consider another example:

Example:

SQL > select ename from emp where ename like '- - - - -';

ENAME
WARD
KING
FORD

The above-mentioned statement gives the name of all employees with total length 4.

Note: % cannot be used to match a Null character.

Example:

SQL> select ename from emp where ename like '_A%';

```
ENAME
-------
WARD
MARTIN
JAMES
```

The above example gives the name of employees, with second character 'A', with one character before 'A' and any number of characters after 'A'.

(iii) Logical operators: A logical operator is used to combine the results of two conditions to produce a single result. The logical operators are AND, NOT and OR.

Consider the example given below:

Example:

SQL> select ename from emp where sal>3000 **and** deptno = 10;

```
ENAME
-------
KING
RIKTESH
rajiv
```

We have now gone through the various operators supported by SQL*Plus. Now let us have a look at the order in which these operators are evaluated.

Operator precedence

The precedence of the operators discussed above is given below:

Arithmetic operator's →*highest precedence*
Comparison operators
NOT logic operator
AND logic operator
OR logic operator →*lowest precedence*

- The order of precedence could be altered using parenthesis.

7.6 PRIVILEGE COMMANDS

Privilege is the right to access another user's objects (table, view...). We can grant privileges (insert, select ...) to others and can also withdraw the granted privilege by using the privilege commands – grant and revoke.

Grant privilege command: For example, if a user creates a table named EMP_DETAILS, there is no necessity for the user to be given any privilege to use it. He becomes the owner of the table. In case, the user wants to share an object with others, the appropriate privileges can be granted on that particular object to others. Objects are logical data storage structures like tables, views, sequences, indexes, synonyms etc.

Object privileges can be granted to others using the SQL command GRANT. The syntax is given below:

```
Grant privileges on <object_name> to <username>;
```

The following example grants privileges like select, insert, delete to a single user. We can also specify ALL to grant all the privileges.

SQL > grant select, insert: delete on emp_details to user2;

After successful execution of the above command, the message "grant succeeded" displayed.

The following example grants the select privilege on emp_details table to user2 along with "with grant option", so that user2 can pass the respective privileges to others.

Example:

SQL > grant select on emp_details to user2 with grant option;

Revoke privilege command: To withdraw the privilege, which has been granted to a user, we use the revoke command. This command is closely similar to that of the grant command in its format. The syntax is given below:

Revoke privileges on<object_name>from<username>;

To withdraw select, insert and delete privileges on the object "emp_details" from user2 can use the following command.

Example:

SQL > revoke select, insert, delete on emp_details from user2;

After successful execution of the above command, the message "revoke succeeded" appear.

7.7 TRANSACTION CONTROL COMMANDS

Transaction Control Commands are the user defined statement or operators to be performed on Oracle table. The transaction is performed on executable SQL statement. This is a group of event, which occurs on the operation in the oracle package as below:

1. Connecting Oracle
2. Disconnecting from Oracle
3. Committing changes in the database
4. Rolling back to previous stage.

The transaction permit the user to decides whether the performed operation is final and to be saved or not to be saved, this operation can be performed by three types of statements.

1. COMMIT, 2. ROLLBACK, and 3. SAVEPOINT

1. Commit

The commit statement ends the current transaction and makes permanent changes during that transaction. It is written as:

COMMIT;

2. Rollback

The rollback statement does a work of rolling back to previous situation. It ends the transaction but removes the changes made during transaction. This is useful for following reasons:

1. It may be possible that there is mistake in operation, therefore the operation should be deleted.
2. The rollback is useful if stated-transaction is not able to complete. Such situation might occur due to logical or SQL not executable successfully. This can be written by a statement.

ROLLBACK;

The rollback command can be used with savepoint command. It is written as

ROLLBACK TO SAVEPOINT SP1;

SP1 is a savepoint at which saving was performed.

3. Savepoint

This marks and saves at any point during processing of transaction. It saves the current work and allows you to Indicate saving point by specific name.

It is written as

SAVEPOINT SP1;

where SP1 is name of save point.

SQL> update emp set sal=5000 where empno = 7788;

1. row updated.

SQL> savepoint one;

Savepoint created.

SQL> update emp set sal = 4500 where empno = 7800;

1 row updated.

SQL> savepoint two;

Savepoint created.

SQL> rollback to savepoint one;

Rollback complete.

In the above example, we have two markers one and two and a rollback statement, which rolls back the SQL statements to the savepoint one.

7.8 ORACLE FUNCTIONS

The previous section dealt with insert and other manipulation commands, which helped us to interact with tables present in the database. It also enlightened us on SQL*Plus operators. This section deals with functions supported by SQL. A function takes one or more arguments and returns a value. One can classify functions into single row functions and group functions. Let us go about discussing them.

Single Row Functions: A single row function or a scalar function returns only one value for every row queried in the table. Single row functions can appear in a select command and can also be included in a "where" clause. The single row functions can be broadly classified as:

- Date functions
- Character functions
- Numeric functions
- Conversion functions
- Miscellaneous functions

The examples that follow mostly use the system table "dual". It is a table, which is automatically created by Oracle along with the data dictionary. Dual table has one column defined to be of varchar2 type and contains only one row with value 'x'.

Example:

```
SQL > select * from dual;
```

Date functions: They operate on date values producing output, which also belongs to date datatype, except for months_between date function, which returns a number. We shall discuss some of the most important date functions with examples.

Add_months

This date function returns a date after adding a specified date with the specified number of months. The format is add_months(d,n), where d is the date and n represents the number of months.

Consider the following example to understand the above concept.

Example:

```
SQL> select add_months (sysdate, 2) from dual;
ADD_MONTH
----------
04-DEC-04
```

Note: The sysdate variable will display system date.

Last_day

The format is last_day(d), which returns the date corresponding to the last day of the month.

Example:

```
SYSDATE          LAST_DAY
-------          -------
04-OCT-04        31-OCT-04
```

The above command will display the system date and last day of the current month.

Months_between

To find out the number of months between two dates, we use the months_between function. Its format is

months_between(d1, d2)

where d1, d2 are dates. The following example returns the number of months between two dates. The output will be a number.

Example:

```
SQL>select months_between ('01-dec-04', '01-oct-04') from dual;
 MONTHS_BETWEEN ('01-DEC-04', '01-OCT-04')
-------------------------------------------
                                        2
```

Next_day

The format for this function is

next_day(d, day)

where d represents date and day implies any weekday. This function can be illustrated with the following example:

Example:

SQL> select next_day (sysdate, 'tuesday') from dual;

NEXT_DAY
- - - - - - -
05-OCT-04

So far we have learnt about the usage of date functions. Now let us go about learning character functions. A tabular column that follows helps us to glance at the character functions.

Character functions: Character functions accept character input and return either character or number values.

The character functions supported by Oracle are listed below:

FUNCTION	INPUT	OUTPUT
initcap(char)	SQL> select initcap ('welcome') from dual;	INITCAP - - - - - Welcome
lower(char)	SQL> select lower ('ENJOY') from dual;	LOWER - - - - - enjoy
upper(char)	SQL> select upper ('enjoy') from dual;	UPPER - - - - - ENJOY
ltrim(char,set)	SQL> select ltrim ('xyzadams', 'xyz') from dual;	LTRIM - - - - - adams
rtrim(char,set)	SQL> select rtrim ('xyzadams', 'ams') from dual;	RTRIM - - - - - xyzad
translate(char,from,to)	SQL> select translate ('jack', 'j', 'b') from dual;	TRAN - - - - - back
replace(char,searchstring, [rep string])	SQL> select replace ('jack and jue', 'j', 'b1') from dual	REPLACE - - - - - - - black and blue
substr(char,m,n)	SQL> select substr ('oracle', 2, 4) from dual;	SUBS - - - - racl

Numeric functions: Numeric function accepts numeric input and returns numeric values as the output. The values that the numeric functions return are accurate up to 38 decimal digits. The following tabular column will enlighten us on numeric functions supported by Oracle.

FUNCTION	INPUT	OUTPUT
Abs	select abs (–15) from dual;	15
Ceil(n)	select ceil (44.778) from dual;	45
Cos(n)	select cos (180) from dual;	–.5984601
Cosh(n)	select cosh (0) from dual;	1
Exp(n)	select exp(4) from dual;	54.59815

Floor(n)	select floor(100.2) from dual;	100
Power(m,n)	select power (4,2) from dual;	16
Mod(m,n)	select mod(10,3) from dual;	1
Round(m,n)	select round (100.256,2) from dual;	100.26
Trunc(m,n)	select trunc (100.256,2) from dual;	100.25
Sqrt(n)	select sqrt(4) from dual;	2

Conversion functions: Conversion functions convert a value from one data type to another. The conversion functions are broadly classified into the following:

- to_char( )
- to_date( )

Apart from to_char( ) and to_date there are more than 10 such conversion functions are available. Let us now discuss to_char( ) and to_date( ).

to_char( )

The function is to_char(d [,fmt]), where d is the date, fmt is the format model, which specifies the format of date. to_char conversion function converts date to a value of varchar2 datatype in a form specified by date format fmt. If fmt is neglected then it converts date to varchar2 in the default date format. Consider the following example:

Example:

```
SQL>select to_char (sysdate,' ddth "of" fmmonth yyyy') from dual:
TO_CHAR(SYSDATE, 'DDTH'
-----------------------
05th of october 2004
```

The above statement displays the date according to the format specified in the format model. As a result, the date will be displayed as 05th of October 2004, if sysdate is '05-oct-04'. In the above example, fill mode(fm) format mask is used to avoid blank padding of characters and zero padding to numeric.

to_date ( )

The format is to_date(char [,fmt]).This converts char or varchar datatype to date datatype. Format model, fmt specifies the form of character. Consider the following example, which returns the date for the string 'October 05 2004'.

```
SQL> select to_date('october 05 2004', 'month-dd-yyyy') from dual;
TO_DATE ('
----------
05-OCT-04
```

Example:

Note:

- The definition for fmt, explained in the to_char conversion function also holds well for to_date conversion function.
- The square braces indicate that the arguments are optional.

Miscellaneous functions: The following are some of the miscellaneous functions supported by Oracle:

- uid
- user

- nvl
- vsize

Let us discuss the functions mentioned above one by one in detail.

Uid

This function returns the integer value corresponding to the user currently logged in. The following example is illustrative.

Example:

```
SQL>select uid from dual;
        UID
     -------
         18
```

The result could be a number.

User

This function returns the login's user name, which is in varchar2 datatype. Consider the following example:

Example:

```
SQL>select user from dual;
       USER
     -------
      SCOTT
```

The result is the name of the current user.

Null value(nvl): The Null value function is mainly used in the case where we want to consider Null values as zero. The syntax is given as nvl(expressionl, expression2).

- If expression1 is Null, nvl will return expression2.
- If expression1 is Not Null, nvl will return expression1.
- If expressions 1 and 2 are of different datatype, then Oracle converts expression2 to the datatype of expression 1 and then compares it.

Consider the following example, which fills up the blanks present in the column "comm" by zeroes, while displaying the rows pertaining to it.

Example:

```
SQL> select sal + nvl (comm,0) from emp;
SAL +NVL (COMM, 0)
-------------------------
              800
             1900
             1750
             2975
             2650
             2850
             2450
             5000
             5000
             1500
             1100
```

```
                    950
                   3000
                   1300
                  15000
                  10000
     16 rows selected.
```

Note

- Null values and zeroes are not equivalent. Null values are represented by blank and zeroes are represented by (0).

Vsize: The function is vsize(expr). It returns the number of bytes in the expression. If expression is Null, it returns Null.

```
SQL> select visze ('enjoy') from dual;
VSIZE ('ENJOY')
---------------
              5
```

Example:

Group functions: A group function returns a result based on group of rows. The group functions supported by Oracle are summarized below:

FUNCTION	EXAMPLE	OUTPUT
avg( )	select avg(sal) from emp;	Average value of sal
min()	select min(sal) from emp;	Lowest value of sal
max()	select max(sal) from emp;	Highest value of sal
sum( )	select sum(sal) from emp;	Summation of total sal

Count function: In order to count the number of rows, count function is used. It can take three different arguments and is discussed below with appropriate examples.

Count(*): It counts all rows, inclusive of duplicates and Nulls. The following example is illustrative which counts all the rows belonging to the EMP table.

Example:

```
SQL>select count from emp;
  COUNT (*)
  ---------
         14
```

Count(col_name): It counts the number of values present in the column without including Nulls. The following example counts the number of rows after eliminating Nulls in the column total.

Example:

```
SQL>select count (comm) from emp;
  COUNT (COMM)
  ------------
             4
```

Group by clause: Simultaneous usage of column name and group function is totally absurd in a select statement. This flaw can be removed by using group by clause in the select statement. If an SQL command consists of a "where" clause and "group" by clause, then the latter should follow the former. The following example lists maximum *sal* for every *deptno*.

Example:

```
SQL>select max(sal), deptno from emp group by deptno;
 MAX(SAL)    DEPTNO
 --------    ------
     5000        10
     5000        20
     2850        30
```

Having clause: HAVING clause is very much similar to WHERE clause except that having clause is applicable only for grouped data. Here the rows are further restricted according to the having clause. For example, If we want to find out the maximum salary for all departments having more than three employees, then the query will be:

```
SQL> select deptno, max(sal) from emp group by
  2  deptno having count (*)>3;

 DEPTNO      MAX(SAL)
 ------      --------
     20          5000
     30          2850
```

7.9 SET OPERATORS

Set operators combine the results of two queries into a single one. The following set operators aid SQL in joining queries to retrieve rows. Now let us discuss them in detail:

- Union
- Union all
- Intersect
- Minus

The columns in the select statements joined using the set operators should adhere strictly to the norms mentioned below.

- The queries, which are related by a set operator, should have the same number of columns and the corresponding columns must be of the same datatype.
- Such a query should not contain any column of type long.
- The labels under which the rows are displayed are those from the first select statement.

Union: The union operator returns all distinct rows selected by either query. The following example combines the result of two queries with the union operator, which eliminates duplicate rows.

Example

```
SQL>  select sal from emp where deptno = 10
2     union
3     select sal from emp where deptno = 20;

 SAL
 ---
 800
1100
1300
2450
2975
```

```
     3000
     5000
7 rows selected.
```

Union all: The 'union all' operator returns all rows selected by either query including duplicates. The following example combines the result with the 'union all' operator, which does not eliminate duplicate rows.

Example

```
SQL>  select sal from emp where deptno = 10
2     union all
3     select sal from emp where deptno = 20;
         SAL
      ------
         2450
         5000
         1300
         800
         2975
         5000
         1100
         3000
8 rows selected.
```

Intersect: Intersect operator returns only rows that are common to both the queries.

The following example is illustrative of the above statement.

Example

```
SQL>  select sal from emp where deptno = 10
2     intersect
3     select sal from emp where deptno = 20;
         SAL
      ------
         5000
```

Minus: Minus operator returns all distinct rows selected only by the first query and not by the second. The following example illustrates this.

Example:

```
SQL>  select sal from emp where deptno = 10
2     minus
3     select sal from emp where deptno = 20;
      SAL
    -----
      1300
      2450
```

7.10 JOINS

The purpose of a join is to combine the data spread across tables. A Join is actually performed by the "where" clause which combines the specified rows of tables. The syntax for joining tables is as follows:

select columns from table1, table2 where logical expression;

The logical expression specifies how the tables are joined. There are basically three different types of joins. They are:

- Simple join
- Outer join
- Self join

Let us discuss them in detail.

Simple join: Simple Join finds the exact match of the common column in both the tables. If match is found then that information will be displayed, otherwise not. The criteria for that is

emp.deptno=dept.deptno

An example of simple join is given as follows:

Example

Find the name and department of every employee.

```
SQL> select sal e.ename, d.dname
 2   from emp e, dept d
 3   where e.deptno=d.deptno;

ENAME       DNAME
------      ---------
SMITH       RESEARCH
ALLEN       SALES
WARD        SALES
JONES       RESEARCH
MARTIN      SALES
BLAKE       SALES
CLARK       ACCOUNTING
SCOTT       RESEARCH
KINGACCOUNTING
TURNER      SALES
ADAMS       RESEARCH
JAMES       SALES
FORD        RESEARCH
MILLER      ACCOUNTING

14 rows selected.
```

The WHERE clause specifies the join condition based on the common attribute, deptno. If a department exists in both the tables then it displays the desired information (dname and ename). For example, if in a particular department, no employee exists then it will not even display that department name.

It is clear from the above examples that, in order to join two tables we need a join condition. Similarly, to join three tables we need two join conditions and so on. A simple rule is

The minimum number of join conditions= The number of tables used minus one

Outer join: In simple join, a matching common column value is checked in both the tables for equality. In outer join, it picks all the records from one table and takes only the matching records from another table, displaying NULL for non-matching values.

In outer join, the statement will display all the employees from EMP table and the matching departments from DEPT table. For example, if there are some employees for whom the department is not assigned even then it will display the name and designation of those employees, leaving the corresponding dname column NULL.

In outer join, both the EMP and DEPT rows (with match and without match) will be displayed.

In Oracle, the syntax for outer join is as follows:

```
SQL>  select e.ename, e.job, d.deptno
  2   from emp e.dept d
  3   where e.deptno (+) = d.deptno;
```

ENAME	JOB	DEPTNO
CLARK	MANAGER	10
KING	PRESIDENT	10
MILLER	CLERK	10
SMITH	CLERK	20
ADAMS	CLERK	20
FORD	ANALYST	20
SCOTT	ANALYST	20
JONES	MANAGER	20
ALLEN	SALESMAN	30
BLAKE	MANAGER	30
MARTIN	SALESMAN	30
JAMES	CLERK	30
TURNER	SALESMAN	30
WARD	SALESMAN	30
		40

15 rows selected.

It uses a (+) sign for outer join. In the above example, it will take all the departments from DEPT table and take only the matching employees from EMP table.

Self-join: Self-join means the joining of a table to itself. Here, two rows from the same table are joined to form a resulting row. To join a table to itself, two copies of the same table have to be opened in the memory. Here we use concept of alias for both the copies of the same table, which will open two identical tables in different memory locations. An example of self-join is given below:

```
SQL > select e.empno, e.ename, m.empno, m.ename
  2   from emp e, emp m;
  3   where e.mgr=m.empno;
```

EMPNO	ENAME	EMPNO	ENAME
7369	SMITH	7902	FORD
7499	ALLEN	7698	BLAKE
7521	WARD	7698	BLAKE
7566	JONES	7839	KING
7654	MARTIN	7698	BLAKE
7698	BLAKE	7839	KING
7782	CLARK	7839	KING
7788	SCOTT	7566	JONES
7844	TURNER	7698	BLAKE
7876	ADAMS	7788	SCOTT
7900	JAMES	7698	BLAKE
7902	FORD	7566	JONES
7934	MILLER	7782	CLARK

13 rows selected.

7.11 SUB-QUERIES

This is a very powerful and flexible feature of SQL. Through sub queries, we can embed a query within an update, delete or select statements. Sub-queries are useful where the desired output is based on some query or when we do not have the predefined list of values. Some examples of sub queries are as given below.

Example

Delete all those employees who are in 'OPERATIONS' department.

If we are not using the sub-query, we will have to follow the two steps. First we will query the *deptno* of 'OPERATIONS' department, as department name is not in EMP table. In second step, we will perform the delete operation based on that department number. However, if we are using the sub-query, we can delete all those records in a single step. The syntax is as

```
SQL> delete from emp where
  2  deptno = (select deptno from dept where dname = 'OPERATIONS');
```

First, it will execute the SELECT statement and then the output of this statement will be used as an input for the DELETE operation, thus doing both the things in one syntax.

Example:

Update the salary of 'TURNER' to the highest salary of the company.

SQL> update emp set sal=(select max(sal) from emp) where ename='TURNER';

1. row updated.

SQL> select * from emp;

EMPNO	ENAME	JOB	MGR	HIREDATE	SAL	COMM	DEPTNO
7369	SMITH	CLERK	7902	17-DEC-80	800		20
7499	ALLEN	SALESMAN	7698	20-FEB-81	1600	300	30
7521	WARD	SALESMAN	7698	22-FEB-81	1250	500	30
7566	JONES	MANAGER	7839	02-APR-81	2975		20
7654	MARTIN	SALESMAN	7698	28-SEP-81	1250	1400	30
7698	BLAKE	MANAGER	7839	01-MAY-81	2850		30
7782	CLARK	MANAGER	7839	09-JUN-81	2450		10
7788	SCOTT	ANALYST	7566	19-APR-87	5000		20
7839	KING	PRESIDENT		17-NOV-81	5000		10
7844	TURNER	SALESMAN	7698	08-SEP-81	5000	5	30
7876	ADAMS	CLERK	7788	23-MAY-87	1100		20
7900	JAMES	CLERK	7698	03-DEC-81	950		30
7902	FORD	ANALYST	7566	03-DEC-81	3000		20
7934	MILLER	CLERK	7782	23-JAN-82	1300		10

14 rows selected.

You can observe the change in *sal* attribute for *ename* 'TURNER'.

Example

Retrieve the second highest salary from the EMP table.

SQL> select max(sal) from emp where sal<>(select max(sal) from emp);

```
MAX (SAL)
---------
     3000
```

OR

SQL> select max(sal) from emp where sal <(select max(sal) from emp);

```
MAX (SAL)
---------
     3000
```

Example

Get the names of all employees who are getting the second highest salary.

```
SQL> select ename from emp where
  2  sal=(select max(sal) from emp where
  3  sal<>(select max(sal) from emp));
```

```
ENAME
------
FORD
```

Example

List all the employees of 'ACCOUNTING' department.

```
SQL>    select ename from emp where
        2 deptno = (select deptno from dept where dname = 'ACCOUNTING');

ENAME
------
CLARK
KING
MILLER
```

Example

Display the name and hiredate of all employees whose salary is more than the average salary.

```
SQL> select ename, hiredate from emp
  2  where sal>(select avg(sal) from emp);
ENAME      HIREDATE
-----      --------
JONES      02-APR-81
BLAKE      01-MAY-81
SCOTT      19-APR-87
KING       17-NOV-81
TURNER     08-SEP-81
FORD       03-DEC-81
6 rows selected.
```

Correlated query: In normal sub-query, SELECT statements can be nested in the WHERE clause of the outer query. Correlated sub query is a nested sub-query, which is executed once for each row considered by the main query and which on execution uses a candidate row. This causes the correlated sub query to value from a column in the outer query be processed in a different way from the ordinary nested sub query. For example:

```
SQL> select ename, sal, job, deptno from emp e
2       where sal>(select avg(sal) from emp
3       where deptno = e. deptno) order by deptno;

ENAME         SAL   JOB                DEPTNO
-----         ---   ---------          ------
KING         5000   PRESIDENT              10
JONES        2975   MANAGER                20
SCOTT        5000   ANALYST                20
FORD         3000   ANALYST                20
BLAKE        2850   MANAGER                30
TURNER       5000   SALESMAN               30
6 rows selected
```

The above query gives the details of employees who earn a salary greater than the average salary for their department. However, this query has an unusual thing and that is *e.deptno* column of outer query used in the inner query. So why it is executing? The reason is that it is a correlated sub-query. In correlated sub query, a sub query may refer to a column in a table used in its main query.

In the above example, it takes a row from EMP table for outer query and compares the *sal* of this row against value returned by inner query. Inner query uses the *deptno* of the outer query to get the average salary of that department. If the candidate row (salary from outer query) meet the condition *(sal>avg(sal) of that department)* then it displays the information, otherwise not.

The correlated sub-query is one way of reading every row in the table, and comparing values in each row against related data. The inner SELECT statement is executed once for each candidate row.

REVIEW QUESTIONS

Consider the relations EMP and DEPT discussed in this chapter and write the following SQL queries:

1. List the employees in Dept 'Accounting' with the same designation as anyone in department 20.
2. Find all the employees who earn more than the average salary of employees in their own departments and list them in department order.
3. Display information about employees who have at least one other employee reporting to them (consider the table used in self join section).
4. List each salesperson and the location where they work.
5. Display the salary in the Dollar format (Like $5,000).
6. Consider the commission column in the emp table and list employees whose commission is greater than 25% of their salaries.
7. Calculate the total annual compensation of employees who are not managers.
8. Find the average annual compensation of all salespeople.
9. Count the number of different designations held by employees in department 20.
10. Compute SAL+COMM treating null commissions as zero.
11. Compute years of service for each employee in department 10 treating an employee with a null date as if hiredate were DEC 18, 1989.
12. List the name and year of joining for each salesperson.
13. Sort the details of employees by designation and in the descending sequence of salary.
14. List the highest, second highest and third highest salaries in the proper sequence.
15. Display the name of the employees along with their department names who are getting above three salaries.
16. Create a view in the emp table, which consists of only those employees who are either managers or CEO.
17. Write a query to display an * along with the highest salary. Other records should be displayed as usual.
18. Write a query to display the department, which have only 2 employees.
19. Write a query to display the department, which has maximum employees.
20. Find the department with maximum salary.

CHAPTER 8

PL/SQL

In this chapter, you will learn

8.0 INTRODUCTION

SQL is a natural language of the DBA. It does not have any procedural capabilities such as looping and branching. For this, Oracle provides the PL/SQL language.

PL/SQL is really an extension of SQL. PL/SQL adds to the power of SQL and provides the user with all the facilities of a programming environment. PL/SQL is a procedural language that ORACLE developed as an extension to standard SQL in order to provide a way to execute procedural logic on the database.

PL/SQL is an ORACLE's procedural language extension to SQL. Unlike SQL, PL/SQL is a procedural, not declarative. This means that PL/SQL code specifies exactly how things get done. PL/SQL also enables you to embed SQL statements within its procedural code.

PL/SQL bridges the gap between database technology and procedural programming languages. It can be thought of as a development tool that extends the facilities of ORACLE's SQL database language. Programmers can use it to create programs for validation and manipulation of table data. Via PL/SQL they can insert, delete, update and retrieve table data as well as use procedural techniques such as writing loops or branching to another block of code. It allows them to use all the SQL data manipulation statements as well as transaction processing and cursor control operations. PL/SQL blocks can contain any numbers of SQL statements. It allows you to logically group a number of SQL sentences and parse them to DBA as a single block.

Performance: Without PL/SQL the DBA has to process SQL statements one at a time. This results in calls being made to the DBA each time an SQL statement is executed. It slow downs table data processing considerably. With a PL/SQL, an entire block of statements can be sent to the RDBMS engine at any one time. It reduces the traffic on the network.

PL/SQL can also be used in SQL* forms. Its procedural capabilities can be used for writing complex triggers that will validate data before it is placed in the table.

Portability: Applications written in PL/SQL are portable to any computer hardware and operating system. Where ORACLE is operational, hence PL/SQL code blocks written for the DOS version of ORACLE will run on its UNIX version, without any modifications made to it.

What PL/SQL can do for Programmers?

PL/SQL offers procedural methods of code writing for accessing the database and manipulating the data with flexibility and ease. This is because PL/SQL supports the following:

- SQL data manipulation statements, by using which table data can be manipulated.
- SQL transaction processing statements, which are treated as a single block by the DBA, so that all changes made to the data in the table, are done or undone all at once.
- SQL functions can be called from within PL/SQL. These functions can be numeric, character, date or data conversion functions. The functions available in the SQL can be used in PL/SQL blocks.
- ***SQL predicates:*** are used in the where conditions of SQL sentences, for data manipulation. The predicate to a where condition can consist of a simple comparison or of multiple comparisons using the logical operations AND, OR and NOT. Other comparison operators like BETWEEN, IS NULL, LIKE, EXISTS, etc., can also be used to form predicates.

PL/SQL allows you to declare variables and then use them in blocks of code. It is quite possible to use variables to store the results of a query for later processing or calculate values and insert them into an ORACLE table later. PL/SQL variable can be used anywhere, either in SQL statements or in PL/SQL blocks.

This section provides an overview of PL/SQL program structure, data types, operators, functions, procedures, keywords and cursors etc.

8.1 PL/SQL SYNTAX

PL/SQL Block Structure

PL/SQL is a block-structured language. A PL/SQL block defines a unit of processing, which can include its own local variables, SQL statements, cursors, and exception handlers. The blocks can be nested. The simplest block structure is given below:

```
DECLARE
        Variable declarations
BEGIN
        Program statements
EXCEPTION
        WHEN exception THEN
         Program    statements
END;
```

In the above PL/SQL block, block parts are logical. Blocks starts with DECLARATION section in which memory variables and other oracle objects can be declared. The next section contains SQL executable statements for manipulating table data by using the variables and constants declared in the DECLARE section. EXCEPTIONS is the last sections of the PL/SQL block which contains SQL and/or

PL/SQL code to handle errors that may crop up during the execution of the above code block. EXCEPTION section is optional.

Each block can contain other blocks, i.e., blocks can be nested. Blocks of the code cannot be nested in the DECLARATION section.

PL/SQL Character Set

PL/SQL uses the standard ASCII set. The basic character set includes the following:

Uppercase alphabets	**A** to **Z.**
Lowercase alphabets	**a** to **z.**
Numbers	**0** to **9**
Symbols	( ) + - * / < > = ! ; : , . @ ‘ % “ # $ ^ & _ \ { } ? [ ]

Words used in a PL/SQL blocks are called ***lexical units***. We can freely insert blank spaces between lexical units in a PL/SQL blocks. The spaces have no effect on the PL/SQL block.

The ordinary symbols used in PL/SQL blocks are:

( ) + – * / < > = ; % , “ [ ] :

Compound symbols used in PL/SQL block are:

<> != ~= ^= <= >= := ** || << >>

Variables: Variables may be used to store the result of a query or calculations. Variables must be declared before being used. Variables in PL/SQL block are named variables. A variable name must begin with a character and can be followed by a maximum of 29 other characters (variable length is 30 characters).

Reserved words cannot be used as variable names unless enclosed within the double quotes. Variables must be separated from each other by at least one space or by a punctuation mark.

The case (upper/lower) is insignificant when declaring variable names. Space cannot be used in a variable name.

Literals: A literal is a numeric value or a character string used to represent itself. So, literals can be classified into two types.

- Numeric literals
- Non-numeric literals (string literals)

Numeric literals: These can be either integers or floating-point numbers. If a float is being represented, then the integer part must be separated from the float part by a period (**.**).

Integers	25	43	437	–57	etc.
Floating-point	6.34	25E-03	0.1	+17.1	etc.

Non-numeric literals: These are represented by one or more legal characters and must be enclosed within single quotes.

Example: ‘Hello world’

‘EMPLOYEE NAME’

‘ ******* ’

‘A’

‘* ’

We can represent single quote character itself in a non-numeric literal by writing it twice.
Example: 'Don''t go without saving the program'

PL/SQL will also have literals, which are called as logical (***boolean***) literals. These are predetermined constants. The value it can take are TRUE, FALSE, and NULL.

COMMENTS

- A comment line begins with a double hyphen (--). In this case, the entire line will be treated as a comment.

  Example: --This section performs salary updation.

- The comment line begins with a slash followed by an asterisk (/*) until the occurrence of an asterisk followed by a slash (*/). In this case, comment lines can be extended to more than one line.

  Example:

  /* This is only for user purpose which calculates the total salary temporarily and stores the value in temp_sal */

  Example:

  /* This takes rows from /* table EMPLOYEE */ and put on another table */

In the above comment, there is a comment within an another comment line, this is ***not allowed*** in PL/SQL.

8.2 PL/SQL DATA TYPES AND DECLARATIONS

PL/SQL supports the standard ORACLE SQL data types. The default data types that can be declared in PL/SQL are

- **NUMBER** : For storing numeric data
  Syntax: *variable_ name NUMBER (precision, [scale])*
  Precision determines the number of significant digits that NUMBER can contain. Scale determines the number of digits to the right of the decimal point.
  Example: *NUMBER (4,2) stores 4234.60*
  NUMBER (10) stores 3289473348
- **CHAR** : This data type stores fixed length character data.
  Syntax: *variable_name CHAR (size)*
  where size specifies fixed length of the variable name.
  Example: *CHAR (10) stores MASTERFILE*
- **VARCHAR2** : It stores variable length character string data.
  Syntax: *Variable name VARCHAR 2 (size)*
  where size specifies the maximum length of the variable name.
  Example: *VARCHAR2 (20) stores TRANSACTIONFILE*
- **DATE** : The date data types store a date and time.
  Syntax: variable_name DATE
  Example: date_of_birth DATE
- **BOOLEAN** : This data type stores only TRUE, FALSE or NULL values.
  Syntax: *variable name BOOLEAN*
  Example: flag BOOLEAN.

%TYPE declares a variable or constant to have the same data type as that of a previously defined variable or of a column in a table or in a view.

NOT NULL causes creation of a variable or a constant that cannot have a NULL value. If you attempt to assign the value NULL to a variable or a constant that has been assigned a NOT NULL constraint, causes an error.

> **Note:** As soon as a variable or constant has been declared as NOT NULL, it must be assigned a value. Hence, every NOT NULL declaration of variable or constant needs to be followed by PL/SQL expression that loads a value into the variable or constant declared.

Declaring variables: We can declare a variable of any data type either native to the ORACLE or native to PL/SQL. Variables are declared in the DECLARE section of the PL/SQL block. Declaration involves the name of the variable followed by its data type. All statement must end with a semicolon (;) which is the delimiter in PL/SQL. To assign a value to the variable the assignment operator (:=) is used.

The general syntax is <Variable name> <type> [:=<value>];

Examples:

```
pay                 NUMBER (6,2);
in_stack            BOOLEAN;
name                VARCHAR2 (30);
room                CHAR (2);
date_of_purchase    DATE;
```

Assigning a value to a variable

A value can be assigned to the variable in any one of the following two ways:

- Using the assignment operator :=

  Example:

  ```
  tax := price * tax_rate
  pay := basic + da
  ```

- Selecting or fetching table data values into variables.

  Example:

  ```
  SELECT sal INTO pay
  FROM EMP
  WHERE emp_name = 'SMITH';
  ```

Declaring a constant: Declaring a constant is similar to declaring a variable except that you have to add the key word CONSTANT and immediately assign a value to it. Thereafter, no further assignment to the constants is possible,

Example: *pf_percent CONSTANT NUMBER (3,2) := 8.33;*

Picking up a variable's parameters from a table cell: The basic building block of a table is a cell (i.e., table's column). While creating a table user attaches certain attributes like data type and constraints. These attributes can be passed on to the variables being created in PL/SQL. This simplifies the declaration of variables and constants.

For this purpose, the %TYPE attribute is used in the declaration of a variable when the variable's attributes must be picked from a table field (i.e., column).

Example: *current_sal emp.sal %TYPE*

In the above example, current_sal is the variable of PL/SQL block. It gets the data type and constraints of the column (field) ***sal*** belong to the table ***Employee***. Declaring a variable with the %TYPE attribute has two advantages.

- You do not need to know the data type of the table column.
- If you change the parameters of the table column, the variable's parameters will change as well.

PL/SQL allows you to use the %TYPE attribute in a nesting variable declaration. The following example illustrates several variables defined on earlier %TYPE declarations in a nesting fashion.

Examples:

Dept_sales	*INTEGER;*
Area_sales	*dept_sales %TYPE;*
Group_sales	*area_sales %TYPE;*
Regional_sales	*area_sales %TYPE;*
Corporate_sales	*regional_sales %TYPE;*

In case, variables for the entire row of a table need to be declared, then instead of declaring them individually, %ROWTYPE is used

Example: *emp_row_var employee %ROWTYPE;*

Here, the variable emp_row_var will be a composite variable, consisting of the column names of the table as its member. To refer to a specific, say 'sal'; the following statement will be used.

emp_row_var.sal := 5000;

An Identifier in PL/SQL block: The name of any ORACLE object (variable, memory variable, constant, record, cursor etc.) is known as an ***Identifier***. The following laws have to be followed while working with identifiers.

- An identifier cannot be declared twice in the same block.
- The same identifier can be declared in two different blocks.

In the second law, the two identifiers are unique and any change in one does not affect the other.

8.3 PL/SQL OPERATORS

Operators are the glue that holds expressions together. PL/SQL operators can be divided into the following categories:

- Arithmetic operators
- Comparison operators
- Logical operators
- String operators

PL/SQL operators are either unary (i.e., they act on one value/variable) or binary (they act on two values/variables).

Arithmetic operators: Arithmetic operators are used for mathematical computations. They are:

Operator	Description
+	Addition
–	Subtraction or Negation (Example: –5)
*	Multiplication
/	Division
**	Exponentiation operator (Example 10**5 = 10^5)

Comparison operators: Comparison operators return a BOOLEAN result, either TRUE or FALSE. They are:

=	Equality operator	a=b
!=	Inequality operator	a!=b
<>	Inequality operator	5<>3
-=	Inequality operator	'john' - = 'johny'
<	Less than operator	a<b
>	Greater than operator	a>b
<=	Less than or equal to	a<=b
>=	Greater than or equal to	a>=b

In addition to this PL/SQL also provides some other comparison operators like LIKE, IN, BETWEEN, IS NULL etc.

LIKE: Pattern-matching operator.
It is used to compare a character string against a pattern. Two wildcard characters are defined for use with LIKE, the **(%)** percentage sign and (_) underscore. The % sign matches any number of characters in a string and (_) matches exactly one.
Example: new%matches with newdelhi, newyork etc. (i.e., any string beginning with the word new).
Example: '_ _ _day' matches with Sunday, Monday and Friday and it will not match with other days like 'Tuesday', 'Wednesday', 'Thursday' and 'Saturday'.

IN: Checks to see if a value lies within a specified list of values. The syntax is
Syntax: The_value [NOT] IN (value1, value2, value3……)
Example: 3 IN (4, 8, 7, 5, 3, and 2) Returns TRUE.
sun NOT IN ('sat', 'mon', 'tue', 'wed', 'sun') Returns TRUE.

BETWEEN: Checks to see if a value lies with in a specified range of value.
Syntax: The_value [NOT] BETWEEN low_end AND high_end.
Example: 5 BETWEEN –5 AND 10. Returns TRUE
4 NOT BETWEEN 3 AND 4 Returns FALSE.

IS NULL: Checks to see if a value IS NULL.
Syntax: The_value IS [NOT] NULL
Example: if balance IS NULL then
if acc_id IS NOT NULL then

Logical operators: PL/SQL implements 3 logical operations AND, OR and NOT. The NOT operator is unary operator and is typically used to negate the result of a comparison expression, where as the AND and OR operators are typically used to link together multiple comparisons.

- *A AND B* is true only if A returns TRUE and B returns TRUE else it is FALSE.
- *A OR B* is TRUE if either of A or B is TRUE. And it is FALSE if both A and B are FALSE.
- *NOT A* Returns TRUE if A is FALSE
  Returns FALSE if A is TRUE.

Example: *(5 = 5) AND (4<20) AND (2>=2) Returns TRUE*
(5=5) OR (5!=4) Returns TRUE.

'mon' IN ('sun', 'sat') OR (2 = 2) Returns TRUE.

String operators: PL/SQL has two operators specially designed to operate only on character string type data. These are ***LIKE*** and (||) concatenation operator. ***LIKE*** is a comparison operator and is used to compare strings and it is discussed in the previous session. Concatenation operator has following syntax:

Syntax: String_1 || String_2

String_1 and String_2 both are strings and can be a string constants, string variables or string expressions. The concatenation operator returns a resultant string consisting of all the characters in String_1 followed by all the characters in String_2.

Example: *'Chandra' || 'shekhar'* *Returns 'Chandrashekhar'*
A='Engineering' *B='College'* *C=VARCHAR2 (50)*
C=A || ' ' || B *Returns a value to variable C as 'Engineering College'.*

Note 1: PL/SQL string comparisons are always case sensitive, i.e., 'aaa' not equal to 'AAA'.
Note 2: ORACLE has some built in functions that are designed to convert from one data type to another data type.

to_date: *Converts a character string into date.*
to_number: *Converts a character string to a number.*
to_char: *Converts either a number or date to character string.*

Examples:

to_date ('1/1/04', 'mm/dd/yy/'); *Returns 01-jan-2004.*
to_date ('1-1-2004', 'mm-dd-yyyy'); *Returns 01/01/2004.*
to_date ('Jan 1, 2001','mm dd, yyyy'); *Returns Saturday, January 01, 2001.*
to_date ('1/1/02', 'mm/dd/rr'); *Returns Tue, Jan 01, 2002.*
to_number ('123.99', '999D99'); *Returns 123.99*
to_number ('$1,232.95', '$9G999D99'); *Returns $1, 232.99*
to_char (123.99, '999D99'); *Returns 123.99.*

8.4 CONDITIONAL CONTROL IN PL/SQL

In PL/SQL, then if statement allows you to control the execution of a block of code. In PL/SQL we can use the following if forms:

- *IF condition THEN statements END IF;*
- *IF condition THEN statements*
  ELSE statements;
  END IF;
- *IF condition THEN statements;*
  ELSIF condition THEN
  Statements;
  ELSE statements;
  END IF;
  END IF;

8.5 ITERATIVE CONTROL IN PL/SQL

PL/SQL provides iterative control and execution of PL/SQL statements in the block. This is the ability to repeat or skip sections of a code block. Following are the four types of iterative statements provided by the PL/SQL:

- *The Loop statement*
- *The WHILE Loop statement*
- *The GOTO statement*
- *FOR Loop*

Loop statement: A loop repeats a sequence of statements. The format is as follows:

```
LOOP
Statements
END LOOP;
```

The one or more PL/SQL statements can be written between the key words LOOP and END LOOP. Once a LOOP begins to run, it will go on forever. Hence loops are always accompanied by conditional statements that keep control on the number of times it is executed. We can also build user defined exists from a loop, where required.

Example:

```
LOOP
        cntr := cntr + 1;
        IF cntr < 100
            EXIT;
                END IF;
            END LOOP;
```

EXIT statement brings the control out of loop if the condition is satisfied.

While loop: The WHILE loop enables you to evaluate a condition before a sequence of statements would be executed. If condition is TRUE then sequence of statements are executed. This is different from the FOR loop where you must execute the loop at least once. The syntax for the WHILE loop is as follows:

Syntax:

```
WHILE < Condition is TRUE >
LOOP
< Statements >
END LOOP;
```

Example:

```
DECLARE
Count   NUMBER(2):= 0;
BEGIN
WHILE count <= 10
LOOP
Count := Count + 1;
Message('while loop executes');
END LOOP;
END;
```

EXIT and EXIT WHEN statement: EXIT and EXIT WHEN statements enable you to escape out of the control of a loop. The format of the EXIT statement is as follows:

Syntax: *EXIT;*

EXIT WHEN statement has following syntax:

Syntax: *EXIT WHEN <condition is true >;*

EXIT WHEN statement enables you to specify the condition required to exit the execution of the loop. In this case no if statement is required.

Example: *IF count >= 10 EXIT;*

Example: *EXIT WHEN count >= 10;*

The GOTO statement: The GOTO statement allows you to change the flow of control within a PL/SQL block. The syntax is as follows:

Syntax: *GOTO <label name> ;*

The label is surrounded by double brackets (<< >>) and label must not have a semicolon after the label name. The label name does not contain a semicolon because it is not a PL/SQL statement. But rather an identifier of a block of PL/SQL code. You must have at least one statement after the label otherwise an error will result. The GOTO destination must be in the same block, at the same level as or higher than the GOTO statement itself.

Example:

```
IF result = 'fail' THEN
GOTO failed_stud
END IF;
<<failed_stud>>
Message ('student is failed');
```

The entry point of the destination block is defined within << >> as shown above, i.e., labels are written within the symbol << >>. Notice that <<failed_stud>> is a label and it is not ended with semicolon (;).

For Loop: FOR loop will allow you to execute a block of code repeatedly until some condition occurs. The syntax of FOR loop is as follows:

Syntax:

```
FOR loop_index IN [REVERSE] low_value ..
High_value
LOOP
Statements to execute
END LOOP;
```

The loop_index is defined by oracle as a local variable of type integer. REVERSE allows you to execute the loop in reverse order. The low_value .. High_value is the range to execute the loop. These can be constants or variables. The line must be terminated with loop with no semicolon at the end of this line. You can list the statements to be executed until the loop is executed is evaluated to false.

Example:

```
FOR v_count IN 1 .. 5 LOOP
Message ('for loop executes');
END LOOP;
```

In the above example, the message 'for loop executes' is displayed five times.

We can terminate the FOR loop permanently using EXIT statement based on some BOOLEAN condition. Nesting of FOR loop can also be allowed in PL/SQL. The outer loop executed once, and then the inner loop is executed as many times as the range indicates, and then the control is returned to the outer loop until its range expires.

Example:

```
FOR out_count IN 1..2  LOOP
FOR in_count  IN  1..2   LOOP
Message ('nested for loop');
END LOOP;
END LOOP;
```

In the above example, the message 'nested for loop' is displayed four times.

Let us discuss some examples from the understanding how to write a PL/SQL block structure. Here we assume that a table called "EMP" is created and the data's are already inserted into it.

Table name: *EMP*

```
create table EMP
    ( emp_no        NUMBER (3),
    name            VARCHAR2 (15),
    salary          NUMBER (6,2),
    dept            VARCHAR2 (15),
    div             VARCHAR2 (2) );
```

Example:

```
DECLARE
    num             NUMBER (3);
    sal             emp.salary %TYPE;
    emp_name        emp.name %TYPE;
    count           NUMBER (2):= 1;
    starting_emp    CONSTANT  NUMBER(3) := 134;
BEGIN
    SELECT name, salary INTO emp_name, sal
            FROM  EMP
            WHERE  emp_no = starting_emp;
    WHILE sal < 4000.00
        LOOP
            Count := count + 1;
            SELECT emp_no, name, salary INTO
                        Num, emp_name, sal  FROM  EMP
            WHERE emp_no > 2150;
        END LOOP;
    Commit;
END;
```

In the above example there are five statements in the declaration part. The ***num*** is a integer type, ***sal*** and ***emp_name*** takes the similar data type of the ***salary*** and ***name*** columns of EMP table respectively.

Count is a variable of type integer and takes initial value 1. ***Starting_emp*** is a constant and it is of integer type with immediately assigned value 134.

Between BEGIN and END key words, there are some SQL executable statements used for manipulating the table data. The SELECT statement extracts data stored in ***name*** and ***salary*** columns of EMP table corresponding to the employee having employee number 134. It stores those values in the variables ***emp_name*** and ***sal*** respectively.

If ***sal*** less than 4000 then the statements within the loop will be executed. Within the loop, there are two SQL statements, the first one increments the count value by 1 and the second statement is a SELECT statement. The commit statement commits the changes made to that table. The END statement terminates the PL/SQL block.

Example:

This example assumes the existence of table accounts created by using the following SQL statements:

```
create table Accounts
        (accnt_id          NUMBER(3),
         name              VARCHAR2(25),
         bal               NUMBER(6,2) );
```

PL/SQL block:

```
DECLARE
        acct_balance    NUMBER(6,2);
        acct            CONSTANT    NUMBER(3) := 312;
        debit_amt       CONSTANT  NUMBER(5,2) := 500.00;
BEGIN
        SELECT bal INTO acct_balance FROM Accounts
        WHERE accnt_id = acct;
        IF acct_balance = debit_amt     THEN
        UPDATE Accounts
          SET bal := bal - debit_amt WHERE  accnt_id = acct;
        ELSE
              Message ('insufficient amount in account');
        END IF;
END;
```

The above example, illustrates the use of IF.. THEN.. ELSE.. END IF condition control statements.

Declaration part declares one variable and two constants. The SELECT statement extracts the amount in the ***bal*** column of ***Accounts*** table corresponding to account number 312, and stores that in a variable ***acct_balance***.

If statement checks ***acct_balance*** for sufficient amount before debiting. It updates the table ***Accounts*** if it has sufficient amount in the balance, else it displays a message intimating insufficient fund in the account of specified ***accnt_id***.

Example:

This example assumes two tables, which are created by following statements:

```
create table Inventory
        ( prod_no          NUMBER (6),
          product          VARCHAR2 (15),
          quantity         NUMBER (5) );

create table Purchase_record
        ( mesg             VARCHAR2 (50),
          d_ate            DATE );
```

PL/SQL block:

```
DECLARE
        num_in_stack              NUMBER(5);
BEGIN
        SELECT quantity INTO num_in_stack
                FROM Inventory WHERE product = 'gasket';
        IF num_in_stack > 0 THEN
          UPDATE Inventory SET quantity := quantity - 1
                WHERE product = 'gasket';
          INSERT INTO Purchase_record
                VALUES ('One gasket purchased', sysdate);
        ELSE
          INSERT INTO Purchase_record
                VALUES ('no gasket available',sysdate);
          Message ( 'there are no more gasket in stack');
        END IF;
          Commit;
END;
```

The above block of PL/SQL code does the following;

- It determines how many gaskets are left in stack.
- If the number left in staff is greater than zero, it updates the inventory to reflect the sale of a gasket.
- It stores the fact that a gasket was purchased on a certain date.
- If the stock available is zero, it stores the fact that there are no more gaskets for sale on the date on which such a situation occurred.

8.6 ERROR HANDLING IN PL/SQL

PL/SQL has the capability of dealing with the errors that arise while executing a PL/SQL block of code. It has a number of conditions that are pre programmed into it that are recognized as error conditions. These are called ***internally defined exceptions***. You can also program PL/SQL to recognize user-defined exceptions.

There are two different types Error conditions (Exceptions).

- User defined error conditions/exceptions.
- Predetermined internal PL/SQL exceptions.

User defined exceptions: User can write a set of code, which is to be executed while error occurs when executing a PL/SQL block of code. These set of code are called ***user-defined exceptions***, and these are placed in the last section of PL/SQL block called EXCEPTIONS.

The method used to recognize user-defined exceptions is as follows:

- Declare a user defined exception in the declaration section of PL/SQL block.
- In the main program block for the conditions that needs special attention, execute a RAISE statement.
- Reference the declared exception with an error handling routine in EXCEPTION section of PL/SQL block.

RAISE statement acts like CALL statement of high level languages. It has general format

RAISE < name of exception >

When RAISE statement is executed, it stops the normal processing of PL/SQL block of code and control passes to an error handler block of the code at the end of PL/SQL program block (EXCEPTION section).

An exception declaration declares a name for user defined error conditions that the PL/SQL code block recognizes. It can only appear in the DECLARE section of the PL/SQL code which precedes the key word BEGIN.

Example:

```
DECLARE
        ----------------------
        zero_commission    Exception;
        ----------------------
BEGIN
        ----------------------
        IF commission = 0 THEN
                RAISE   zero_commission;
        ----------------------------
EXCEPTION
                WHEN zero_commission THEN
        Process the error
END;
```

Exception handler (error handler block) is written between the key words EXCEPTION and END. The exception handling part of a PL/SQL code is optional. This block of code specifies what action has to be taken when the named exception condition occurs.

The naming convention for exception name is exactly the same as those for variables or constants. All the rules for accessing an exception from PL/SQL blocks are same as those for variables and constants. However, it should be noted that exceptions cannot be passed as arguments to functions or procedures like variables or constants.

Pre-determined internal PL/SQL exceptions: The ORACLE server defines several errors with standard names. Although every ORACLE error has a number, the error must be referred by name. PL/SQL has predefined some common ORACLE errors and exceptions. Some of them are given below:

Exception Names	Exception Details
NO_DATA_FOUND	Raised when a select statement returns zero rows.
TOO_MANY_ROWS	Raised when a select statement returns more than one rows.
VALUE_ERROR	Raised when there is either a data type mismatch or if the size is smaller than required size.
INVALID_NUMBER	Raised when conversion of a number to a character string failed.
ZERO_DIVIDE	Raised when attempted to divide by zero.
PROGRAM_ERROR	Raised if PL/SQL encounters an internal problem.
STORAGE_ERROR	Raised if PL/SQL runs out of memory or if memory is corrupted.
DUP_VAL_ON_INDEX	Raised when attempted to insert or update a duplicate into a column that has unique index.
INVALID_CURSOR	Raised when illegal cursor operation was attempted.
CURSOR_ALREADY_OPEN	Raised when attempted to open a cursor that was previously opened.
NOT_LOGGED_ON	Raised when a database call was made without being logged into ORACLE.
LOGIN_DENIED	Raised when login to ORACLE failed because of invalid username and password.
OTHERS	This will be raised when the all other exceptions failed to catch the errors.

It is possible to use WHEN OTHERS clause in the exception handling part of the PL/SQL block. It will take care of all exceptions that are not taken care of in the code.

The syntax for exception handling portion of PL/SQL block is as follows:

```
EXCEPTION
        WHEN exception_1 THEN Statements;
        WHEN exception_2 THEN Statements;
              ------------------------
        END;
```

In this syntax, exception_1 and exception_2 are the name of exceptions (may be pre-defined or user-defined). Statements in the PL/SQL code that will be executed if the exception name is satisfied.

Example:

This example writes PL/SQL code for validating ***accnt_id*** of ***Accounts*** table so that it must not be left blank, if it is blank cursor should not be allowed to move to the next field.

```
DECLARE
      no_value exception;
```

```
BEGIN
        IF: Accounts.accnt_id IS NULL THEN
            RAISE no_value;
        ELSE
            next_field;
        END IF;

EXCEPTION
        WHEN no_value THEN
        Message ('account id cannot be, blank Please enter valid
        data !!! ');
        go_field ( : system.cursor_field );
END;
```

In the above example, ***accnt_id*** field of ***Accounts*** table is checked for NULL value. If it is NULL, then RAISE statement calls exception handler ***no_value***. This exception name ***no_value*** is declared in DECLARE section and defined in the EXCEPTION section of PL/SQL block by using WHEN statement ***no_value*** is a user-defined exception.

Example:

```
DECLARE
        balance         Accounts.bal %TYPE;
        account_num     Accounts.accnt_id %TYPE;
BEGIN
        SELECT accnt_id bal INTO account_num, balance
        FROM Accounts WHERE accnt_id > 0000;
EXCEPTION
        WHEN no_data_found THEN
        Message ('empty table');
END;
```

In the above example, exception is used in the PL/SQL block. This exception is predefined internal PL/SQL exception (NO_DATA_FOUND).

Therefore, it does not require declaration in DECLARE section and RAISE statement in BEGIN … END portion of the block. Even though it is not raised, the ORACLE server will raise this exception when there is no data in ***bal*** and ***accnt_id*** field.

8.7 PL/SQL FUNCTIONS AND PROCEDURES

PL/SQL allows you to define functions and procedures. These are similar to functions and procedures defined in any other languages, and they are defined as one PL/SQL block.

Functions: The syntax for defining a function is as follows:

```
FUNCTION name [(argument-list)] RETURN data-type {IS, AS}
        Variable-declarations
BEGIN
        Program-code
```

```
[EXCEPTION]
        error-handling-code
END;
```

In this syntax,

name	The name you want to give the function.
argument-list	List of input and/or output parameters for the functions.
data-type.	The data type of the function's return value.
variable-declarations	Where you declare any variables that are local to the function.
program-code	Where you write PL/SQL statements that make up the function.
error-handling-code	Where you write any error handling routine.

Notice that the function block is similar to the PL/SQL block that we discussed earlier.

The keyword DECLARE has been replaced by FUNCTION header, which names the function, describes the parameter and indicates the return type.

Functions can be called by using name (argument list)

Example:

```
FUNCTION check(b_exp in BOOLEAN,
        True_number    in    NUMBER,
         False_number   in    NUMBER)
RETURN NUMBER IS
BEGIN
    IF b_exp THEN RETURN true_number;
ELSE
        RETURN  false_number;
    END IF;
END;
```

The above function can be called as follows:

```
Check ( 2 > 1, 1, 0)
Check (5 = 0, 1, 0)
```

Procedures: The declaration of procedures is almost identical to that of function and the syntax is given below.

```
PROCEDURE  name [(argument list)] {IS,AS}
      Variable declaration
BEGIN
      Program code
[EXCEPTION]
      Error handling code
END;
```

Here ***name*** is the name that you want to give the procedure and all other are similar to function declaration. Procedure declaration resembles a function declaration except that there is no data type and key word PROCEDURE is used instead of FUNCTION.

Example:

```
PROCEDURE swapn (A IN OUT NUMBER, B IN OUT NUMBER) IS
        Temp_num        NUMBER;
BEGIN
        Temp_num:= A;
        A:= B;
        B:= temp_num;
        END;
```

The above procedure can be called as follows:

```
        Swapn (3,4);
        Swapn (–6,7);
```

8.8 DATABASE TRIGGERS

PL/SQL can be used to write database triggers. Triggers are used to define code that is executed/fired when certain actions or event occurs. At the database level, triggers can be defined for events such as inserting a record into a table, deleting a record, and updating a record.

The trigger definition consists of following basic parts:

- The events that fires the trigger.
- The database table on which event must occur.
- An optional condition controlling when the trigger is executed.
- A PL/SQL block containing the code to be executed when the trigger is fired.

A trigger is a database object, like a table or an index. When you define a trigger, it becomes a part of the database and it is always is executed when the event for which it is defined occurs.

Syntax for creating a database trigger is shown below.

```
CREATE [or REPLACE ] TRIGGER trigger-name
{BEFORE | AFTER } verb-list ON table-name
[FOR EACH ROW [ WHEN condition ] ]
DECLARE
    Declarations
BEGIN
    PL/SQL code
END;
```

In the above syntax

REPLACE	Is used to recreate if trigger already exists.
trigger-name	Is the name of the trigger to be created.
verb-list	The SQL verbs that fire the Create, i.e., it may be INSERT, UPDATE or DELETE.
table-name	The table on which the trigger is defined.
condition	An optional condition placed on the execution of the triggers.

declarations	Consists of any variable, record or cursor declarations needed by this PL/SQL blocks.
PL/SQL code	PL/SQL code that is executed when the trigger fires.

Example:

```
CREATE TRIGGER check_salary
        BEFORE insert or update of SAL, JOB on EMP
FOR EACH ROW WHEN ( new.Job != 'director')
DECLARE
        minsal          NUMBER;
        maxsal          NUMBER;
BEGIN
        SELECT min_sal, max_sal INTO minsal, maxsal
        FROM salary-mast WHERE JOB = :new.job;
IF ( :new-sal < minsal or :new.sal > maxsal ) THEN
        Message ( 'salary out of range' );
END IF;
END;
```

8.9 CURSORS

PL/SQL cursors provide a way for your program to select multiple rows of data from the database and then to process each row individually. Cursors are PL/SQL constructs that enable you to process, one row at a time, the results of a multi row query.

ORACLE uses work areas to execute SQL statements, PL/SQL allows user to name private work areas and access the stored information. The PL/SQL constructs to identify each work area used by SQL is called a ***Cursor***.

There are two types of cursors.

- Implicit cursors
- Explicit cursors

Implicit cursors are declared by ORACLE for each UPDATE, DELETE and INSERT SQL commands. Explicit cursors are declared and used by the user to process multiple row, returned by SELECT statement.

The set of rows returned by a query is called the ***Active Set***. Its size depends on the number of rows that meet the search criteria of the SQL query. The data that is stored in the cursor is called the ***Active Data Set***.

ORACLE cursor is a mechanism used to easily process multiple rows of data. Cursors contain a pointer that keeps track of current row being accessed, which enables your program to process the rows at a time.

Example:

When a user executes the following SELECT statement:

```
SELECT emp_no, emp_name, job, salary
FROM employee
WHERE dept = 'ACCOUNTING'
```

The resultant dataset will be displayed as follows:

1234	Rajiv	Asst. Professor	22,000.00
1345	Shailesh	Senior Lecturer	17,000.00
1400	Prashant	Lab Incharge	9,000.00

Explicit cursor management: The following are the steps to using explicitly defined cursors within PL/SQL:

- Declare the cursor
- Open the cursor
- Fetch data from the cursor
- Close the cursor

Declaring the cursor: Declaring a cursor enables you to define the cursor and assign a name to it. It has following syntax:

CURSOR cursor-name IS SELECT statement

Example:
```
CURSOR c_name IS
SELECT emp_name FROM Emp WHERE dept = 'ACCOUNTING'
```

Opening a cursor: Opening a cursor executes the query and identifies the active set that contains all the rows, which meet the query search criteria.

Syntax:
```
OPEN cursor_name
```

Example:
```
OPEN c_name
```

Open statement retrieves the records from the database and places it in the cursor (private SQL area).

Fetching data from cursor: The fetch statement retrieves the rows from the active set one row at a time. The fetch statement is used usually used in conjunction with iterative process (looping statements). In iterative process the cursor advances to the next row in the active set each time the fetch command is executed. The fetch command is the only means to navigate through the active set.

Syntax: FETCH cursor-name INTO record-list

Record-list is the list of variables that will receive the columns (fields) from the active set.

Example:

```
LOOP
-----------------
-----------------
FETCH c_name INTO name;
-----------------
END LOOP;
```

Closing a cursor: Closing statement closes/deactivates/disables the previously opened cursor and makes the active set undefined. Once it is closed, you cannot perform any operations on it. Once a cursor is closed, the user can reopen the cursor by using Open statement.

Syntax: CLOSE cursor_name

Example: CLOSE c_name;

Example:

The HRD manager has decided to raise the salary for all the employees in the ACCOUNTING department by 0.05, whenever any such raise is given to the employees, a record for the same is maintained in the emp_raise table (the data table definitions are given below). Write a PL/SQL block to update the salary of each employee and insert the record in the emp_raise table.

Table: employee

emp_code	varchar (10)
emp_name	varchar (10)
dept	varchar (15)
job	varchar (15)
salary	number (6,2)

Table: emp_raise

emp_code	Varchar(10)
raise_date	Date
raise_amt	Number(6,2)

Solution:

```
DECLARE
    CURSOR c_emp IS
      SELECT emp_code,  salary  FROM employee
        WHERE dept =    'ACCOUNTING';
    str_emp_code        employee.emp_code %TYPE;
    num_salary          employee.salary %TYPE;
BEGIN
     OPEN  c_emp;
  LOOP
    FETCH c_emp INTO str_emp_code, num_salary;
    UPDATE  employee SET salary:= num_salary + (num_salary * 0.05)
      WHERE emp_code = str_emp_code;
    INSERT INTO emp_raise
       VALUES ( str_emp_code, sysdate, num_salary * 0.05 );
  END LOOP;
    Commit;
    CLOSE c_emp;
END;
```

Explicit cursor attributes: ORACLE provides certain attributes/cursor variables to control the execution of the cursor. Whenever any cursor (explicit or implicit) is opened and used, ORACLE creates a set of four system variables via which ORACLE keep track of the "current status" of the cursor. Programmers can access these variables. They are

- %NOT FOUND: Evaluates to TRUE if the last fetch is failed i.e., no more rows are left.
  Syntax: cursor_name %NOT FOUND
- %FOUND: Evaluates to TRUE, when last fetch succeeded
  Syntax: cursor_name %FOUND
- %ISOPEN: Evaluates to TRUE, if the cursor is opened, otherwise evaluates to FALSE.
  Syntax: cursor_name %ISOPEN
- %ROWCOUNT: Returns the number of rows fetched.
  Syntax: cursor_name %ROWCOUNT.

Example:

```
DECLARE
            v_emp_name          varchar2(32);
            v_salary_rate       number(6,2);
            v_payroll_total     number(9,2);
            v_pay_type          char;
    CURSOR c_emp IS
            SELECT emp_name, pay_rate, pay_type FROM employee
            WHERE emp_dept = 'physics'
    BEGIN
            IF c_name %ISOPEN THEN
                    RAISE
                            not_opened
                    ELSE
                            OPEN c_emp;
            LOOP
        FETCH c_emp INTO       v_emp_name, v_salary_rate, v_pay_type;
                    EXIT WHEN c_emp % NOTFOUND;
                    IF v_pay_type = 'S' THEN
                            v_payroll_total:= (v_salary_rate * 1.25);
                    ELSE
                            v_payroll_total:= (v_salary_rate * 40);
                    END IF;
                INSERT INTO weekly_salary VALUES ( 'v_payroll_total');
            END LOOP;
                CLOSE c_emp;
```

```
EXCEPTION
            WHEN not_opened
                Message ( 'cursor is not opened' );
END;
```

REVIEW QUESTIONS

1. Write a PL/SQL block. Take the salary of an employee into a variable and check if he/she are earning less than 5000. If it is then update that salary to 6000.
2. Write a PL/SQL block. Declare a variable eno and assign it a value 1003. Update the EMP table with salary = 6850 where empno = eno.
3. Write a PL/SQL block to delete all the employees from department 20 and check the number of records deleted. Insert the deleted values in a table log_table, which has the same attributes as EMP table.
4. In a PL/SQL block, declare two variables. Data type should be the same as that in the table. Select the data (for any two fields) from table to these variables change the values of these variable and through a PL/SQL block insert these values back to the table.
5. Write a PL/SQL block to invert a given number. (Try separately by using WHILE LOOP and FOR LOOP).
6. Consider three tables say tablel, table2 and table3; all having a number type field say num. Insert some records in tablel and table2. Now write a PL/SQL block to add the corresponding value of num field of tablel and table2 and insert these values to table, table3 (For example first record of table3 should be equal to the first record of table1 plus first record of table2 and so on).
7. In the above question assume that third table is having some already records. Now write the PL/SQL block to update the corresponding values to the addition of corresponding records of table1 and table2.
8. Declare a cursor that selects all the employees in a given department, raise the salary by 3%, and updates the table.
9. Write a PL/SQL block to display the five highest salaries along with the employee names, which are getting those salaries. (Use cursor concept)
10. Produce a block to delete all rows from the table emp. Define an exception to trap the internal error-1031 (Insufficient privileges), and include a handler, which sends message to the MESSAGE table (assume that table is already created), if the exception occurs.
11. Write a PL/SQL block, which raises a user-defined exception on insertion of invalid departments in DEPT table. (Assume that deptno 40 and 50 are invalid departments).
12. Write a procedure, which accepts a parameter eno and raises the salary of the employee to 3%.
13. Write a function, which calculates the experience of an employee. Now call this function in a program and increase the salary up 5% of that employee if his experience more than 5 years.
14. Write a function that checks if salary is in range or not according to the designation of the employees, (say for CEO between 8000 and 10000, for Managers between 5000 and 8000 and for others below 5000). It should give a meaningful message when called from a program.
15. Write a trigger that maintains the history of the EMP table. When an insert, update or delete operation is applied on EMP table it should insert a related information say empno, date_op, user_name should be inserted in a separate table say HISTORY.

CHAPTER 9

Database Design

In this chapter, you will learn

9.0 DEFINITION OF FUNCTIONAL DEPENDENCY

Given a relation r(R) and two sets of its attributes A and B. We will say that attributes A functionally determines B with respect to r, i.e., $A \rightarrow B$, if for any two tuples t_1 and t_2 whenever $t_1(A) = t_2(A)$, then $t_1(B) = t_2(B)$.

- This means that whenever the two tuples have identical value in A, then, corresponding values in B are also identical. In the notation $A \rightarrow B$, A is called determinant.

  Based on the definition given above, A and B have been defined as a set of attributes. Therefore, A and B can be called composite attributes.

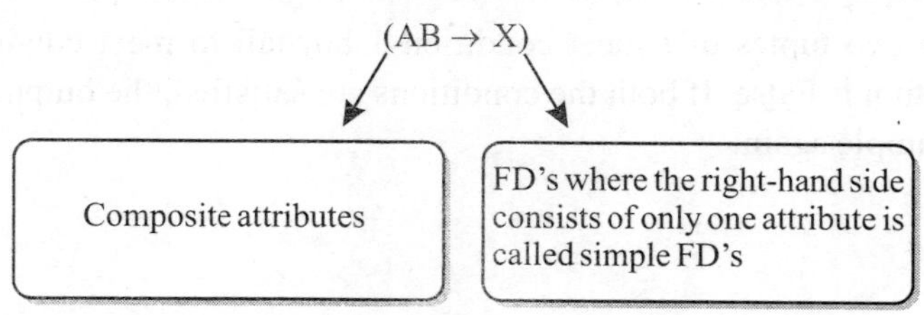

- Given the Lakes_of_the_world, relation shown below, state whether or not the functional dependencies
  (a) Continent → Name
  (b) Name → Length

Lakes_of_the_world

Name	Continent	Area	Length
Caspian Sea	Asia-Europe	143744	760
Superior	North-America	31700	350
Victoria	Africa	26828	250
Aral Sea	Asia	24904	280
Huron	North-America	23000	206
Michigan	North-America	22300	307
Great Sea	Africa	12700	420

Solution:

(a) → Continent → Name

t_1: (Superior, North-America, 31700, 350)

t_2: (Huron, North-America, 22300, 307)

Notice that, t_1(Continent) = t_2(Continent) → North-America, but,

t_1(Name) = Superior & t_2(Name) = Huron ∴ t_1(Name) ≠ t_2(Name)

Since, these two tuples are not same, thus, Continent → Name.

(b) Name → Length is true, because for any Name, there is only one Length attached to it.

From the above-mentioned discussion, it is always possible to determine if a given functional dependency is satisfied or not by an instance of relation. This Satisfies Algorithm can be used to determine whether a given relation r satisfies or not a given functional dependency A → B.

Satisfies Algorithm

The steps of Satisfies Algorithm are as follows:

(1) Sort the tuples of the relation r on the A attribute(s).

(2) Check that tuples with equal values under A also have equal values under B.

(3) If any two tuples of r meet condition 1 but fail to meet condition 2, the output of the algorithm is False. If both the conditions are satisfied, the output of the algorithm is True.

Using the same example again:

Name	Continent	Area	Length
Caspian Sea	Asia-Europe	143744	760
Superior	North-America	31700	350
Victoria	Africa	26828	250
Aral Sea	Asia	24904	280
Huron	North-America	23000	206
Michigan	North-America	22300	307
Great Sea	Africa	12700	420

We have sorted continent.

t_1: (Superior, North-America, 31700, 350)

t_2: (Huron, North-America, 22300, 307)

t_1: (Superior) $\neq t_2$(Huron), Output is False and FD is not true.

9.1 INFERENCE AXIOMS FOR FUNCTIONAL DEPENDENCIES

The Inference Axioms is another method that allows us to define the FD's without any use of algorithms. Given the set of FD's on the relation, inference axioms are the set of rules that lets us to define the set of FD's that is satisfied by relation r.

These defined FD's are called DERIVED or LOGICALLY DEDUCED from the FD's of F. These Inference axioms are complete and sound.

- **Complete** → Complete means that given a set of FD's , we may be able to derive a new set of FD's.
- **Sound** → Sound because that if the axioms are applied correctly, then, we cannot derive false dependencies.

(1) Reflexivity rule:

If α be the set of attributes and $\beta \subseteq \alpha$, then $\alpha \to \beta$ holds.

(2) Augmentation rule:

If $\alpha \to \beta$ and γ be the set of attributes, then, $\gamma\alpha \to \gamma\beta$ holds.

(3) Transitivity rule:

If $\alpha \to \beta$ and $\beta \to \gamma$ holds, then $\alpha \to \gamma$ also holds.

(4) Union rule:

If $\alpha \to \beta$ holds and $\alpha \to \gamma$ holds, then $\alpha \to \beta\gamma$ also holds.

(5) Decomposition rule:

If $\alpha \to \beta\gamma$ holds, then $\alpha \to \beta$ and $\alpha \to \gamma$ also holds.

(6) Pseudotransitivity rule:

If $\alpha \to \beta$ and $\beta\gamma \to \delta$ holds, then, $\alpha\gamma \to \delta$ also holds.

Some of the important examples of Inference Axioms (ARMSTRONG AXIOMS) are as follows:

Example: Given the set of F = {A → B, C → X, BX → Z}, derive AC → Z using inference axioms.

→ Using Pseudotransitivity rule:

$A \rightarrow B$ and $BX \rightarrow Z \rightarrow AX \rightarrow Z$

$C \rightarrow X$ and $AX \rightarrow Z \rightarrow AC \rightarrow Z$ //Proved

Example: Given $F = \{A \rightarrow B, C \rightarrow D\}$ and $C \subset B$, show that $F \mid = A \rightarrow D$.

Using Reflexivity rule: $C \subset B \rightarrow B \rightarrow C$

$A \rightarrow B$ and $B \rightarrow C \rightarrow A \rightarrow C$ (Transitivity rule)

$A \rightarrow C$ and $C \rightarrow D \rightarrow A \rightarrow D$ (Transitivity rule)

9.2 REDUNDANT FUNCTIONAL DEPENDENCIES

Given a set F of FD's, a functional dependency A→ of F is called redundant w.r.t., FD's of F, if $A \rightarrow B$ can be derived from the set of functional dependencies $\rightarrow F - \{A \rightarrow B\}$

We have to determine which of the functional dependency in our relation is redundant; we do it by using Membership Algorithm.

Membership Algorithm:

Assume that F is the set of Functional Dependencies with $A \rightarrow B \in F$. To determine whether $A \rightarrow B$ is redundant, we proceed with the following steps:

(1) Remove temporarily $A \rightarrow B$ from F.

$\therefore G = F - \{A \rightarrow B\}$

If $G \neq \phi$, proceed to step 2 otherwise stop executing.

(2) Initialize the set of attributes $T_i (i = 1)$ with the determinants of A

$T_i = T_1 = \{A\}$

(3) In the set G, search for the functional dependence $X \rightarrow Y$, such that the determinants of the attribute X are the member of T_i. There are two possible outcomes to this search:

(a) If such a functional dependency is found, then the right hand side of $X \rightarrow Y$ is attached:

$$T_{i+1} = T_i \cup Y.$$

Check if all the attributes of B are members if T_{i+1}. If this is the case, stop executing as $A \rightarrow B$ is redundant. If this is not the case, then remove $X \rightarrow Y$ from G and go to step 3.

(b) If $G = \phi$ or G does not have FD's, such that the attributes of its determinants are the members of T_i, then $A \rightarrow B$ is not redundant.

Based on the algorithm given above, let us take into consideration the following example:

Example: Given that the set $F=\{X \rightarrow YW, XW \rightarrow Z, Z \rightarrow Y, XY \rightarrow Z\}$, determine if the functional dependency $XY \rightarrow Z$ is redundant in F.

Step 1: $G = F - \{XY \rightarrow Z\}$

$G = \{X \rightarrow YW, XW \rightarrow Z, Z \rightarrow Y\}$

Step 2: Initialize the set of attributes of T_i

$T_i = T_1 = \{XY\}$

Step 3: $G = \{X \rightarrow YW, XW \rightarrow Z, Z \rightarrow Y\}$

(*1st Time*) If any of the determinants of the given FD's is the member of G.

$X \rightarrow YW$ (X is member)

$\therefore T_{i+1} = T_2 = T_1 \cup (YW) = XY \cup YW \rightarrow (XYW)$

Since 2, $(Z \notin T_2)$ (R.H.S. of $XY \rightarrow Z$)

$\therefore$ Remove $X \rightarrow YW$

$\therefore G = \{XW \rightarrow Z, Z \rightarrow Y\}$

$T_2 = (XYW)$

Step 4:

(*2nd Time*) Since $XW \rightarrow Z$(determinant XW) is the member of T_2

$\therefore T_3 = T_2 \cup Z \rightarrow XYW \cup Z = WXYZ$

Since $Z \in T_3 S$ $\therefore$ the algorithm stops and $XY \rightarrow Z$ is redundant and can be safely removed from the FD's.

To verify whether $XY \rightarrow Z$ is redundant, we can also make use of Inference Axioms, as given under:

$XY \rightarrow Z \rightarrow X \rightarrow Z$ and $Y \rightarrow Z$

$F = \{X \rightarrow YW, XW \rightarrow Z, Z \rightarrow Y\}$

If any one of the functional dependency is defined, $XY \rightarrow Z$ will be considered redundant

* $X \rightarrow YW, XW \rightarrow Z, Z \rightarrow Y$

$X \rightarrow Y, X \rightarrow W, XW \rightarrow Z$

$\therefore XX \rightarrow Z$

$\rightarrow X \rightarrow Z$

$\therefore XY \rightarrow Z$ is redundant.

9.3 CLOSURE OF A SET OF FUNCTIONAL DEPENDENCIES

Given a set of functional dependencies F on relation R, then F^+, the closure of F, defines the set of FD's, which are logically implied by F.

Mathematically,

$$F^+ = \{X \rightarrow Y \mid F \models X \rightarrow Y\}$$

The closure of a set of FD's defines the following properties:

(1) F^+ is the smallest set, which contains F and satisfies property 2.

(2) Any application of the inference axioms on F, gives the FD's, which are already in F^+.

Example: Given set $F = \{XY \rightarrow Z\}$ determine all the element of F^+.

$F^+ = \{X \rightarrow X, Y \rightarrow Y, Z \rightarrow Z, XY \rightarrow X, XY \rightarrow Y, XY \rightarrow XY, YZ \rightarrow Y, YZ \rightarrow Z, YZ \rightarrow YZ, XZ \rightarrow X, XZ \rightarrow Z, XZ \rightarrow XZ, XYZ \rightarrow XY, XYZ \rightarrow YZ, XYZ \rightarrow XZ, XYZ \rightarrow XYZ\}$

9.4 CLOSURE OF A SET OF ATTRIBUTES

Definition:

Given the set of attributes X and the set of functional dependencies F on relation scheme R. Thus, the closure of the set of attributes, hereby denoted as X^+, is the set of attributes A that can be derived from X by applying Inference axioms on functional dependencies F of relation R.

The best way to find X^+ in a given FD F of R is to use Closure Algorithm.

Closure Algorithm

Input → set F of FD

Output → X^+

The steps of algorithm are as follows:

(1) Set G = F.

(2) Initialize set of attributes T_i={X}

(3) In the set G, look for the FD's {X → Y} such that the determinant of its attributes is the elements of T_i. There can be two possible conditions:

(a) If determinant of any of the attribute matches with T_i, the set

$$T_{i+1} = T_i \cup Y \text{ (Y is the R.H.S. of } X \rightarrow Y)$$

and remove X → Y as it no longer contributes new attributes to future T_i's.

(b) If G = ϕ or there are no determinants in FD's, then stop execution of the algorithm.

When the algorithm stops, the final values of $T_{i(i+1)} = X^+$.

Consider the following example:

Example: Given the set of functional dependencies F = {A → B, B → C, BC → D, DA → B}, find X^+ for X={A}.

Using Closure Algorithm

Step 1: Set G = F → G = {A → B, B → C, BC → D, DA → B}

Step 2: T_i = X = {A}

Step 3:/a Since determinant of A → B is in T_i

(1st Time) ∴ $T_2 = T_1 \cup \{B\} = AB$

Remove A → B since it no longer contributes any of the attributes to future T_i's.

Step 3:/a

(2nd Time) T_2={AB} [B → C]

∴ $T_3 = T_2 \cup \{C\} = \{ABC\}$

Remove B → C

Step 3:/a

(3rd Time) T_3={ABC} [BC → D]

∴ $T_4 = T_3 \cup \{D\} = \{ABCD\}$

Remove $BC \rightarrow D$

Step 3:/a

(4th Time) $T_4 = \{ABCD\}$ $[DA \rightarrow B]$

$\therefore T_5 = T_4 \cup \{B\} = \{ABCD\}$

Step 3:/b

(1st Time) Since $G = \phi$, the algorithms stop

$\therefore T_i = T_5 = \{ABCD\} = X^+$.

9.5 COVERS AND EQUIVALENCE OF SET OF FUNCTIONAL DEPENDENCIES

Over the relation R, let us consider that F is the set of FD's. That F^+ contains the large number of elements. Thus, if F is large, then F^+ becomes even larger. We need to find F, which is small, but, even contains all the elements of FD. Such sets are called equivalent set of FD's. We can formalize the definition as follows:

If F and G are the FD of R, then we say F and G are equivalent if $F^+ = G^+$ or $F \equiv G$. Whenever $F^+ = G^+$, we say F covers G or vice versa. When G covers F and no proper subset H of G is such that $H^+ = G^+$, then G is the non-redundant cover of F.

9.6 EXTRANEOUS ATTRIBUTES

If F is a set of non-redundant FD of R, then F cannot be made smaller. Even though, if we are able to remove the left OR right attribute(s) from the FD, then such attributes are called as Extraneous Attributes.

Let F be FD of R and let $A_1A_2 \rightarrow B_1B_2$ exists. Then attribute A_1 is Extraneous attribute if $F \equiv F - \{A_1A_2 \rightarrow B_1B_2\} \cup \{A_2 \rightarrow B_2\}$, if attribute A_1 can be removed from the determinant of $A_1A_2 \rightarrow B_1B_2$ (left redundant)

Similarly, in $A_1A_2 \rightarrow B_1B_2$, B_1 is Extraneous right attribute if

$F \equiv F - \{A_1A_2 \rightarrow B_1B_2\} \cup \{A_1A_2 \rightarrow B_2\}$ (right redundant)

9.7 CANONICAL COVER

For a given set of attribute, a canonical cover, given by F_c is a set of FD's where:

(1) F_C is simple, means R.H.S. of FD contains only one attribute.

(2) F_C is left reduced.

(3) F_C is non-redundant.

9.8 NORMAL PROCESS

In relational databases the name *normalization* refers to a reversible step-by-step process in which an agreed set of relations is replaced by successive collections of relations that have a progressively simpler and more regular structure. Each step, referred to as a *normal form,* and defines a set of criterion (the normal form test) that needs to be met by the different tables of the database. In this sense, to say that a relation is in a particular normal form is an indication of the conditions that the table has met. Since the process is reversible, the original set of relations can be improved with no loss of information. As the normalization progresses to higher forms, the individual collection of relation becomes progressively more restricted on the type of functional dependencies that they can satisfy and the data anomalies that they can experience. Data anomalies will be explained in detail in following Section:

The objectives of the normalization process are:

- To make it feasible to symbolize any relation in the database.
- To find powerful relational retrieval algorithms based on a collection of primitive relational operators.
- To free relations from unwanted insertion, update, and deletion anomalies.
- To decrease the need for restructuring the relations as new data types are introduced.

The first two objectives pertain specifically to the First Normal Form; the last two apply to all normal forms. These terms will be clear shortly.

The entire normalization process is based upon the analysis of relations, their schemes, their primary keys and their functional dependencies. Whenever a relation does not meet a normal form test, the relation must be *decomposed* or broken into some other relations that individually meet the criteria of the normal form test. Initially, E. F. Codd proposed three normal forms that he called first, second, and third normal form. These forms are generally abbreviated and referred to as 1NF, 2NF, and 3NF respectively. In addition to these original normal forms there exist others such as the Boyce-Codd Normal Form (BCNF), Fourth Normal Form (4NF), and Fifth Normal Form (5NF). The relationship between some of these normal forms is shown in Figure 9.1. This figure is sometimes referred to as the normal form *"onion"*. A discussion of these forms follows.

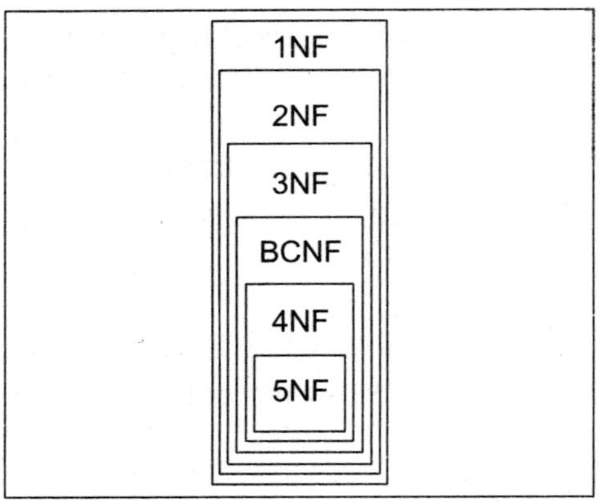

Figure 9.1: *Hierarchy of the Normal Forms*

9.9 FIRST NORMAL FORM

Occasionally, during the procedure of designing a database it may be essential to transform into a relation a given table that in some of its entries (the intersection of a row and a column) may have more than one value. For example, consider the PROJECT table shown in Figure 9.2, where one or more employees may be assigned to a project. Notice that for each Project id (Proj-ID) every *"row"* of the table has more than one value under the columns empno, ename, deptno, Emp-Hrly-Rate, and Total-Hrs.

Proj-ID	Proj-Name	Proj-Mgr-Id	empno	ename	deptno	Emp-Hrly-Rate	Total-Hrs
100	e-Com	7321	7876	ADAMS	20	65	10
			7369	SMITH	20	45	6
			7788	SCOTT	20	35	6
			7844	TURNER	30	30	12
110	DBMS	7962	7698	BLAKE	30	50	5
			7900	JAMES	30	35	12
			7499	ALLEN	30	30	8
125	Web Designing	7391	7521	WARD	30	80	4
			7766	JONES	20	35	11
			7654	MARTIN	30	30	12
			7876	ADAMS	20	65	7
150	AI	7698	7782	CLARK	10	65	7

Figure 9.2: *PROJECT table*

To refer to this type of table and how tables relate to relations some new terms are necessary. Table entries that have more than one value are called *multivalue* entries. Tables with multivalue entries are called *unnormalized* tables. Within an unnormalized table, we will describe a *repeating group* an attribute or group of attributes that might have multivalue entries for single occurrences of the table identifier. This last term refers to the attribute that allows us to distinguish the different rows of the unnormalized table. Using this terminology, we can describe the PROJECT table shown above as an unnormalized table where attributes *empno, ename, deptno, Emp-Hrly-Rate,* and *Total-Hrs* are repeating groups. We already know that this type of table cannot be considered a relation because there are entries with more than one value.

To be able to symbolize this table as a relation and to implement it in a RDBMS, it is necessary *to normalize the table.* In other words, we need to locate the table in first normal form. We can properly define the latter term as follows: A relation r(R) is said to be in *First Normal Form (1NF)* if and only if every entry of the relation (the intersection of a tuple and a column) has at most a single value. A number of authors prefer to state that a relation is in 1NF if and only if all its attributes are based upon a simple domain. These two definitions are equivalent. If all relations of a database are in 1NF we will say that the database is in 1NF.

The objective of normalizing a table is to remove its repeating groups and ensure that all entries of the resulting table have at most a single value. The reader should be aware that by simply removing their repeating groups unnormalized tables do not become relations automatically. Some further manipulation of the resulting table(s) may be necessary to ensure that they are indeed relations. In general, there are two basic approaches to normalize tables. We will consider these two approaches next.

The first approach, known as 'flattening the table', removes repeating groups by filling in the 'missing' entries of each 'incomplete row' of the table with copies of their corresponding nonrepeating attributes.

In the PROJECT table, for each individual project, under the empno, ename, deptno, Emp-Hrly-Rate, and Total-Hrs attributes there is more than one value per entry. To normalize this table, we just fill in the remaining entries by copying the corresponding information from the nonrepeating attributes.

For instance, for the row that contains the employee Jones, we fill in the remaining 'blank' entries by copying the values of the Proj-ID, Proj-Name, and Proj-Mgr-ID columns. This row has now a single value in each of its entries. In the new table shown below, we have grayed all the new set of tuples for the employees of the E-commerce project. We have repeated a similar process for the employees of the remaining two projects. The normalized representation of the PROJECT table is:

Proj-ID	Proj-Name	Proj-Mgr-Id	empno	ename	deptno	Emp-Hrly-Rate	Total-Hrs
100	e-Com	7321	7876	ADAMS	20	65	10
100	e-Com	7321	7369	SMITH	20	45	6
100	e-Com	7321	7788	SCOTT	20	35	6
100	e-Com	7321	7844	TURNER	30	30	12
110	DBMS	7962	7698	BLAKE	30	50	5
110	DBMS	7962	7900	JAMES	30	35	12
110	DBMS	7962	7499	ALLEN	30	30	8
125	Web Designing	7391	7521	WARD	30	80	4
125	Web Designing	7391	7766	JONES	20	35	11
125	Web Designing	7391	7654	MARTIN	30	30	12
125	Web Designing	7391	7876	ADAMS	20	65	7
150	AI	7698	7782	CLARK	10	65	7

This normalized PROJECT table is not a relation because it does not have a primary key. The attribute Proj-ID no longer identifies uniquely any row. Notice that all rows in the grayed area have the same Proj-ID. To transform this table into a relation a primary key needs to be defined. A suitable primary key for this table is the *composite key (Proj-ID, empno)*.

To normalize the PROJECT table we need to replace it by two new tables. The first table contains the table attribute and the nonrepeating groups. The attributes are: Proj-ID (the table identifier), Proj-Name, and Proj-Mgr-ID. The second table contains the table identifier and all the repeating groups. Therefore, the attributes of this table are: Proj-ID, empno, ename, deptno, Emp-Hrly-Rate, and Total-Hrs. To transform the latter table into a relation, it is necessary to assign it a primary key. These two new 1NF relations are shown below. Notice that for the PROJECT-EMPLOYEE table the composite attribute (Proj-ID, empno) is an appropriate primary key.

Project

Proj_id	Proj-Name	Proj-Mgr-ID
100	e-Com	7321
110	DBMS	7962
125	Web Designing	7391
150	AI	7698

Project-Employee

Proj-ID	empno	ename	deptno	Emp-Hrly-Rate	Total-Hrs
100	7876	ADAMS	20	65	10
100	7369	SMITH	20	45	6
100	7788	SCOTT	20	35	6
100	7844	TURNER	30	30	12
110	7698	BLAKE	30	50	5
110	7900	JAMES	30	35	12
110	7499	ALLEN	30	30	8
125	7521	WARD	30	80	4
125	7766	JONES	20	35	11
125	7654	MARTIN	30	30	12
125	7876	ADAMS	20	65	7
150	7782	CLARK	10	65	7

Data Anomalies in 1NF Relations

Redundancies in 1NF relations lead to a variety of *data anomalies.* By this latter term we mean side effects that the data experience as a result of some relational operations. Data anomalies are divided into three general categories: *insertion, deletion* and *update* anomalies. They are named respectively after the relational operations of INSERT, DELETE and UPDATE because it is during the application of these operations that a relation may experience anomalies. In realism there are only two types of anomalies: update and insertion/deletion anomalies. The latter category can be considered as only one category because a relation that experiences deletion anomalies will also have insertion anomalies. One cannot exist without the other. However, for explanation purposes we will consider these data anomalies as divided into three categories.

To help us appreciate the concept of data anomalies in 1NF relations, let's consider the functional dependency empno $\rightarrow$ deptno of the PROJECT-EMPLOYEE relation of the preceding section, *Insertion anomalies* occur in this relation because we cannot insert information about any new employee that is going to work for a particular department unless that employee is already assigned to a project. Remember that the composite key of this relation is *(Proj-ID, empno).* Notice also that the integrity constraint prevents any attribute of a composite key from being NULL. Likewise, the relation experiences *deletion anomalies* whenever we delete the last tuple of a particular employee. In this case, we not only delete the project information that connects that employee to a particular project but also lose other information about the department for which this employee works. Consider the information that is lost if employee Shaw is deleted. In addition to these two types of anomalies, the relation is also susceptible to *update anomalies* because the department for which an employee works may appear many times in the table. It is this redundancy of information that causes the anomaly because if an employee moves to another department, we are now faced with two problems: we either search the entire table looking for that employee and update his or her deptno value or we miss one or more tuples of that employee and end up with an inconsistent database. For small tables, this type of anomaly may not seem to be much of a problem, but it is easy to imagine situations where there may be thousands of tuples that experience similar anomaly.

9.10 PARTIAL DEPENDENCIES

Given a relation r(R), the sets of attributes X and Y (X, Y $\subset$ R), and X $\rightarrow$ Y, we will say that attribute *Y is fully dependent on attribute X* if and only if there is no proper subset W of X such that W $\rightarrow$ Y. If there is a proper subset W of X such that W $\rightarrow$ Y then attribute Y is said to be *partially dependent on attribute X.* Another way of expressing the concept of partial and full dependency is as follows:

Given $A_1A_2A_3$........A_m $\rightarrow B_1B_2$............B_n with (m > n), the set of attributes B_1B_2.......B_n is said to be partially dependent on attributes $A_1A_2A_3$......A_m if and only if there exists a proper subset of attributes $A_cA_dA_e$......$A_k \subset A_1A_2A_3$ ...A_m such that $A_cA_dA_e$......$A_k \subset B_1B_2$.......B_n. In other words, attributes B_1B_2.......B_n are partially dependent on the determinant if there is a subset of the attributes of the determinant that functionally determine the right-hand side of the FD. If no such a subset of attributes of the determinant exist then we say that attributes B_1B_2.......B_n are fully dependent on the determinant of the FD.

The identification of partial dependencies is a critical aspect of transforming relations to 2NF.

As indicated before, the PK of this relation is formed by the attributes *Proj-ID* and *ename.* This implies that *Proj-ID, ename* functionally determines any individual attribute or any combination of attributes of the relation. However, we only need attribute *empno* to functionally determine the following attributes: *ename, deptno, Emp-Hrly-Rate,* and *Total-Hrs*. In other words, attributes *ename, deptno,* and *Emp-Hrly-Rate* are partially dependent on the key. Figure 9.3 represents the partial dependency of these attributes on the composite key is shown below:

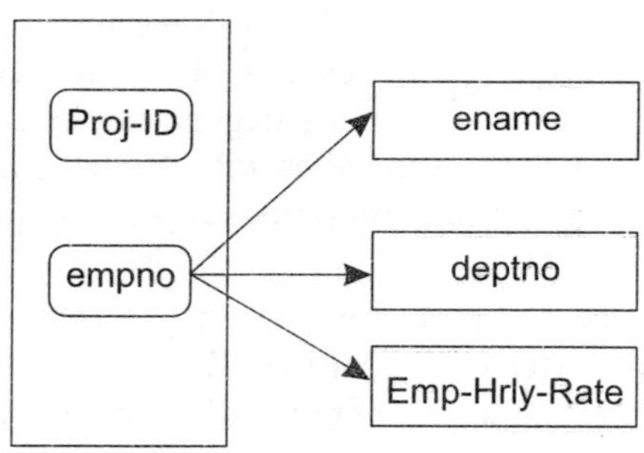

Figure 9.3: *Partial Dependency*

There are no partial dependencies in this table because the determinant of the key only has a single attribute.

9.11 SECOND NORMAL FORM

A relation r(R) is in *Second Normal Form* (2NF) if and only if the following two conditions are met simultaneously:

(1) r(R) is already in 1NF.

(2) No nonprime attribute is partially dependent on any key or, equivalently, each nonprime attribute in R is fully dependent upon every key (including candidate keys).

Notice that in order to find the nonprime attributes of R we need to identify *all* prime attributes of R. As a result of this we need to recognize first *all* possible keys of the relation. The nonprime attributes are then calculated as R-P where P is the set of all prime attributes and R is the relational scheme of R.

If all relations of a database are in 2NF we will say that the database is in 2NF.

To convert a relation into a 2NF relation we will follow the approach illustrated in Figure 9.4. In this Figure, the prime attributes are indicated with asterisks and functional dependencies with arrows. The composite key is indicated with a curly bracket.

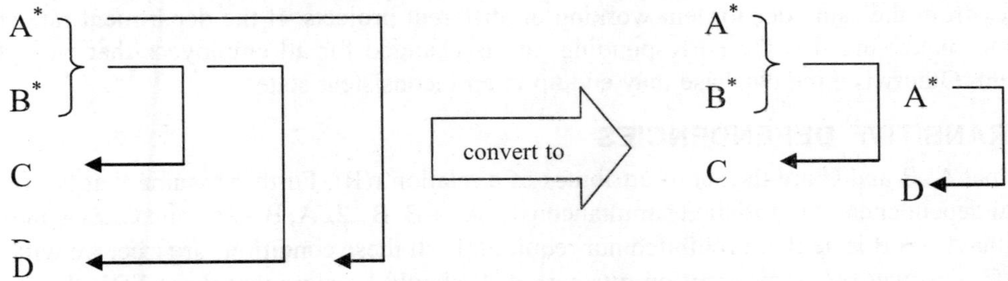

Figure 9.4: *Conversion to 2NF*

Notice that in Figure 9.4, the primary key consists of attributes A and B. These two attributes determine all other attributes. Attributes A and B are the only prime attributes. Attribute C is fully dependent on the key. Attribute D is partially dependent on the key because we only need attribute A to functionally determine it. Attributes C and D are nonprime. Observe that in the Figure the original relation gets replaced by two new relations. The first new relation has three attributes: A, B and C. The primary key of this relation is AB (the primary key of the original relation). The second relation has A and D as its only two attributes. Observe that attribute A has been designated as the PK of the second relation and that attribute D is now fully dependent on the key. Although the Figure only shows four attributes, we can generalize this procedure for any relation that we need to transform to 2NF if we assume that C stands for the collection of attributes that are fully dependent on the key and D stands for the collection of attributes that are partially dependent on the key. The example now illustrates how to transform a relation into 2NF using this general procedure.

The general procedure calls for breaking this relation into two new relations. The first relation has as its primary key the primary key of

PROJECT-EMPLOYEE (Proj-ID, empno)

and the remaining attributes of this relation are all the attributes that fully depend on this key. In this case, the only attribute that fully depends on this composite key is Total-Hours. The scheme of this new relation that we have named *HOURS-ASSIGNED* is as follows:

HOURS-ASSIGNED (Proj-ID, empno, Total-Hours)

The second relation contains as its key the empno attribute since this attribute fully determines the *ename, deptno,* and *Emp-Hrly-Rate.* The scheme of this relation is as follows:

EMPLOYEE(empno, ename, deptno, Emp-Hrly-Rate)

Data Anomalies in 2NF Relations

Relations in 2NF are still subject to data anomalies. For sake of clarification, let us suppose that the department in which an employee works functionally determines the hourly rate charged by that employee. That is, *deptno→Emp-Hrly-Rate*. This fact was not considered in the explanation of the previous normal form but it is not an improbable situation. *Insertion anomalies* occur in the *EMPLOYEE* relation. For example, consider a situation where we would like to set in advance the rate to be charged by the employees of a new department. We cannot insert this information until there is an employee assigned to that department. Notice that the rate that a department charges is independent of whether or not it has employees. The *EMPLOYEE* relation is also susceptible to *deletion anomalies.* This type of anomaly occurs whenever we delete the tuple of an employee who happens to be the only employee left in a department. In this case, we will also lose the information about the rate that the department charges. *Update anomalies* will also occur in the *EMPLOYEE* relation because there may be several employees from the same department working on different projects. If the department rate changes, we need to make sure that the corresponding rate is changed for all employees that work for that department. Otherwise, the database may end up in an inconsistent state.

9.12 TRANSITIVE DEPENDENCIES

Assume that A, B and C are the set of attributes of a relation r(R). Further assume that the following functional dependencies are satisfied simultaneously: $A \rightarrow B$, $B \not\rightarrow A$, $B \rightarrow C$, and $C \not\rightarrow A$ and $A \rightarrow C$. Observe that $C \rightarrow B$ is neither prohibited nor required. If all these conditions are true, we will say that attribute C *is transitively dependent on attribute A.* It should be clear that these FD's determine the conditions for *having* a transitive dependency of attribute C on A. If any of these FD's are not satisfied then attribute C is not transitively dependent on attribute A. Figure 9.5 summarizes these conditions. In this Figure, the arrows are equivalent to the symbol '$\rightarrow$' that we use for denoting FD's. Notice that the functional dependency $A \rightarrow C$ may not be explicitly indicated but it holds true due to the Transitivity axiom. The requirements that $B \not\rightarrow C$ and $C \not\rightarrow A$ are necessary to ensure that attributes A and B are nonprime attributes.

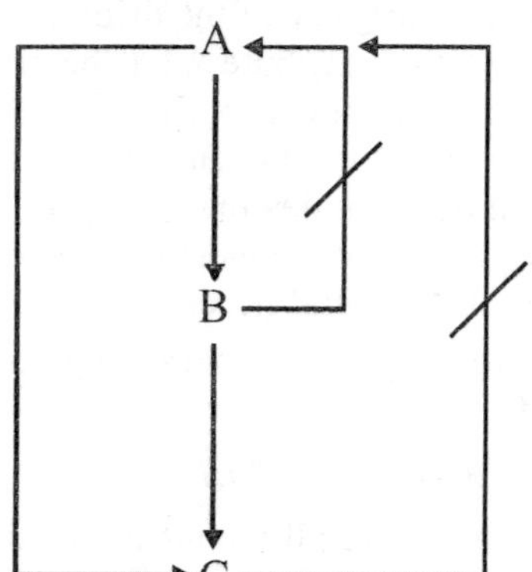

Figure 9.5: *Conditions to define the transitive dependency of attribute C on attribute A*

9.13 THIRD NORMAL FORM

A relation r(R) is in Third Normal Form (3NF) if and only if the following conditions are satisfied simultaneously:

(1) r(R) is already in 2NF.

(2) No nonprime attribute is transitively dependent on the key.

The reader should not get confused with the conditions stated in Figure 9.5 and the second condition of the definition of 3NF. Notice that Figure 9.5 states the conditions that need to be met so that the nonprime attribute C can be transitively dependent on key A. The definition of 3NF requires that these conditions are not met if A is the key attribute and C is a nonprime attribute.

Another method of expressing the conditions for Third Normal Form is as follows:

(1) r(R) is already in 2NF.

(2) No nonprime attribute functionally determines any other nonprime attribute.

Since these two sets of conditions are equivalent, we will use the one that is most convenient for the particular problem at hand.

As these two definitions of 3NF imply, the objective of transforming relations into 3NF is to remove all transitive dependencies. To transform a 2NF relation into a 3NF we will follow the approach indicated by Figure 9.6. In this Figure, assume that any FD not implicitly indicated does not hold. An asterisk indicates the key attribute and the arrows denote functional dependencies. The dotted line indicates that the FD A — C may not be explicitly given but it is always present because it can be derived using the inference axioms.

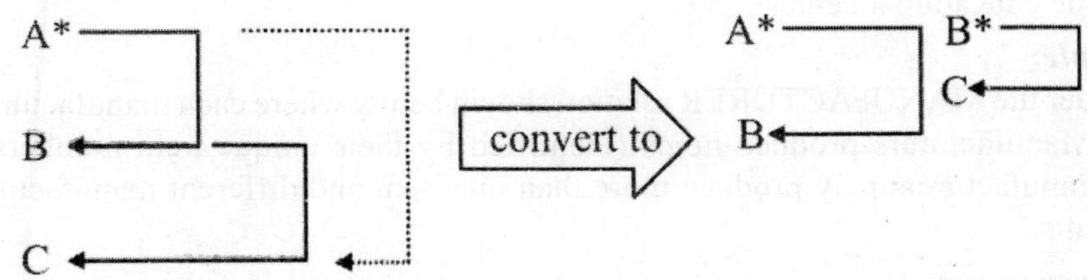

Figure 9.6: *Conversion to Third Normal Form*

Now, we have to convert EMPLOYEE relation into 3NF using the first definition of 3NF.

The relation *EMPLOYEE* is not in 3NF because there is transitive dependency of a nonprime attribute on the primary key of the relation. In this case, the nonprime attribute *Emp-Hrly-Rate* is transitively dependent on the key through the functional dependency *deptno* $\rightarrow$ *Emp-Hrly-Rate*. Notice that all other conditions required by the definition are met by this set of FD's. In particular, we have that *deptno* $\not\rightarrow$ *empno* and *Emp-Hrly-Rate* $\not\rightarrow$ *empno*. To transform this relation into a 3NF relation, it is necessary to remove any transitive dependency of a nonprime attribute on the key. According to the Figure 9.6, it is necessary to create two new relations. The scheme of the first relation is *EMPLOYEE(<u>empno</u>, ename, deptno)*. The scheme of the second relation is *CHARGES(deptno, Emp-Hrly-Rate)*. Observe that in the Second relation, the *deptno* attribute has been made the primary of the relation as required by the Figure.

Data Anomalies in 3NF Relations

The Third Normal Form helped us to get rid of the data anomalies caused either by transitive dependencies on the primary key (PK) or by dependencies of a nonprime attribute on another nonprime attribute. However, relations in 3NF are still susceptible to data anomalies particularly when the relations have two overlapping candidate keys or when a nonprime attribute functionally determines a prime attribute. The following two examples will illustrate this:

Example:

Consider the *CERT-PROG (<u>Area</u>, <u>Course</u>, <u>Section</u>, Time, Location)*

Area	Course	Section	Time	Location
NewDelhi	RDBMS	Introduction	8:00 – 10:00	Advance Training Center
NewDelhi	RDBMS	Introduction	10:00 – 12:00	DBMS Training Center
Lucknow	RDBMS	Professional	8:00 – 10:00	Professional Training Center

This relation is in 3NF because neither of the nonprime attributes functionally determines the other attributes. However, if there is only one instructional center per city then we will have that Location ® Area. This dependency does not violate the 3NF condition but there are some anomalies in the data. For example, assume that if we delete the last tuple of the relation we may lose information about the location of the educational center.

Example:

Consider the MANUFACTURER relation shown below where each manufacturer has a *unique ID* and *name*. Manufacturers produce items (identified by their unique item numbers) in the amounts indicated. Manufacturers may produce more than one item and different manufacturers may produce the same items.

MANUFACTURER

ID	Name	Item-No	Quantity
C110	EC, India	R2345	2300
C110	EC, India	H0987	1200
C110	EC, India	E0009	800
C233	SC, India	W4564	235

This *MANUFACTURER* relation has two candidate keys: *(ID, Item-No)* and *(Name, Item-No)* that overlap on the attribute *Item-No*. The relation is in because there is only one nonprime attributeand therefore it is impossible this attribute can determine another nonprime attribute.

The relation *MANUFACTURER* is susceptible to update anomalies. Consider for example the case in which one of the manufacturers changes its name. If the value of this attribute is not changed in all of the corresponding tuples there is the possibility of having an inconsistent state.

9.14 BOYCE-CODD NORMAL FORM

To eradicate these anomalies in 3NF relations, it is essential to carry out normalization process to the next higher step, the Boyce-Codd Normal Form. This idea is formalized next.

A relation r(R) is in Boyce-Codd Normal Form (BCNF) if and only if the subsequent conditions are met concurrently:

(1) The relation is in 1NF.

(2) For every functional dependency of the form $X \rightarrow A$, we have that either $A \subset X$ or X is a superkey of r. In other words, every functional dependency is either a trivial dependency or in the case that the functional dependency is not trivial then X must be superkey.

Observe that the explanation of BCNF does not make any orientation to the concepts of full or partial dependency. However, from this characterization, we can make the following assertions about the prime and nonprime attributes of the relational scheme:

- All nonprime attributes must be fully dependent on every key.
- All prime attributes must be fully dependent on all keys of which they are not part.

In Figure 9.1, we can observe that the set of 3NF relations are a proper subset of the BCNF relations. That is, all BCNF are in 3NF but not all 3NF are in BCNF. In this sense, the definition of BCNF is said to be more restrictive. The following example illustrates this.

Example:

Using the MANUFACTURER relation of the previous example, transform it to BCNF. To convert this relation into BCNF we can decompose it into the subsequent set of relational schemes:

Set No. 1

MANUFACTURER(ID, Name)

MANUFACTURER-PART(ID, Item-No, Quantity) .

or

Set No. 2

MANUFACTURER(ID, Name)

MANUFACTURER-PART(Name, Item-No, Quantity)

Observe that both relations are in BCNF and that the update data anomaly be no longer present. In this instance, we have decomposed the relation in a manner that is suitable for purpose of the clarification.

9.15 MULTI-VALUED DEPENDENCIES

Consider the database of an 'Institute' where we have the information about the faculties, their subjects and the committees for which they are the in charge. For example, faculty *'Rajiv'* is teaching *RDBMS, Java* and *Electronic-Commerce* and is *Coordinator of Training & Placement* and *Admissions* committees. Now we can store this information in many ways as given below:

Faculty	Subject	Committee
Rajiv	RDBMS	Training & Placement
Rajiv	Java	Admissions
Rajiv	Electronic Commerce	Admissions

Figure 9.7(a): *Minimal number of records with repetitions*

Faculty	Subject	Committee
Rajiv	RDBMS	Training & Placement
Rajiv	Java	Admissions
Rajiv	Electronic Commerce	

Figure 9.7(b): *Minimal number of records with NULL values*

Faculty	Subject	Committee
Rajiv	RDBMS	
Rajiv	Java	
Rajiv	Electronic Commerce	
Rajiv		Training & Placement
Rajiv		Admissions

Figure 9.7(c): *Minimal number of records with no repetition*

Each explanation seems unsatisfactory in some way or the other. It requires more time for DBMS optimizer to process the null values or redundant data. Moreover it is not clear that Committee and Subject attributes are independent to each other or not. For example, in first case RDBMS subject in some way connected to Training & Placement committee. However in case (iv) this apparent relationship between independent attributes is eliminated by requiring that every value of one attribute appears in at least with one row with every value of the other attribute. In this case, Training & Placement and Admissions committees appear in rows with all three subjects. This leads to the redundancy in data. The fact that 'Rajiv' can teach 'RDBMS' is recorded once per committee, which John is Coordinating. A condition that enforces attribute independence by requiring this duplication of values is called multi-valued dependency.

Faculty	Subject	Committee
Rajiv	RDBMS	Training & Placement
Rajiv	Java	Training & Placement
Rajiv	Electronic Commerce	Training & Placement
Rajiv	RDBMS	Admissions
Rajiv	Java	Admissions
Rajiv	Electronic Commerce	Admissions

Figure 9.8: *Relation with Multi-valued Dependency*

Multi-valued dependency (MVD) occurs when two or more independent multi-valued facts about the same attribute occur within the same relation. More generally, MVD can be defined as:

Let R be a relational scheme and let X and Y be the subsets of attributes of R. Intuitively the MVD $X \rightarrow \rightarrow Y$ is said to hold over R if, in every legal instance r of R, each X value is associated with a set of Y values and this set is independent of the values in the other attributes.

Intuitively, a multi-valued dependency is denoted by $X \rightarrow \rightarrow Y$ and will be read as "there is a multi-valued dependency of Y on X" or 'X multi determines Y'.

We can infer several MVD's from a given set of MVD by using the Armstrong axioms. These axioms are given below:

- Complementation: If $X \rightarrow \rightarrow Y$, then, $X \rightarrow \rightarrow R\text{-}XY$.
- Augmentation: If $X \rightarrow \rightarrow Y$ and $Z \subseteq W$, then $WX \rightarrow \rightarrow YZ$

- Transitivity: If $X \rightarrow \rightarrow Y$ and $Y \rightarrow \rightarrow Z$ then $X \rightarrow \rightarrow Z - Y$

There are two more rules, which relate FD's and MVD's.

- Replication: If $X \rightarrow Y$, then $X \rightarrow \rightarrow Y$
- Coalescence: If $X \rightarrow \rightarrow Y$ and there is a W such that $W \cap Y$ is empty, $W \rightarrow Z$, and $Z \subseteq Y$ then $X \rightarrow Z$.

9.16 FOURTH NORMAL FORM

A table is in fourth normal form *if it is in BCNF and it contains no multi-valued dependencies*.

Consider again the same Faculty relation with MVD. Clearly a faculty has multiple courses to teach and he is heading several committees. This relation is in BCNF, since all the three attributes concatenated together constitutes its key, yet it is clearly wrong and requires decomposition. The rule for decomposition is to decompose the offending table into two, with the multi-determinant attribute or attributes as part of the key of both. In this case, to put the relation in 4NF, two separate relations are formed as follows:

FACULTY_COURSE (FACULTY, COURSE)
FACULTY COMMITTEE (FACULTY, COMMITTEE)

Faculty	**Subject**
Rajiv	RDBMS
Rajiv	Java
Rajiv	Electronic Commerce

FACULTY_COURSE Relation

Faculty	**Committee**
Rajiv	Training & Placement
Rajiv	Admissions

FACULTY_COMMITTEE Relation

Figure 9.9: *Relations in 4NF*

Now these relations are in 4NF, because all multi-valued attributes (Course and Committee) have been placed in relations by themselves. Moreover this approach overcomes the problems of the various approaches discussed in MVD section.

9.17 JOIN DEPENDENCY AND FIFTH NORMAL FORM

5NF is of little practical use to the database designer, but may be important from theoretical point of view. For a relation to be in a particular normal form, we generally decompose the relation into two separate relations in such a way that there should not be any loss of information. No-loss decomposition is possible because of the availability of the join operator as part of the relational model.

More technically, in 5NF we use the concept of **Join Dependency**, which is a generalized form of Multi-valued dependency. A join dependency (JD), denoted by $JD(R_1, R_2, \ldots, R_n)$ specified on relation scheme R, specifies a constraint on the states r of R. The constraint states that every legal state r of R should have a loss-less join decomposition into $R_1, R_2, \ldots, R_n$.

A relation is in 5NF if it is in 4NF and cannot be further non-loss decomposed.

No loss decomposition is possible because of the availability of the join operator in Relational model. Such decomposition can only be achieved by decomposing into three or more separate tables. Such decomposition is not always possible as in some cases we can loose some information if we do the decomposition. Taking the following example, we can show this:

Consider the relation COMPANY_PRODUCT_SUPPLIER

Company	Product	Supplier
Sony	CD	Rohan
Sony	Cell phone	Rohan
Sony	Cell phone	Rakesh
Sony	Cell phone	Shashi
Samsung	CD	Rohan
Samsung	CD	Rakesh
Samsung	Cell phone	Rakesh

Figure 9.10: *COMPANY_PRODUCT_SUPPLIER Relation*

The table is in fourth normal form as there is no multi-valued dependency. It does, however have a lot of redundancies. For example 'Rohan' is a supplier for 'Sony' for twice and 'Rakesh' is also supplier for 'Samsung' twice. But if we decompose the table then we will loose information, which can be shown as follows:

Suppose the table is decomposed into two parts as:

COMPANY_PRODUCT

Company	Product
Sony	CD
Sony	Cell phone
Sony	Cell phone
Sony	Cell phone
Samsung	CD
Samsung	CD
Samsung	Cell phone

COMPANY_SUPPLIER

Company	Supplier
Sony	Rohan
Sony	Rakesh
Sony	Shashi
Samsung	Rohan
Samsung	Rakesh

The above said redundancy has been eliminated but we have lost the information. For example, if we want to display the products and their suppliers, then we will have to use the join based on the company attribute. The result will display some spurious records. For Shashi, it will display both the products, CD and Cell phone as the company for which Shashi is the supplier (Sony) is producing CD and Cell phone, which is incorrect.

Now suppose that the original tables were to be decomposed in three parts, COMPANY_PRODUCT, COMPANY_SUPPLIER and one more PRODUCT_SUPPLIER, which is as given below:

PRODUCT_SUPPLIER

Product	**Supplier**
CD	Rohan
CD	Rakesh
Cell phone	Rohan
Cell phone	Rakesh
Cell phone	Shashi

If a join is taken of all the projections, again we will get wrong results. So it is not possible to decompose the original table without loosing information. Thus using the normalization techniques cannot eliminate all redundancies, because it cannot be assumed that all decompositions will be non-loss. So it is clear that if a table is in 4NF and cannot be further non-loss decomposed, it is said to be in 5NF

It can be revealed that if a table is in 5NF then it should also be in 4NF because join dependency is the ultimate form of all the dependencies, thus confirming to all the further normal forms.

9.18 INCLUSION DEPENDENCIES

Definition:

An **inclusion dependency** $R.X < S.Y$ between two sets of attribute–X of relation schema R, and Y of relation schema S–specifies the constraint that, at any specific time when γ is a relation state of R and s a relation state of S, we must have:

$$\Pi_X(\gamma(R)) \subseteq \Pi_{\gamma}(s(S))$$

The $\subseteq$ (subset) relationship does not necessarily have to be a proper subset. Obviously, the sets of attributes on which the inclusion dependency is specified–X of R and Y of S–must have the same number of attributes. In addition, the domains for each pair of corresponding attributes should be compatible. For example, if $X=\{A_1,A_2,\dots A_n\}$ and $Y=\{B_1,B_2,\dots B_n\}$, one possible correspondence is to have $dom(A_i)$ compatible with $dom(B_i)$ for $1 \le i \le n$. In this case, we say that A_i **corresponds** to B_i.

To understand in detail about the concept of Inclusion Dependencies, consider COMPANY relational schema given below:

EMPLOYEE

Ename	SSN (PK)	Bdate	Address	Dnumber (FK)

DEPARTMENT

Dname	Dnumber (PK)	Dmgrssn (FK)

DEPT_LOCATIONS

Dnumber	Dlocation

PK (Dnumber, Dlocation)

PROJECT

Pname	Pnumber	Plocation	Dnum
	PK		FK

WORKS_ON

SSN	Pnumber	Hours
FK	FK	

PK (SSN, Pnumber)

We can specify the following inclusion dependencies on the relational schema:

DEPARTMENT.Dmgrssn < EMPLOYEE.SSN

WORKS_ON.SSN < EMPLOYEE.SSN

EMPLOYEE.Dnumber < DEPARTMENT.Dnumber

PROJECT.Dnum < DEPARTMENT.Dnumber

WORKS_ON.Pnumber < PROJECT.Pnumber

DEPT_LOCATIONS.Dnumber < DEPARTMENT.Dnumber

All the preceding inclusion dependencies represent **referential integrity constraints.**

The inclusion dependency inference rules (IDIR) are as follows:

(1) *Reflexivity*: R.X < R.X.

(2) *Attribute Correspondence:* If R.X < S.Y, whee X={A_1, A_2,......A_n} and Y={B_1,B_2,......B_n} and A_i corresponds to B_i, then R.A_i < S.B_i for $1 \leq i \leq n$.

(3) *Transitivity:* If R.X < S.Y and S.Y < T.Z, then R.X < T.Z.

The preceding inference axioms are sound and complete for inclusion dependencies.

9.19 LOSSLESS OR LOSSY DECOMPOSITIONS

So far we have decomposed a relation using either a general procedure or an ad-hoc method. However, whenever a relation is decomposed it is necessary to ensure that the data in the original relation is represented faithfully by the data in the relations that are the result of the decomposition; that is, we need to make sure that we can recover the original relation from the new relations that have replaced it. Generally the original relation is recovered by forming the natural join of the new relations. If we can recover the original relation we say that the decomposition is lossless with respect to D or that the relation has lossless-join decomposition with respect to D where D is a set of FD's satisfied by the original relation. If the relation cannot be recovered we say that the decomposition is lossy. We can formalize this concept as follows:

Assume that a relation $r(R)$ has been replaced by a collection or relation $r_1(R_1)$, $r_2(R_2)$, ... $r_n(R_n)$ such that $R = R_1 \cup R_2 \cup \ldots\ldots\ldots\ldots \cup R_n$ and D is a set of dependencies satisfied by r. We say that the decomposition is *lossless with respect to D or is a lossless-join decomposition with respect to D* if and only if $r = \pi_{R1}(r)$ join $\pi_{R2}(r)$ join . . .join $\pi_{Rn}(r)$. That is, the relation r is lossless if it is the natural join of its projections onto the Ri's. If the relation cannot be recovered from the natural projection the decomposition is said to be lossy with respect to D. The following example illustrates this concept.

Example:

Consider the relation r shown below and its decomposition R_1 and R_2. Assume that $X \rightarrow Y$ and $Z \rightarrow Y$. Is this decomposition lossless or lossy?

r

X	Y	Z
x_1	y_1	z_1
x_2	y_2	z_2
x_3	y_2	z_3
x_4	y_3	z_4

Decompose

R_1

X	Y
x_1	y_1
x_2	y_2
x_3	y_2
x_4	y_3

R_2

Y	Z
y_1	z_1
y_2	z_2
y_2	z_3
y_3	z_4

R_1 join R_2

X	Y	Z
x_1	y_1	z_1
x_2	y_2	z_2
x_2	y_2	z_3
x_3	y_2	z_2
x_3	y_2	z_3
x_4	y_3	z_4

Notice that the natural join of relations R_1 and R_2 has tuples that were not present in the original relations. These additional tuples that were not in the original relation are called *spurious tuples* because they represent spurious or false information that is not valid. We have grayed the spurious tuples in the join relation. Since the natural join of relation R_1 and R_2 does not recover the original relation the decomposition is lossy.

Testing for Lossless Joins

As indicated before, lossless-join decomposition is necessary to ensure that the relation is recoverable. Determining whether or not decomposition is lossless or lossy with respect to a set of FD's is a fairly easy procedure if we use the Lossless Join Algorithm. This algorithm is shown next.

The Lossless-Join Algorithm

The algorithm has two inputs. The first input is a set of relations $r_1 (R_1), r_2(R_2), ..., r_n (R_k)$ that have replaced a relation $r(A_1,A_2, A_3,..., A_n)$ where $R = \{A_1, A_2, A_3,..., A_n\} = R_1 \cup R_2 \cup ... \cup R_k$. The second input to the algorithm is a set F of functional dependencies satisfied by r. The output of the algorithm is a decision staling that the decomposition is lossless or lossy. To apply this algorithm proceeds as follows:

(1) Construct a table with n columns (n is the number of attributes of the original relation) and k rows (k is the number of relations in which the original relation has been decomposed). Label the columns of this table $A_1, A_2, A_3,..., An$ respectively. Label the rows $R_1, R_2, R_3,..., R_k$.

(2) Fill in the entries of this table as follows:

For each attribute A_i check if this attribute is one of the attributes of the scheme of the relation R_j. If attribute A_i is in the scheme of R_j, then in the entry (A_i, R_j) of the table write a_i. If attribute A_i is not one of the attributes in the scheme of relation R_j then in the entry (A_i, R_j) write b_{ij}.

(3) For each of the functional dependencies $X \rightarrow Y$ of F do the following *until* it is not possible to make any more changes to the table. When the table no longer changes, continue with step 4.

Look for two or more rows that have the same value under the attribute or attributes that comprise X (the determinant of the FD under consideration). There are two possible outcomes to this search:

(a) If there are two or more rows with the same value under the attribute or attributes of the determinant X then make equal their entries under attribute Y (the right-hand side of the FD under consideration). When making equal two or more symbols under any column, if one of them is a_j, make all of them a_j. If they are b_{ij} and b_{kl}, choose one of these two values as the representative value and make the other values equal to it. Continue with Step 3.

(b) If there are no two rows with the same value under the attribute or attributes of the determinant X continue with step 3.

(4) Check the rows of the table. If there is a row with its entries equal to $a_1, a_2,......,a_n$ then the decomposition is lossless. Otherwise, the decomposition is lossy.

Example:

Consider the relation r(X, Y, Z, W, Q=), the set $F = \{X \rightarrow Z, Y \rightarrow Z, Z \rightarrow W, WQ \rightarrow Z, ZQ \rightarrow X\}$ and the decomposition of r into relations $R_1(X,W)$, $R_2(X,Y)$, $R_3(Y,Q)$, $R_4(Z,W,Q)$, and $R_5(X,Q)$. Using the Lossless-Join Algorithm determine if the decomposition is lossless or lossy.

Steps 1-2: Since the original relation has 5 attributes and the original relation has been decomposed into 5 relations, we need to create a table with 5 columns and 5 rows. The columns of the table are named X, Y, Z, W and Q respectively. The rows of the table are named R_1, R_2, R_3, R_4 and R_5 respectively. For explanation purposes we have renamed the attributes A_1, A_2,..., A_5. The table is shown below:

	X(A_1)	Y(A_2)	Z(A_3)	W(A_4)	Q(A_5)
R_1					
R_2					
R_3					
R_4					
R_5					

Since X is one of the attributes of relation R_1 we write ai the entry (R_1, A_1) or its equivalent (R_1, X). In other words, under column A_1 (or X) and row R_1 we write ai as seen in the row pointed to by the arrow (see below). Likewise, we write a_4 in the entry corresponding to (R_1, A_4) or its equivalent (R_1, W) because W is also an attribute of relation R_1. That is, under column A_4 (or W) and row R_1 we write a_4 as seen in the row pointed to by the arrow (see below). In the remaining entries of row R_1 we write the values b_{ij} where i is the column number and j is the row number. These entries (from left to right) are b_{12}, b_{13} and b_{15} respectively as seen in the row pointed to by the arrow in the following table:

	X(A_1)	Y(A_2)	Z(A_3)	W(A_4)	Q(A_5)
→ R_1	a_1	b_{12}	b_{13}	a_4	b_{15}
R_2					
R_3					
R_4					
R_5					

Proceeding in this fashion we fill in the remaining entries in the table. After filling in all entries the table looks like this.

	X(A_1)	Y(A_2)	Z(A_3)	W(A_4)	Q(A_5)
R_1	a_1	b_{12}	b_{13}	a_4	b_{15}
R_2	a_1	a_2	b_{23}	b_{24}	b_{25}
R_3	b_{31}	a_2	b_{33}	b_{34}	a_5
R_4	b_{41}	b_{42}	a_3	a_4	a_5
R_5	a_1	b_{52}	b_{53}	b_{54}	a_5

Steps 3/3-a: (1*st* Time) Considering $X \rightarrow Z$ or its equivalent $A_1 \rightarrow A_3$ we look for tuples that have the same value under column X (or A_i). In this case, rows R_1, R_2 and R_5 have the same value a_1.

Therefore, we equate or make equal the values under attribute Z (or A_3). Remember that Z (or A_3) is the right-hand side of the functional dependency that we are considering. Notice that the corresponding entries for rows R_1, R_2 and R_5 under the Z column are b_{13}, b_{23} and b_{53} respectively. To equate these entries to the same value we need to choose one of them arbitrarily and make the other two entries the same. Choosing b_{13} as the representative value and changing the remaining two entries to this value, we have that the table looks like the one shown next. Notice that we have grayed the entries that were made equal to the value b_{13} of row R_1. Repeat step 3.

	$X(A_1)$	$Y(A_2)$	$Z(A_3)$	$W(A_4)$	$Q(A_5)$
R_1	a_1	b_{12}	b_{13}	a_4	b_{15}
R_2	a_1	a_2	b_{13}	b_{24}	b_{25}
R_3	b_{31}	a_2	b_{33}	b_{34}	a_5
R_4	b_{41}	b_{42}	a_3	a_4	a_5
R_5	a_1	b_{52}	b_{13}	b_{52}	a_5

Steps 3/3-a: (2*nd* Time) Considering $Y \rightarrow Z$ or its equivalent $A_2 \rightarrow A_3$, we now look for rows that have the same value in the column Y (or A_2). In this case, rows R_2 and R_3 have the same value a_2. Therefore, we need to equate the corresponding entries under column Z (or A_3). Choosing b_{13} as the representative value we can change the b_{33} entry to b_{13}. After this change the table looks like the one shown below. Notice that we have grayed the row whose entry changed. Repeat step 3.

	$X(A_1)$	$Y(A_2)$	$Z(A_3)$	$W(A_4)$	Q(A)
R_1	a_1	b_{12}	b_{13}	a_4	B_{15}
R_2	a_1	a_2	b_{13}	b_{24}	B_{25}
R_3	b_{31}	a_2	b_{33}	b_{34}	a_5
R_4	b_{41}	b_{42}	a_3	a_4	a_5
R_5	a_1	b_{52}	b_{13}	b_{52}	a_5

Steps 3/3-a: (3*rd* Time) Considering $Z \rightarrow W$ or its equivalent $A_3 \rightarrow A_4$,we look for tuples that have identical values under column Z (or A_3). In this case rows R_1, R_2, R_3 and R_5 have the same value, b_{13}, under this column. Therefore, we need to make equal all entries under column W (or A_4). Since one of the values under column W (or A_4) is a, (for row R_1), we make all the b_{ij}'s entries equal to a_4. The resulting table is shown next. As before we have grayed all entries that were changed. Repeat step 3.

	X(A_1)	Y(A_2)	Z(A_3)	W(A_4)	Q(A_5)
R_1	a_1	b_{12}	b_{13}	a_4	b_{15}
R_2	a_1	a_2	a_3	a_4	b_{25}
R_3	b_{31}	a_2	a_3	a_4	a_5
R_4	b_{41}	b_{42}	a_3	a_4	a_5
R_5	a_1	b_{52}	a_3	a_4	a_5

Steps 3/3-a: (4*th* Time) Considering WQ $\rightarrow$ Z or its equivalent $A_4 A_5 \rightarrow A_3$, we now look for rows that have identical values under columns A_4 and A_5 simultaneously. Rows R_3, R_4, and R_5 have values of a_4 and a_5 under columns WQ (or a_4 and a_5) respectively. Therefore, we need to equate all the corresponding entries for these rows under column Z (or A_3). Since all the values under column Z (or A_3) are already equal no changes are necessary. Repeat step 3.

Steps 3/3-a: (5*th* Time) Considering ZQ $\rightarrow$ X or its equivalent $A_3 A_5 \rightarrow A_1$, we look for rows that have equal values under columns ZQ (or $A_3 A_5$) simultaneously. Rows R_3, R_4 and R_5 have values equal to a_3 and a_5 under columns A_3 and A_5 respectively. Therefore, it is necessary to equate their corresponding entries under column X (or A_1). Since one of the entries is a_1 (for row R_5),we make all the remaining b_{ij}'s equal to a_1. The resulting table, after all the corresponding changes are made, looks like the one shown below. As in all cases before, we have grayed the entries that were affected by the changes. Repeat step 3.

	X(A_1)	Y(A_2)	Z(A_3)	W(A_4)	Q(A_5)
R_1	a_i	b_{12}	b_{13}	a_4	b_{15}
R_2	a_1	a_2	a_3	a_4	b_{25}
R_3	a_1	a_2	a_3	a_4	a_5
R_4	a_1	b_{42}	a_3	a_4	a_5
R_5	a_1	b_{52}	a_3	a_4	a_5

Steps 3/3-a: (6*th* time) There are no more FD's to consider and the table cannot undergo any more changes. Therefore, we are through with step 3 and move to step 4.

Step 4: (1*st* Time) We now look for a row that has all a_i's. Since row R_3 has become $a_1 a_2 a_3 a_4 a_5$ (see below) the decomposition is lossless.

	X(A_1)	Y(A_2)	Z(A_3)	W(A_4)	Q(A_5)
R_1	a_1	b_{12}	b_{13}	a_4	b_{15}
R_2	a_1	a_2	a_3	a_4	b_{25}
R_3	a_1	a_2	a_3	a_4	a_5
R_4	a_1	b_{42}	a_3	a_4	a_5
R_5	a_1	b_{52}	a_3	a_4	a_5

REVIEW QUESTIONS

1. What do you mean by Normalization? Why normalization is required in database designing?
2. Discuss the various problems, which we have to face without normalizing the database.
3. Explain functional dependency with suitable example.
4. Explain why BCNF is stronger than Third Normal Form.
5. Explain the following Normal Forms. Take the appropriate examples for each normal form to convert the relation into a particular normal form.
   (*a*) 1NF (*b*) 2NF
   (*c*) 3NF (*d*) BCNF
   (*e*) 4NF (*f*) 5NF
6. Define the following:
   (*a*) Multi-valued dependency
   (*b*) Join dependency
   (*c*) Lossless dependency
   (*d*) Closure of a set of functional dependency.
7. A relation R satisfies the following FDs:
   $ABD \rightarrow E, AB \rightarrow G, B \rightarrow F, C \rightarrow J, CJ \rightarrow I, G \rightarrow H.$

   Find the closure (A, B, C, J)* of the set of attributes (A, B, C, J) under the set of given FDs.

CHAPTER 10

Query Processing

In this chapter, you will learn

10.0 Introduction

10.1 Phases of Query Processing

10.2 Query Optimization

10.3 Algorithms for Algebra Operations

Review Questions

10.0 INTRODUCTION

In this chapter, we will discuss in detail about the query processing in DBMS and you will find many repetitions from the previous chapters. That is included in this chapter purposefully in order to maintain the continuity and meaningfulness of the topic, which we are going to deal with.

10.1 PHASES OF QUERY PROCESSING

In most database systems, queries are posed in a non-procedural language like SQL and as we have noted earlier such queries do not involve any reference to access paths or the order of evaluation of operations. The query processing of such queries by a DBMS usually involves the following four phases (Figure 10.1):

1. Parsing
2. Optimization
3. Code Generation
4. Execution

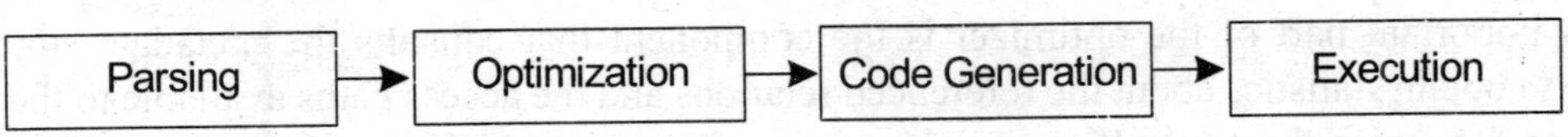

Figure 10.1: *Phases of Query Processing*

The parser checks the query for correct syntax and translates it into a conventional parse-tree (often called a *query-tree*) or some other internal representation.

If the parser returns with no errors, and the query uses some user-defined views, it is necessary to expand the query by making appropriate substitutions for the views. It is then necessary to check the query for semantic correctness by consulting the system catalogues and check for semantic errors and type compatibility in both expressions and predicate comparisons. The optimizer is then invoked with the internal representation of the query as input so that a *query plan* or *execution plan* may be devised for retrieving the information that is required. The optimizer carries out a number of operations. It relates the symbolic names in the query to data base objects, checks their existence, and further checks if the user is authorized to perform the operations that the query specifies.

In formulating the plans, the query optimizer obtains relevant information from the metadata that the system maintains and attempts to model the estimated costs of performing many alternative query plans and then selects the best amongst them. The metadata or system catalog consists of descriptions of all the databases that a DBMS maintains. Often, the query optimizer would at least retrieve the following information:

1. Cardinality of each relation of interest.
2. The number of pages in each relation of interest.
3. The number of distinct keys in each index of interest.
4. The number of pages in each index of interest.

The above information and perhaps other information will be used by the optimizer in modeling the cost estimation for each alternative query plan.

Considerable other information is normally available in the system catalog:

1. Name of each relation, all its attributes, and their domains.
2. Information about the primary key and foreign keys of each relation.
3. Descriptions of views.
4. Descriptions of storage structures.
5. Other information including information about ownership and security issues.

Often this information is updated only periodically and not at every update/insert/delete. In addition, the system catalog is often stored as a relational database itself making it easy to query the catalog if a user is authorized to do so.

Information in the catalog is very important of course since query processing makes use of this information extensively. Therefore, more comprehensive and more accurate information a database maintains the better optimization it can carry out but maintaining more comprehensive and more accurate information also introduces additional overheads and a good balance therefore must be found.

The catalog information is also used by the optimizer in access path selection. These statistics are often updated only periodically and therefore are not always accurate.

An important part of the optimizer is the component that consults the metadata stored in the database to obtain statistics about the referenced relations and the access paths available to them. These are used to determine the most efficient order of the relational operations and the most efficient access paths. The order of operations and the access paths are selected from a number of alternate possibilities that normally exist so that the cost of query processing is minimized. More details of query optimization are presented in the next section (Section 10.2).

If the optimizer finds no errors and outputs an execution plan, the code generator is then invoked. The execution plan is used by the code generator to generate the machine language code and any associated data structures. This code may now be stored if the code is likely to be executed more than once. To execute the code, the machine transfers control to the code which is then executed.

10.2 QUERY OPTIMIZATION

Query processing and query optimization are almost the same. Before query optimization is carried out, one would ofcourse need to decide what needs to be optimized. The goal of achieving efficiency itself may be different in different situations. For example, one may wish to minimize the processing time but in many situations one would wish to minimize the response time. In other situations, one may wish to minimize the I/O, network time, memory used or some sort of combination of these e.g., total resources used. Generally, a query processing algorithm A will be considered more efficient than an algorithm B if the measure of cost being minimized for processing the same query given the same resources using A is generally less than that for B.

To illustrate the desirability of optimization, we now present an example of a simple query that may be processed in several different ways. The following query retrieves subject names and instructor names of all current subjects in Computer Science that Rohan is enrolled in.

SELECT *subject.name, instructor*
FROM *student, enrolment, subject*
WHERE *student.student_id* = *enrolment.student_id*
AND *subject.subject_id* = *enrolment.subject_id*
AND *subject.department* = *'Computer Science'*
AND *student.name* = *'Rohan'*

To process the above query, two joins and two restrictions need to be performed. There are a number of different ways by which these may be performed including the following:

1. Join the relations *student* and *enrolment*, join the result with *subject* and then do the restrictions.
2. Join the relations *student* and *enrolment*, do the restrictions, join the result with *subject*.
3. Do the restrictions, join the relations *student* and *enrolment*, join the result with *subject*.
4. Join the relations *enrolment* and *subject*, join the result with *student* and then do the restrictions.

Here we are, talking about the cost estimates. Before we attempt to compare the costs of the above four alternatives, it is necessary to understand that estimating the cost of a plan is often non-trivial. Since normally a database is disk-resident, often the cost of reading and writing to disk dominates the cost of processing a query. We would therefore estimate the cost of processing a query in terms of disk accesses or block accesses. Estimating the number of block accesses to process even a simple query is not necessarily straight forward since it would depend on how the data is stored and which, if any, indexes are available. In some database systems, relations are stored in packed form, that is, each block only has tuples of the same relation while other systems may store tuples from several relations in each block making it much more expensive to scan all of a relation.

Let us now compare the costs of the above four options. Since exact cost computations are difficult, we will use simple estimates of the cost. We consider a situation where the enrolment database consists of 10,000 tuples in the relation *student*, 50,000 in *enrolment*, and 1,000 in the relation *subject*. For simplicity, let us assume that the relations *student* and *subject* have tuples of similar size of around 100 bytes each and therefore we can accommodate 10 tuples per block if the block is assumed to be 1 Kbytes in size. For the relation *enrolment*, we assume a tuple size of 40 bytes and thus we use a figure of 25 tuples/block. In addition, let John Smith be enrolled in 10 subjects and let there be 20 subjects offered by Computer Science. We can now estimate the costs of the four plans listed above.

The cost of query plan (1) above may now be computed. Let the join be computed by reading a block of the first relation followed by a scan of the second relation to identify matching tuples (this method is called *nested-scan* and is not particularly efficient. We will discuss the issue of efficiency of algebraic operators in later section). This is then followed by the reading of the second block of the first relation followed by a scan of the second relation and so on. The cost of *R* |X| *S* may therefore be estimated as the number of blocks in *R* times the number of blocks in *S*. Since the number of blocks in *student* is 1000 and in *enrolment* 2,000, the total number of blocks read in computing the join of *student* and *enrolment* is 1000 * 2000=2,000,000 block accesses. The result of the join is 50,000 tuples since each tuple from *enrolment* matches with a tuple from *student*. The joined tuples will be of size approximately 140 bytes since each tuple in the join is a tuple from *student* joined with another from *enrolment*. Given the tuple size of 140 bytes, we can only fit 7 tuples in a block and therefore we need about 7,000 blocks to store all 50,000 joined tuples. The cost of computing the join of this result with *subject* is 7000 * 100=700,000 block accesses. Therefore the total cost of plan (1) is approximately 2,700,000 block accesses.

To estimate the cost of plan (2), we know the cost of computing the join of *student* and *enrolment* has been estimated above as 2,000,000 block accesses. The result is 7000 blocks in size. Now the result of applying the restrictions to the result of the join reduces this result to about 5-10 tuples i.e., about 1-2 blocks. The cost of this restriction is about 7000 disk accesses. Also the result of applying the restriction to the relation *subject* reduces that relation to 20 tuples (2 blocks). The cost of this restriction is about 100 block accesses. The join now only requires about 4 block accesses. The total cost therefore is approximately 2,004,604.

To estimate the cost of plan (3), we need to estimate the size of the results of restrictions and their cost. The cost of the restrictions is reading the relations *student* and *subject* and writing the results. The reading costs are 1,100 block accesses. The writing costs are very small since the size of the results is 1 tuple for *student* and 20 tuples for *subject*. The cost of computing the join of *student* and *enrolment* primarily involves the cost of reading *enrolment*. This is 2,000 block accesses. The result is quite small in size and therefore the cost of writing the result back is small. The total cost of plan (3) is therefore 3,100 block accesses.

Similar estimates may be obtained for processing plan (4). We will not estimate this cost, since the above estimates are sufficient to illustrate that *brute force* method of query processing is unlikely to be efficient. The cost can be significantly reduced if the query plan is optimized. The issue of optimization is ofcourse much more complex than estimating the costs like we have done above since in the above estimation we did not consider the various alternative access paths that might be available to the system to access each relation.

The above cost estimates assumed that the secondary storage access costs dominate the query processing costs. This is often a reasonable assumption although the cost of communication is often quite important if we are dealing with a distributed system. The cost of storage can be important in large databases since some queries may require large intermediate results. The cost of CPU of course is always important and it is not uncommon for database applications to be CPU bound than I/O bound as is normally assumed. In the present chapter we assume a centralized system where the cost of secondary storage access is assumed to dominate other costs although we recognize that this is not always true. For example, system *R* uses

$$\boxed{cost = page\ fetches + w\ X\ CPU\ utilization}$$

When a query is specified to a DBMS, it must choose the best way to process it gives the information it has about the database. The optimization part of query processing generally involves the following operations:

1. A suitable internal representation.
2. Logical transformation of the query.
3. Access path selection of the alternatives.
4. Estimate costs and select best.

We will discuss the above steps in detail in the sections to follow:

Internal Representation

As noted earlier, a query posed in a query language like SQL must first be translated to a internal representation suitable for machine representation. Any internal query representation must be sufficiently powerful to represent all queries in the query language (e.g., SQL). The internal representation could be relational algebra or relational calculus since these languages are powerful enough (they have been shown to be *relationally complete* by E.F. Codd) although it will be necessary to modify them from what was discussed in earlier chapters so that features like Group By and aggregations may be represented. A representation like relational algebra is procedural and therefore once the query is represented in that representation, a sequence of operations is clearly indicated.

Logical Transformations

At the beginning of this chapter, we showed that the same query may be formulated in a number of different ways that are semantically equivalent. It is clearly desirable that all such queries be transformed into the same query representation. To do this, we need to translate each query to some canonical form and then simplify.

This involves transformations of the query and selection of an optimal sequence of operations. The transformations that we discuss in this section donot consider the physical representation of the database and are designed to improve the efficiency of query processing whatever access methods might be available. An example of such transformation has already been discussed in the examples given. If a query involves one or more joins and a restriction, it is always going to be more efficient to carry out the restriction first since that will reduce the size of one of the relations (assuming that the restriction applies to only one relation) and therefore the cost of the join, often quite significantly.

- ***Heuristic optimization:*** In the heuristic approach, the sequence of operations in a query is reorganized so that the query execution time improves.
- ***Deterministic optimization:*** In the deterministic approach, cost of all possible forms of a query are evaluated and the best one is selected.
- ***Common subexpression:*** In this technique, common subexpressions in the query, if any, are recognised so as to avoid executing the same sequence of operations more than once.

Heuristic Optimization

Heuristic optimization often includes making transformations to the query tree by moving operators up and down the tree so that the transformed tree is equivalent to the tree before the transformations. Before we discuss these heuristics, it is necessary to discuss the following rules governing the manipulation of relational algebraic expressions:

1. ***Joins and products are commutative***

Example:

$$R \times S = S \times R$$
$$R \mid X \mid S = S \mid X \mid R$$

where |X| may be a θ join or a natural join. The order of attributes in the two products or joins may not be quite the same but the ordering of attributes is not considered significant in the relational model since the attributes are referred to by their name not by their position in the list of attributes.

2. ***Restriction is commutative***

Example:

$$\sigma_p(\sigma_q(R)) = \sigma_q(\sigma_p(R))$$

3. ***Joins and products are associative***

Example:

$$(R \times S) \times T = R \times (S \times T)$$
$$(R \backslash X \backslash S) \backslash X \backslash T = R \backslash X \backslash (S \backslash X \backslash T)$$

The associativity of the above operations guarantees that we will obtain the same results whatever be the ordering of computations of the operations product and join. Union and intersection are also associative.

4. ***Cascade of projections***

Example:

$$\pi_A(\pi_B(R)) = \pi_A(R)$$

where the attributes *A* is a subset of the attributes *B*. The above expression formalizes the obvious that there is no need to take the projection with attributes *B* if there is going to be another projection which is a subset *of B* that follows it.

5. ***Cascade of restrictions***

Example:

$$\sigma_p(\sigma_q(R)) = \sigma_{p \wedge q}(R)$$

The above expression also formalizes the obvious that if there are two restrictions one after the other, then there is no need to carry out the restrictions one at a time (since each will require processing a relation) and instead both restrictions could be combined.

6. ***Commuting restrictions and projections***

Example:

$$\sigma_p(\pi_A(R)) = \pi_A \sigma_p(R)$$

or

$$\pi_A \sigma_p(R) = \sigma_p(\pi_A(R))$$

There is no difficulty in computing restriction with a projection since we are then doing the restriction before the projection. However, if we wish to commute the projection and the restriction, that is possible only if the restriction used no attributes other than those that are in the projection.

7. *Commuting restrictions with cartesian product. In some cases, it is possible to apply commutative law to restrictions and a product.*

Example:

$$\sigma_p(RXS) = \sigma_p(R)XS$$

or

$$\sigma_{p \wedge q}(RXS) = \sigma_p(R)X\sigma_q(S)$$

In the above expressions we have assumed that the predicate p has only attributes from R and the predicate q has attributes from S only.

8. *Commuting restriction with a union.*

9. *Commuting restriction with a set difference.*

10. *Commuting projection with a cartesian product or a join:* We assume that the projection includes the join predicate attributes.

11. *Commuting Projection with a Union.*

We now use the above rules to transform the query tree to minimize the query cost. Since the cost is assumed to be closely related to the size of the relations on which the operation is being carried out, one of the primary aims of the transformations that we discuss is to reduce the size of intermediate relations.

The basic transformations include the following:

(a) *Moving restrictions down the tree as far as possible:* The idea is to carry out restrictions as early as possible. If the query involves joins as well as restrictions, moving the restrictions down is likely to lead to substantial savings since the relations that are joined after restrictions are likely to be smaller (in some cases much smaller) than earlier restrictions. This is clearly shown by the example that we used earlier in this chapter to show that some query plans can be much more expensive than others. The query plans that cost the least were those in which the restriction was carried out first. There are ofcourse situations where a restriction does not reduce the relation significantly, for example, a restriction selecting only women from a large relation of customers or clients.

(b) *Projections are executed as early as possible:* In real-life databases, a relation may have one hundred or more attributes and therefore the size of each tuple is relatively large. Some relations can even have attributes that are images making each tuple in such relations very large. In such situations, if a projection is executed early and it leads to elimination of many attributes so that the resulting relation has tuples of much smaller size, the amount of data that needs to be read in from the disk for the operations that follow could be reduced substantially leading to cost savings. It should be noted that only attributes that we need to retain from the relations are those that are either needed for the result or those that are to be used in one of the operations that is to be carried out on the relation.

(c) *Optimal ordering of the joins:* We have noted earlier that the join operator is associative and therefore when a query involves more than one join, it is necessary to find an efficient ordering for carrying out the joins. An ordering is likely to be efficient if we carry out those joins first that are likely to lead to small results rather than carrying out those joins that are likely to lead to large results.

(d) *Cascading restrictions and projections:* Sometimes it is convenient to carry out more than one operation together. When restrictions and projections have the same operand, the operations may be carried out together thereby saving the cost of scanning the relations more than once.

(e) *Projections of projections are merged into one projection:* Clearly, if more than one projection is to be carried out on the same operand relation, the projections should be merged and this could lead to substantial savings since no intermediate results need to be written on the disk and read from the disk.

(f) *Combining certain restrictions and Cartesian product to form a Join:* A query may involve a Cartesian product followed by a restriction rather than specifying a join. The optimizer should recognize this and execute a join which is usually much cheaper to perform.

(g) *Sorting is deferred as much as possible:* Sorting is normally an *nlogn* operation and by deferring sorting, we may need to sort a relation that is much smaller than it would have been if the sorting was carried out earlier.

(h) A set of operations is reorganized using commutativity and distribution if a reorganized form is more efficient.

Estimating Size of Results

The cost of a query evaluation plan depends on the sizes of the basic relations referenced as well as the sizes of the intermediate results. To obtain reasonable cost estimates of alternate plans, the query optimizer needs estimates of the various intermediate results.

To estimate sizes of the intermediate results, we define the concept of selectivity factor. The selectivity factor roughly corresponds to the expected fraction of tuples which will satisfy the predicates. For the restriction operation, the selectivity factor is the ratio of the cardinality of the result to the base relation. Selectivity of a restriction is estimated by the DBMS by maintaining profiles of attribute value distribution or by making suitable assumptions of the distribution. The selectivity of projection is the ratio of tuple size reduction. Often however it is not only that some attributes are being removed in a projection, the duplicates are also removed. The join selectivity of one relation with another defines the ratio of the attribute values that are selected in one of the relations.

We now consider methods of estimating the cost of several relational operations. Let us consider relations *R* and *S* with n_R and n_S number of tuples respectively. Let b_R and b_S be the number of tuples per block for the relations *R* and *S* respectively. Also, assume further, that ***D(A,S)*** be the number of distinct values of attribute *A* in relation *S*".

Size of a Restriction

A restriction may involve a number of types of predicates as given under:

1. attribute = value
2. attribute1 = attribute2
3. attribute > value
4. attribute between value1 and value 2
5. attribute IN (list of values)
6. attribute IN sub-query
7. predicate expression OR predicate expression
8. predicate expression AND predicate expression

Let us first consider the simplest restriction (1) and a relation *R* that has an attribute *A* on which an equality condition has been specified. If we assume that values of attribute *A* are distributed uniformly, we would expect the result of the restriction (1) above to have approximately $n_R/D(A,R)$ tuples where *D(A,R),* as noted above, is the number of different values that attribute *A* takes in relation *R.* Although the assumption of uniform distribution is almost always unrealistic, the above estimate is easily obtained and is often quite useful.

It is useful to define *selectivity* as the ratio of the number of tuples satisfying the restriction condition to the total number of tuples in the relation.

Size of a Projection

The projection operation removes a number of attributes and the DBMS has enough information to estimate the size of the projected relation if it had no duplicates. When duplicates occur, as often is the case, estimation of the size of the projected relation is difficult.

Cartesian Product

Estimating the size of a cartesian product is quite simple since the number of tuples in the cartesian product is $n_R * n_S$.

Join

It is often necessary to estimate the size of the result of a join *R* \X\ *S.* If the join attribute(s) of one of the relation *R* is the key of the relation, the cardinality of the join cannot be bigger than the cardinality of the other relation 5. When neither of the join attributes are a key for their relation, finding the size of the resulting relation is more difficult. One approach that is then often used is to make use of the statistics from metadata, for example, information like *D(A, R)* which is an estimate of the number of different values of the attribute *A* in relation *R. If A* is the join attribute between relations *R* and *S,* we may be able to assume that each value of join attribute in *R* also appears in *S* and given that there are "tuples in *S* and there are *D(A, S)* distinct values of *A* in *S,* we can assume uniform distribution and conclude that for each value of *A* in *R* there will be $n_S / D(\wedge, S)$ matching tuples in *S.* Therefore an estimate of the size of the join is $n_R n_S/D(\wedge, S)$. Another estimate would ofcourse be $n_R n_S/D(\wedge, R)$. Often the two estimates are not identical since the assumption of all tuples from one relation participating in the join does not apply equally well to both relations. For example, only 80 tuples in *R* might be participating in the join while only 50 are participating from *S.*

Although the cardinality of the join of *n* relations is the same regardless of the join order, the cost of joining in different order can be substantially different. If we are dealing with relations *R(A, B)* and *S(B, C),* we need to find how many tuples of *S* on the average match with each tuple of *R* (i.e., have the same value).

Access Paths

[image size = size of index = size of different values] A software component of the DBMS maintains the physical storage of relations and provides access paths to these relations. Often relations in a database are stored as collection of tuples which may be accessed a tuple at a time along a given access path. The access paths may involve an index on one or more attributes of the relation. The indexes are often implemented as B-trees. An index may be scanned tuple by tuple providing a sequential read along the attribute or attributes in the index. The tuples may ofcourse be scanned using a sequential scan.

This involves selection of suitable access paths.

B-tree better for range queries. Hashing is useless.

A relation may have one or more indexes available on it. In fact, a relation with many attributes could well have many indexes such that the storage occupied by the indexes becomes as large as the storage occupied by the relation. Indexes may use hashing or B-tree. They allow very efficient search when the tuple with a given value of an attribute needs to be found.

The two steps are not separate and are often carried out together. The logical transformations may involve using one or more of the following techniques:

A query may involve a number of operations and would often be a number of different ways these operations could be processed. The DBMS must therefore estimate the cost of the different alternatives and choose the alternative with the least estimate. The estimates of costs are often based on statistics about the sizes of the relations and distribution of key values (or ranges).

Consider the task of estimating the cost of one of the options, for example, (2) above. The query optimizer needs to estimate the cost of join of student and enrolment, the cost of restriction and the cost of joining the result with subject. To estimate these costs, a DBMS would normally maintain statistics about the sizes of relations and a histogram of the number of tuples within various key ranges. Given the statistics, the size of the join of *student* and *subject* can be estimated as

$$n_{join} = S_{student,\ subject}(n_{student}\ X\ n_{subject})$$

where $n_{student}$ and $n_{subject}$ are the number of tuples in *student* and *subject* respectively and $S_{student,\ subject}$ is called the *selectivity* of the join. It is clearly very difficult to estimate $S_{student,\ subject}$ and most query optimizers use quite crude estimates. Fortunately, experiments have shown that selection of optimal plan for processing a plan is not very sensitive to inaccurate estimation of join selectivities.

Query optimization in a DBMS is carried out by a piece of software often called a *query planner*. The query planner is given:

1. The query in canonical form
2. Information about cardinalities and degrees of relations involved in the query.
3. Information about the indexes
4. Information about any fields on which relations have been sorted
5. Estimates of selectivities of joins involved in the query.

The planner then produces a plan that presents a suggested sequence of operations as well as details of how the operations should be carried out (for example, when an index is to be used).

Estimating Costs

It should be now clear that most queries could be translated to a number of semantically equivalent query plans. The process followed so far should eliminate most alternatives that are unlikely to be efficient but one is still likely to have a number of plans that could well be reasonably efficient. The cost of these alternatives must be estimated and the best plan selected. The cost estimation will ofcourse require the optimizer to consult the metadata.

The metadata or system catalog (sometime also called *data dictionary*) consists of descriptions of the databases that a DBMS maintains. The following information is often available in the system catalog:

1. Name of each relation and all its attributes and their domains.

2. Information about primary key and foreign keys of each relation.
3. Cardinality of each relation.
4. The number of pages in each relation.
5. Descriptions of views.
6. Descriptions of storage structures.
7. The number of distinct keys in each index.
8. The number of pages in an index.
9. Other information including ownership and security issues.

Often there statistics are updated only periodically and not at every update/insert/delete. Also, the system catalog is often stored as a relational database itself making it easy to query the catalog if a user is authorized to do so.

Information in the catalog is very important of course since query processing makes use of this information extensively. Therefore more comprehensive and more accurate information is desirable but maintaining more comprehensive and more accurate information also introduces additional overheads and a balance must be found.

10.3 ALGORITHMS FOR ALGEBRA OPERATIONS

The efficiency of query processing in a relational database system depends on the efficiency of the relational operators. Even the simplest operations can often be executed in several different ways and the costs of the different ways could well be quite different. Although the join is a frequently used and the most costly operator and therefore worthy of detailed study, we also discuss other operators to show that careful thought is needed in efficiently carrying out the simpler operators as well.

Selection

Let us consider the following simple query:

SELECT A
FROM R
WHERE p

The above query may involve any of a number of types of predicates. The list is given as under: [could have a query with specifying WHERE condition in different ways]

1. attribute = value
2. attribute1 = attribute2
3. attribute > value
4. attribute between value1 and value2
5. attribute IN (list of values)
6. attribute IN subquery
7. predicate expression OR predicate expression
8. predicate expression AND predicate expression.

Even in the simple case of equality, two or three different approaches may be possible depending on how the relation has been stored. Traversing a file to find the information of interest is often called a *file scan* even if the whole file is not being scanned. For example, if the predicate involves an equality condition on a single attribute and there is an index on that attribute, it is most efficient to search that index and find the tuple where the attribute value is equal to the value given. That should be very efficient since it will only require accessing the index and then one block to access the tuple. Ofcourse, it is possible that there is no index on the attribute of interest or the condition in the WHERE clause is not quite as simple as an equality condition on a single attribute. For example, the condition might be an inequality or specify a range. The index may still be useful if one exists but the usefulness would depend on the condition that is posed in the WHERE clause. In some situations it will be necessary to scan the whole relation R to find the tuples that satisfy the given condition. This may not be so expensive if the relation is not so large and the tuples are stored in packed form but could be very expensive if the relation is large and the tuples are stored such that block has tuples from several different relations. Another possibility is of course that the relation R is stored as a hash file using the attribute of interest and then again one would be able to hash on the value specifies and find the record very efficiently.

As noted above, often the condition may be a conjunction or disjunction of several different conditions i.e., it may be like p_1 and p_2 or p_1 or p_2. Sometime such conjunctive queries can be efficiently processed if there is a composite index based on the attributes that are involved in the two conditions but this is an exception rather than a rule. Often however, it is necessary to access which one of the two or more conditions can be processed efficiently. Perhaps one of the conditions can be processed using an index. As a first step then, those tuples that satisfy the condition that involves the most efficient search (or perhaps that which retrieves the smallest number of tuples) are retrieved and the remaining conditions are then tested on the tuples that are retrieved. Processing disjunctive queries of course requires somewhat different techniques since in this case we are looking at a union of all tuples that satisfy any one of the conditions and therefore each condition will need to be processed separately. It is therefore going to be of little concern which of the conditions is satisfied first since all must be satisfied independently of the other. Of course, if any one of the conditions requires a scan of the whole relation then we can test all the conditions during the scan and retrieve all tuples that satisfy any one or more conditions.

Projection

A projection would of course require a scan of the whole relation but if the projection includes a candidate key of the relation then no duplicate removal is necessary since each tuple in the projection is then guaranteed to be unique. Of course, more often the projection would not include any candidate key and may then have duplicates. Although many database systems do not remove duplicates unless the user specifies so, duplicates may be removed by sorting the projected relation and then identifying the duplicates and eliminating them. It is also possible to use hashing which may be desirable if the relations are particularly large since hashing would hash identical tuples to the same bucket and would therefore only require sorting the relations in each bucket to find the duplicates if any. Often of course one needs to compute a restriction and a join together. It is then often appropriate to compute the restriction first by using the best access paths available (example, an index).

Join

We assume that we wish to carry out an equi-join of two relations *R* and *S* that are to be joined on attributes *a* in *R* and *b* in *S*. Let the cardinality of *R* and *S* be *m* and *n* respectively. We do not count join output costs since these are identical for all methods. We assume $|R| \leq |S|$. We further assume that all restrictions and projections of *R* and *S* have already been carried out and neither *R* nor 5 is ordered or indexed unless explicitly noted.

Because of the importance of the join operator in relational database systems and the fact that the join operator is considerably more expensive than operators like selection and projection, a number of algorithms have been suggested for processing the join. The more commonly used algorithms are:

1. The Nested Scan Method
2. The Sort-Merge algorithm
3. Hashing algorithm (hashing no good if not equi-join?)
4. Variants of hashing
5. Semi-joins
6. Filters
7. Links
8. Indexes
9. More recently, the concept of join indices has been proposed by Valduriez (1987). Hashing methods are not good when the join is not an equi-join.

Nested Iteration

Before discussing the methods listed above, we briefly disçuss the naive nested iteration method that accesses every pair of tuples and concatenates them if the equi-join condition (or for that matter, any other condition) is satisfied. The cost of the naive algorithm is *O(mn)* assuming that *R* and *S* both are not ordered. The cost obviously can be large when *m* and *n* are large.

We will assume that the relation *R* is the *outer relation,* that is, *R* is the relation whose tuples are retrieved first. The relation *S* is then the *inner relation* since in the nested iteration loop, tuples of 5 will only be retrieved when a tuple of *R* has been read. A predicate which related the join attributes is called *the Join predicate.*

The algorithm may be v tten as:

```
for i = 1 to m do
access ith tuple of R;
for j = 1 to n do
access jth tuple of S,
compare ith tuple of R and the jth tuple of S,
if equi-join condition is satisfied
then concatenate and save;
end
end.
```

This method basically scans the outer relation *(R)* first and retrieves the first tuple. The entire inner relation *S* is then scanned and all the tuples of 5 that satisfy the join predicate with the first tuple of *R* are combined with that tuple of *R* and output as result. The process then continues with fee next tuple *of R* until *R* is exhausted.

This has cost *(m + mn)* which is order *(mn)*. If the memory buffers can store two blocks, one from *R* and one from *S,* the cost will go down by a factor *rs* where *r* and *s* are the number of tuples per block in *R* and *S* respectively. The technique is sometimes called the *nested block* method. Some cost saving is achieved by reading the smaller relation in the outer block since this reduces *(m + mn)*. The cost of the method would of course be much higher if the relations are not stored in a packed form since then we might need to retrieve many more tuples.

Efficiency of the nested iteration (or nested block iteration) would improve significantly if an index was available on one of the join attributes. If the average number of blocks of relation *S* accessed for each tuple of *R* was *c* then the cost of the join would be $(m + mc)$ where $c \ll n$.

Using Indexes

The nested iteration method can be made more efficient if indexes are available on both join columns in the relations *R* and *S*.

Assume that we have available indexes on both join columns *a* and *b* in the relations *R* and *S* respectively. We may now scan both the indexes to determine whether a pair of tuples has the same value of the join attribute. If the value is the same, the tuple from *R* is selected and then all the tuples from *S* are selected that have the same join attribute value. This is done by scanning the index on the join attribute in *S*. The index on the join attribute in *R* is now scanned to check if there are more than the one tuple with the same value of the attribute. All the tuples of *R* that have the same join attribute value are then selected and combined with the tuples of *S* that have already been selected. The process then continues with the next value for which tuples are available in *R* and *S*.

Clearly this method requires substantial storage so that we may store all the attributes from *R* and *S* that have the same join attribute value.

The cost of the join when the indexes are used may be estimated as follows. Let the cost of reading the indexes be αN_1 and βN_2, then the total cost is $\alpha N_1 + \beta N_2 + N_1 + N_2$.

Cost savings by using indexes can be large enough to justify building an index when a join needs to be computed.

The Sort Merge Method

The nested scan technique is simple but involves matching each block of *R* with every block of *S*. This can be avoided if both relations were ordered on the join attribute. The sort-merge algorithm was introduced by Blasgen and Eswaran in 1977. It is a classical technique that has been the choice for joining relations that have no index on either of the two attributes.

This method involves sorting the relations *R* and *S* on the join attributes (if not already sorted), storing them as temporary lists and then scanning them block by block and merging those tuples that satisfy the join condition. The advantage of this scheme is that all of the inner relation (in the nested iteration) does not need to be read in for each tuple of the outer relation. This saving can be substantial if the outer relation is large.

Let the cost of sorting *R* and *S* be C_s and C_r and let the cost of reading the two relations in main memory be N_s and N_r respectively. The total cost of the join is then

$$C_s + C_r + N_s + N_r$$

If one or both the relations are already sorted on the join attribute then the cost of the join reduces.

The algorithm can be improved if we use Multiway Merge-Sort.

The cost of sorting is *nlogn*.

Simple Hash Join Method

This method involves building a hash table of the smaller relation *R* by hashing each tuple on its hash attribute. Since we have assumed that the relation *R* is too large to fit in the main memory, the hash table would in general not fit into the main memory. The hash table therefore must be built in stages. A number of addresses of the hash table are first selected such that the tuples hashed to those addresses can be stored in the main memory. The tuples of R that do not hash to these addresses are written back to the disk. Let these tuples be relation R. Now the algorithm works as follows:

(a) Scan relation R and hash each tuple on its join attribute. If the hashed value is equal to one of the addresses that are in the main memory, store the tuple in the hash table. Otherwise write the tuple back to disk in a new relation R'.

(b) Scan the relation S and hash each tuple of S on its join attribute. One of the following three conditions must hold:

1. The hashed value is equal to one of the selected values, and one or more tuple of R with same attribute value exists. We combine the tuples of R that match with the tuple of S and output as the next tuples in the join.
2. The hashed value is equal to one of the selected values, but there is no tuple in R with same join attribute value. These tuple of S are rejected.
3. The hashed value is not equal to one of the selected values. These tuples are written back to disk as a new relation S'.

The above step continues till S is finished.

(c) Repeat steps (*a*) and (*b*) until either relation R' or S' or both are exhausted.

Grace Hash-Join Method

This method is a modification of the Simple Hash Join method in that the partitioning of R is completed before S is scanned and partitioning of S is completed before the joining phase. The method consists of the following three phases:

1. **Partition R:** Since R is assumed to be too large to fit in the main memory, a hash table for it cannot be built in the main memory. The first phase of the algorithm involves partitioning the relation into n buckets, each bucket corresponding to a hash table entry. The number of buckets n is chosen to be large enough so that each bucket will comfortably fit in the main memory.
2. **Partition S:** The second phase of the algorithm involves partitioning the relation S into the same number (n) of buckets, each bucket corresponding to a hash table entry. The same hashing function as for R is used.
3. **Compute the Join:** *A* bucket of R is read in and the corresponding bucket of S is read in. Matching tuples from the two buckets are combined and output as part of the join.

Hybrid Hash-Join Method

The hybrid hash join algorithm is a modification of the Grace hash join method.

Aggregation: Aggregation is often found in queries given the frequency of requirements of finding an average, the maximum or how many times something happens. The functions supported in SQL are average, minimum, maximum, count, and sum. Aggregation can itself be of different types including aggregation that only requires one relation, for example, finding the maximum mark in a subject, or it may involve a relation but require something like finding the number of students in each class. The latter aggregation would obviously require some grouping of the tuples in the relation before aggregation can be applied.

REVIEW QUESTIONS

1. Discuss the rules governing the manipulation of relational algebraic expressions.
2. Explain the algorithms used for the processing of join operations?
3. Explain how could you estimate costs while performing query processing?

CHAPTER 11

Transaction Processing Concepts

In this chapter, you will learn

11.0 INTRODUCTION

This chapter begins with the introduction to the concept of transaction-which is an easy way of encapsulating the various logical operations on the database. It is presumed that each of these transactions do operate on a common database to produce the desired results. Since a large number of transactions keep operating on the database, the need for concurrent operations and interleaving of their operations is brought out. Concurrency brings with it several problems of data integrity maintenance. To solve these problems, to begin with, the transactions themselves are expected to obey certain properties—called ACID properties with, such transactions we set out to solve the commonly found problems normally the dirty read problem, lost update problem, incorrect summary problem etc.

You are then introduced to the concept of a system log, which is a case history of system updating. The concept of commit point of a transaction is also introduced.

Next, the concept of schedules (which is a collection of transactions presently operating) is introduced and we see that "serializability" of the schedules is the key to control errors due to concurrent operations. You will be introduced to the methods of testing the serializability of schedules and the limitations of such tests.

11.1 TRANSACTION AND SYSTEM PRELIMINARIES

The concept of transaction has been devised as a convenient and precise way of describing the various logical units that form a database system. We have transaction systems which are systems that operate on very large databases, on which several (sometimes running into hundreds) of users concurrently operate—i.e., they manipulate the database transaction. There are several such systems presently in operation in our country also. If you consider the railway reservation system, wherein thousands of stations–each with multiple numbers of computers operate on a huge database, the database containing the reservation details of all trains of our country for the next several days. There are many other such systems like the airlines reservation systems, distance banking systems, stock market systems etc. In all these cases apart from the accuracy and integrity of the data provided by the database (note that money is involved in almost all the cases–either directly or indirectly), the systems should provide instant availability and fast response to these hundreds of concurrent users. In this block, we discuss the concept of transaction, the problems involved in controlling concurrently operated systems and several other related concepts. We repeat–a transaction is a logical operation on a database and the users intend to operate with these logical units trying to get information either from the database or in some cases modify them. Before we look into the problem of concurrency, we view the concept of multiuser systems from another point of view–the view of the database designer.

11.2 A TYPICAL MULTIUSER SYSTEM

We remind ourselves that a multiuser computer system is a system that can be used by a number of persons simultaneously as against a single user system, which is used by one person at a time. (Note however, that the same system can be used by different persons at different periods). Now extending this concept to a database, a multiuser database is one, which can be accessed and modified by a number of users simultaneously–whereas a single user database is one, which can be used by only one person at a time. Note that multiuser databases essentially mean there is a concept of multiprogramming but the converse is not true. Several users may be operating simultaneously, but not all of them may be operating on the database simultaneously.

Now, before we see what problems can arise because of concurrency, we see what operations can be done on the database. Such operations can be single line commands or can be a set of commands meant to be operated sequentially. Those operations are invariably limited by the "begin transaction" and "end transaction" statements and the implication is that all operations in between them are to be done on a given transaction.

Another concept is the "granularity" of the transaction. Assume each field in a database is named. The smallest such named item of the database can be called a field of a record. The unit on which we operate can be one such "grain" or a number of such grains collectively defining some data unit. However, in this course, unless specified otherwise, we use of "single grain" operations, but without loss of generality. To facilitate discussions, we presume a database package in which the following operations are available:

(i) read_tr(X): The operation reads the item X and stores it into an assigned variable. The name of the variable into which it is read can be anything, but we would give it the same name X, so that confusions are avoided. i.e., whenever this command is executed, the system reads the element required from the database and stores it into a program variable called X.

(ii) write_tr(X): This writes the value of the program variable currently stored in X into a database item called X.

Once the read_tr(X) is encountered, the system will have to perform the following operations:

1. Find the address of the block on the disk where X is stored.
2. Copy that block into a buffer in the memory.
3. Copy it into a variable (of the program) called X.

A write_tr(X) performs the converse sequence of operations.

1. Find the address of the disk block where the database variable X is stored.
2. Copy the block into a buffer in the memory.
3. Copy the value of X from the program variable to this X.
4. Store this updated block back to the disk.

Normally however, the operation (4) is not performed every time a write_tr is executed. It would be a wasteful operation to keep writing back to the disk every time. So the system maintains one/more buffers in the memory which keep getting updated during the operations and this updated buffer is moved on to the disk at regular intervals. This would save a lot of computational time, but is at the heart of some of the problems of concurrency that we will have to encounter.

11.3 THE NEED FOR CONCURRENCY CONTROL

Let us visualize a situation wherein a large number of users (probably spread over vast geographical areas) are operating on a concurrent system. Several problems can occur if they are allowed to execute their transactions operations in an uncontrolled manner.

Consider a simple example of a railway reservation system. Since a number of people are accessing the database simultaneously, it is obvious that multiple copies of the transactions are to be provided so that each user can go ahead with his operations. Let us make the concept a little more specific. Suppose we are considering the number of reservations in a particular train of a particular date. Two persons at two different places are trying to reserve for this train. By the very definition of concurrency, each of them should be able to perform the operations irrespective of the fact that the other person is also doing the same. In fact, they will not even know that the other person is also booking for the same train. The only way of ensuring the same is to make available to each of these users their own copies to operate upon and finally update the master database at the end of their operation.

Now suppose there are 10 seats are available. Both the persons, say A and B want to get this information and book their seats. Since they are to be accommodated concurrently, the system provides them two copies of the data. The simple way is to perform a read_tr(X) so that the value of X is copied on to the variable X of person A (let us call it XA) and of the person B (XB). So each of them know that there are 10 seats available.

Suppose A wants to book 8 seats. Since the number of seats he wants is (say Y) less than the available seats, the program can allot him the seats, change the number of available seats (X) to X-Y and can even give him the seat numbers that have been booked for him.

The problem is that a similar operation can be performed by B also. Suppose he needs 7 seats. Therefore, he gets his seven seats, replaces the value of X to 3 (10 – 7) and gets his reservation.

The problem is noticed only when these blocks are returned to main database (the disk in the above case).

Before we can analyze these problems, we look at the problem from a more technical view.

11.3.1 The Lost Update Problem

This problem occurs when two transactions that access the same database items have their operations interleaved in such a way as to make the value of some database incorrect. Suppose the transactions T_1 and T_2 are submitted at the (approximately) same time. Because of the concept of interleaving, each operation is executed for some period and then the control is passed on to the other transaction and this sequence continues. Because of the delay in updating, this creates a problem. This was what happened in the previous example. Let the transactions be called T_A and T_B.

T_A	T_B	
read_tr(X)		
	read_tr(X)	Time
$X = X - N_A$		
	$X = X - N_B$	
write_tr(X)		
	write_tr(X)	

Note that the problem occurred because the transaction T_B failed to record the transactions T_A. i.e., T_B lost on T_A. Similarly, since T_A did the writing later on, T_A lost the updating of T_B.

11.3.2 The Temporary Update (Dirty Read) Problem

This happens when a transaction T_A updates a data item, but later on (for some reason) the transaction fails. It could be due to a system failure or any other operational reason. Alternatively, the system may have later on noticed that the operation should not have been done and cancels it. To be fair, it also ensures that the original value is restored.

In the meanwhile, another transaction T_B has accessed the data and since it has no indication as to what happened later on, it makes use of this data and goes ahead. Once the original value is restored by T_A, the values generated by T_B are obviously invalid.

T_A	T_B	
read_tr(X)		Time
$X = X - N$		
write_tr(X)		
	read_tr(X)	
	$X = X - N$	
	write_tr(X)	
Failure		
$X = X + N$		
write_tr(X)		

The value generated by T_A out of a non-sustainable transaction is a "dirty data" which is read by T_B, produces an illegal value. Hence, the problem is called a dirty read problem.

11.3.3 The Incorrect Summary Problem

Consider two concurrent operations, again called T_A and T_B. T_B is calculating a summary (average, standard deviation or some such operation) by accessing all elements of a database (note that it is not updating any of them, only is reading them and is using the resultant data to calculate some values). In the meanwhile, T_A is updating these values. In case, since the operations are interleaved, T_A, for some of its operations will be using the not updated data, whereas for the other operations will be using the updated data. This is called the incorrect summary problem.

T_A	T_B
	Sum = 0
	read_tr(A)
	Sum = Sum + A
read_tr(X)	
X = X – N	
write_tr(X)	
	read_tr(X)
	Sum = Sum + X
	read_tr(Y)
	Sum = Sum + Y
read (Y)	
Y = Y – N	
write_tr(Y)	

In the above example, both T_A will be updating both X and Y. However, since it first updates X and then Y and the operations are so interleaved that the transaction T_B uses both of them in between the operations, it ends up using the old value of Y with the new value of X. In the process, the sum we got does not either refer to the old set of values or to the new set of values.

11.3.4 Unrepeatable Read

This can happen when an item is read by a transaction twice, (in quick succession) but the item has been changed in the meanwhile, though the transaction has no reason to expect such a change. Consider the case of a reservation system, where a passenger gets a reservation detail and before he decides on the aspect of reservation, the value is updated at the request of some other passenger at another place.

11.4 THE CONCEPT OF FAILURES AND RECOVERY

Any database operation cannot be immune to the system on which it operates (both the hardware and the software, including the operating systems). The system should ensure that any transaction submitted to it is terminated in one of the following ways:

(a) All the operations listed in the transaction are completed, the changes are recorded permanently back to the database and the database is indicated that the operations are complete.

(b) In case the transaction has failed to achieve its desired objective, the system should ensure that no change, whatsoever, is reflected onto the database. Any intermediate changes made to the database are restored to their original values, before calling off the transaction and intimating the same to the database.

In the second case, we say the system should be able to "Recover" from the failure. Failures can occur in a variety of ways.

(a) **A System crash:** A hardware, software or network error can make the completion of the transaction impossibility.

(b) **A transaction or system error:** The transaction submitted may be faulty – like creating a situation of division by zero or creating a negative numbers, which cannot be handled (for example, in a reservation system, negative number of seats conveys no meaning). In such cases, the system simply discontinue the transaction by reporting an error.

(c) **Some programs provide for the user to interrupt during execution:** If the user changes his mind during execution, (but before the transactions are completed), he may opt out of the operation.

(d) **Local exceptions:** Certain conditions during operation may force the system to rise that are known as 'exceptions'. For example, a bank account holder may not have sufficient balance for some transaction to be done or special instructions might have been given in a bank transaction that prevents further continuation of the process. In all such cases, the transactions are terminated.

(e) **Concurrency control enforcement:** In certain cases when concurrency constrains are violated, the enforcement regime simply aborts the process to restart later.

The other reasons can be physical problems like theft, fire etc., or system problems like disk failure, viruses etc. In all such cases of failure, a recovery mechanism is to be in place.

11.5 TRANSACTION STATES AND ADDITIONAL OPERATIONS

Though the read_tr and write_tr operations described above the most fundamental operations, they are seldom sufficient. Though most operations on databases comprise of only the read and write operations, the system needs several additional operations for its purposes. One simple example is the concept of recovery discussed in the previous section. If the system were to recover from a crash or any other catastrophe, it should first be able to keep track of the transactions – when they start, when they terminate or when they abort. Hence, the following operations come into picture.

(i) **Begin Trans:** This marks the beginning of an execution process.

(ii) **End trans:** This marks the end of an execution process.

(iii) **Commit trans:** This indicates that transaction is successful and the changes brought about by the transaction may be incorporated onto the database and will not be undone later.

(iv) **Rollback:** Indicates that the transaction is unsuccessful (for whatever reason) and the changes made to the database, if any, by the transaction need to be undone.

Most systems also keep track of the present status of all the transactions at the present instant of time (note that in a real multiprogramming environment, more than one transaction may be in various stages of execution). The system should not only be able to keep a tag on the present status of the transactions, but also should know what are the next possibilities for the transaction to proceed and in case of a failure, how to roll it back. The whole concept takes the state transition diagram. A simple state transition diagram, in view of what we have seen so for can appear as follows:

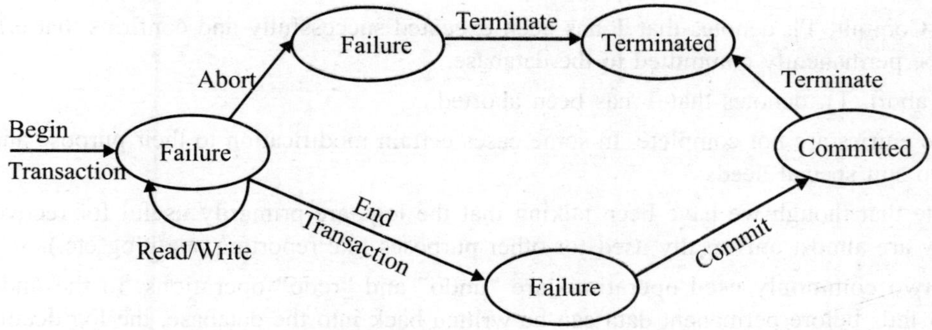

The arrow marks indicate how a state of a transaction can change to a next state. A transaction is in an active state immediately after the beginning of execution. Then it will be performing the read and write operations. At this state, the system protocols begin ensuring that a system failure at this juncture does not make erroneous recordings on to the database. Once this is done, the system "Commits" itself to the results and thus enters the "Committed state". Once in the committed state, a transaction automatically proceeds to the terminated state.

The transaction may also fail due to a variety of reasons discussed in a previous section. Once it fails, the system may have to take up error control exercises like rolling back the effects of the previous write operations of the transaction. Once this is completed, the transaction enters the terminated state to pass out of the system.

A failed transaction may be restarted later – either by the intervention of the user or automatically.

11.5.1 The Concept of System Log

To be able to recover from failures of the transaction operations the system needs to essentially maintain a track record of all transaction operations that are taking place and that are likely to affect the status of the database. This information is called a "System log" (similar to the concept of logbooks) and may become useful when the system is trying to recover from failures. The log information is kept on the disk, such that it is not likely to be affected by the normal system crashes, power failures etc. (Otherwise, when the system crashes, if the disk also crashes, then the entire concept fails). The log is also periodically backed up into removable devices (like tape) and is kept in archives.

The question is, what type of data or information needs to be logged into the system log?

Let T refer to a unique transaction–id, generated automatically whenever a new transaction is encountered and this can be used to uniquely identify the transaction. Then the following entries are made with respect to the transaction T.

(i) [start_trans, T]: denotes that T has started execution.

(ii) [write_tr, T, X, old, new]: denotes that the transaction T has changed the old value of the data X to a new value.

(iii) [read_tr, T, X]: denotes that the transaction T has read the value of the X from the database.

(iv) [Commit, T]: denotes that T has been executed successfully and confirms that effects can be permanently committed to the database.

(v) [abort, T]: denotes that T has been aborted.

These entries are not complete. In some cases certain modification to their purpose and format are made to suit special needs.

(Note that though we have been talking that the logs are primarily useful for recovery from errors, they are almost universally used for other purposes like reporting, auditing etc.).

The two commonly used operations are "undo" and "redo" operations. In the undo, if the transaction fails before permanent data can be written back into the database, the log details can be used to sequentially trace back the updating and return them to their old values. Similarly, if the transaction fails just before the commit operation is complete, one need not report a transaction failure. One can use the old, new values of all write operation on the log and ensure that the same is entered onto the database.

11.5.2 Commit Point of a Transaction

The next question to be tackled is when should one commit to the results of a transaction? Note that unless a transaction is committed, its operations do not get reflected in the database. We say a transaction reaches a "Commit point" when all operations that access the database have been successfully executed and the effects of all such transactions have been included in the log. Once a transaction T reaches a commit point, the transaction is said to be committed – i.e., the changes that the transaction had sought to make in the database are assumed to have been recorded into the database. The transaction indicates this state by writing a [commit, T] record into its log. At this point, the log contains a complete sequence of changes brought about by the transaction to the database and has the capacity to both undo it (in case of a crash) and redo it (if a doubt arises as to whether the modifications have actually been recorded onto the database).

Before we close this discussion on logs, one small clarification. The records of the log are on the disk (secondary memory). When a log record is to be written, a secondary device access is to be made, which slows down the system operations. So normally, a copy of the most recent log records are kept in the memory and the updating are made there. At regular intervals, these are copied back to the disk. In case of a system crash, only those records that have been written onto the disk will survive. Thus, when a transaction reaches commit stage, all records must be forcefully written back to the disk and then commit is to be executed. This concept is called 'forceful writing' of the log file.

11.6 DESIRABLE TRANSACTION PROPERTIES (ACID PROPERTIES)

For the effective and smooth database operations, transactions should possess several properties. These properties are – Atomicity, consistency preservation, isolation and durability. Often by combining their first letters, they are called ACID properties.

(i) **Atomicity:** A transaction is an atomic unit of processing i.e., it cannot be broken down further into a combination of transactions. Looking other way, a given transaction either will get executed or is not performed at all. There cannot be a possibility of a transaction getting partially executed.

(ii) **Consistency preservation:** A transaction is said to be consistency preserving if its complete execution takes the database from one consistent state to another.

We shall slightly elaborate on this. In steady state a database is expected to be consistent i.e., there are not anomalies in the values of the items. For example, if a database stores N values and also their sum, the database is said to be consistent if the addition of these N values actually leads to the value of the sum. This will be the normal case.

Now consider the situation when a few of these N values are being changed. Immediately after one/more values are changed, the database becomes inconsistent. The sum value no more corresponds to the actual sum. Only after all the updating are done and the new sum is calculated that the system becomes consistent.

A transaction should always ensure that once it starts operating on a database, its values are made consistent before the transaction ends.

(iii) **Isolation:** Every transaction should appear as if it is being executed in isolation. However, in a practical sense, a large number of such transactions keep executing concurrently no transaction should get affected by the operation of other transactions. Then only is it possible to operate on the transaction accurately.

(iv) **Durability:** The changes effected to the database by the transaction should be permanent – should not vanish once the transaction is removed. These changes should also not be lost due to any other failures at later stages.

Now how does one enforce these desirable properties on the transactions? The atomicity concept is taken care of, while designing and implementing the transaction. If, however, a transaction fails even before it can complete its assigned task, the recovery software should be able to undo the partial effects inflicted by the transactions onto the database.

The preservation of consistency is normally considered as the duty of the database programmer. A "consistent state" of a database is that state which satisfies the constraints specified by the schema. Other external constraint may also be included to make the rules more effective. The database programmer writes his programs in such a way that a transaction enters a database only when it is in a consistent state and also leaves the state in the same or any other consistent state. This, ofcourse implies that no other transaction "interferes" with the action of the transaction in question.

This leads us to the next concept of isolation i.e., every transaction goes about doing its job, without being bogged down by any other transaction, which may also be working on the same database. One simple mechanism to ensure this is to make sure that no transaction makes its partial updates available to the other transactions, until the commit state is reached. This also eliminates the temporary update problem. However, this has been found to be inadequate to take care of several other problems. Most database transaction today come with several levels of isolation. A transaction is said to have a level zero (0) isolation, if it does not overwrite the dirty reads of higher-level transactions (level zero is the lowest level of isolation). A transaction is said to have level 1 isolation, if it does not lose any updates. At level 3, the transaction neither loses updates nor has any dirty reads. At level 3, the highest level of isolation, a transaction does not have any lost updates, does not have any dirty reads, but has repeatable reads.

11.7 THE CONCEPT OF SCHEDULES

When transactions are executing concurrently in an interleaved fashion, not only does the action of each transaction becomes important, but also the order of execution of operations from each of these transactions. As an example, in some of the problems that we have discussed earlier in this section, the problem may get itself converted to some other form (or may even vanish) if the order of operations becomes different. Hence, for analyzing any problem, it is not just the history of previous transactions that one should be worrying about, but also the "schedule" of operations.

11.7.1 Schedule (History of Transaction)

We formally define a schedule *S* of *n* transactions T_1, T_2 ...T_n as on ordering of operations of the transactions subject to the constraint that, for each transaction, T_i that participates in *S*, the operations of T_i must appear in the same order in which they appear in T_i. i.e., if two operations T_{i1} and T_{i2} are listed in T_i such that T_{i1} is earlier to T_{i2}, then in the schedule also T_{i1} should appear before T_{i2}. However, if T_{i2} appears immediately after T_{i1} in T_i, the same may not be true in *S*, because some other operations T_{j1} (of a transaction T_j) may be interleaved between them. In short, a schedule lists the sequence of operations on the database in the same order in which it was affected in the first place.

For the recovery and concurrency control operations, we concentrate mainly on readtr and writetr operations, because these operations actually effect changes to the database. The other two (equally) important operations are commit and abort, since they decide when the changes effected have actually become active on the database.

Since listing each of these operations becomes a lengthy process, we make a notation for describing the schedule. The operations of readtr, writetr, commit and abort, we indicate by r, w, c and a and each of them come with a subscript to indicate the transaction number

For example: SA : r1(x); y2(y); w2(y); r1(y), w1(x); a1

indicates the following operations in the same order:

read_tr(x)	transaction 1
read_tr(y)	transaction 2
write_tr(y)	transaction 2
read_tr(y)	transaction 1
write_tr(x)	transaction 1
Abort	transaction 1

Conflicting operations: Two operations in a schedule are said to be in conflict if they satisfy these conditions

(i) The operations belong to different transactions

(ii) They access the same item x

(iii) At least one of the operations is a write operation.

Example: r1(x); w2(x)

w1(x); r2(x)

w1(y); w2(y)

Conflict because both of them try to write on the same item.

But r1(x); w2(y) and r1(x) and r2(x) do not conflict, because in the first case the read and write are on different data items, in the second case both are trying read the same data item, which they can do without any conflict.

A complete schedule: A schedule *S* of *n* transactions T_1, T_2……. T_n is said to be a "Complete Schedule" if the following conditions are satisfied:

(i) The operations listed in S are exactly the same operations as in T_1, T_2 …..T_n, including the commit or abort operations. Each transaction is terminated by either a commit or an abort operation.

(ii) The operations in any transaction. T_i appears in the schedule in the same order in which they appear in the Transaction.

(iii) Whenever there are conflicting operations, one of two will occur before the other in the schedule.

A 'Partial order' of the schedule is said to occur, if the first two conditions of the complete schedule are satisfied, but whenever there are non-conflicting operations in the schedule, they can occur without indicating which should appear first.

This can happen because non-conflicting operations any way can be executed in any order without affecting the actual outcome.

However, in a practical situation, it is very difficult to come across complete schedules. This is because new transactions keep getting included into the schedule. Hence, often one works with a "committed projection" C(*S*) of a schedule *S*. This set includes only those operations in *S* that have committed transactions i.e., transaction T_i whose commit operation C_i is in *S*.

Put in simpler terms, since non-committed operations do not get reflected in the actual outcome of the schedule, only those transactions, who have completed their commit operations contribute to the set and this schedule is good enough in most cases.

11.7.2 Schedules and Recoverability

Recoverability is the ability to recover from transaction failures. The success or otherwise of recoverability depends on the schedule of transactions. If fairly straightforward operations without much interleaving of transactions are involved, error recovery is a straightforward process. On the other hand, if lot of interleaving of different transactions has taken place, then recovering from the failure of any one of these transactions could be an involved affair. In certain cases, it may not be possible to recover at all. Thus, it would be desirable to characterize the schedules based on their recovery capabilities.

To do this, we observe certain features of the recoverability and also of schedules. To begin with, we note that any recovery process, most often involves a "roll back" operation, wherein the operations of the failed transaction will have to be undone. However, we also note that the roll back needs to go only as long as the transaction T has not committed. If the transaction T has committed once, it need not be rolled back. The schedules that satisfy this criterion are called "recoverable schedules" and those that do not, are called "non-recoverable schedules". As a rule, such non-recoverable schedules should not be permitted.

Formally, a schedule *S* is recoverable if no transaction T that appears is *S* commits, until all transactions T_1 that have written an item, which is read by T, have committed.

The concept is a simple one. Suppose the transaction T reads an item X from the database, completes its operations (based on this and other values) and commits the values, i.e., the output values of T become permanent values of database.

But suppose, this value X is written by another transaction T (before it is read by T), but aborts after T has committed. What happens? The values committed by T are no more valid, because the basis of these values (namely X) itself has been changed. Obviously, T also needs to be rolled back (if possible), leading to other rollbacks and so on.

The other aspect to note is that in a recoverable schedule, no committed transaction needs to be rolled back. However, it is possible that a cascading roll back scheme may have to be effected, in which an uncommitted transaction has to be rolled back, because it read from a value contributed by a transaction, which later aborted. However, such cascading rollbacks can be very time consuming because at any instant of time, a large number of uncommitted transactions may be operating. Thus, it is desirable to have 'cascadeless' schedules, which avoid cascading rollbacks.

This can be ensured by ensuring that transactions read only those values, which are written by committed transactions i.e., there is no fear of any aborted or failed transactions later on. If the schedule has a sequence wherein a transaction T_1 has to read a value X by an uncommitted transaction T_2, then the sequence is altered, so that the reading is postponed, till T_2 either commits or aborts.

This delays T_1, but avoids any possibility of cascading rollbacks.

The third type of schedule is a 'strict schedule', which as the name suggests is highly restrictive in nature. Here, transactions are allowed neither to read nor write a value X until the last transaction that wrote X has committed or aborted. Note that the strict schedules largely simplify the recovery process, but the many cases, it may not be possible device strict schedules.

It may be noted that the recoverable schedule, cascadeless schedules and strict schedules each is more stringent than its predecessor. It facilitates the recovery process, but sometimes the process may get delayed or even may become impossible to schedule.

11.8 SERIALIZABILITY

Given two transaction T_1 and T_2 are to be scheduled, they can be scheduled in a number of ways. The simplest way is to schedule them without in that bothering about interleaving them, i.e., schedule all operation of the transaction T_1 followed by all operations of T_2 or alternatively schedule all operations of T_2 followed by all operations of T_1.

T_1	T_2
read_tr(X)	
X=X+N	
write_tr(X)	
read_tr(Y)	
Y=Y+N	
write_tr(Y)	
Time ↓	read_tr(X)
	X=X+P
	write_tr(X)

Non-interleaved (Serial Schedule): A

T_1	T_2	T_2	T_2
read_tr(X)	read_tr(X)		read_tr(X)
X=X+N	X=X+P	→	X=X+P
write_tr(X)	write_tr(X)		write_tr(X)
read_tr(Y)		read_tr(X)	
Y=Y+N			
write_tr(Y)			

Non-interleaved (Serial Schedule):B

These now can be termed as serial schedules, since the entire sequence of operation in one transaction is completed before, the next sequence of transactions is started.

In the interleaved mode, the operations of T_1 are mixed with the operations of T_2. This can be done in a number of ways. Two such sequences are given below:

T_1	T_2
read_tr(X)	
X=X+N	
	read_tr(X)
	X=X+P
write_tr(X)	
read_tr(Y)	
	write_tr(X)
Y=Y+N	
write_tr(Y)	

Interleaved (non-serial schedule):C

T_1	T_2
read_tr(X)	
X=X+N	
write_tr(X)	
	read_tr(X)
	X=X+P
	write_tr(X)
read_tr(Y)	
Y=Y+N	
write_tr(Y)	

Interleaved (non-serial schedule): D.

Formally, a schedule *S* is serial if, for every transaction, T in the schedule, all operations of T are executed consecutively, otherwise it is called non-serial. In such a non-interleaved schedule, if the transactions are independent, one can also presume that the schedule will be correct, since each transaction commits or aborts before the next transaction begins. As long as the transactions individually are error free, such a sequence of events is guaranteed to give a correct results.

The problem with such a situation is the wastage of resources. If in a serial schedule, one of the transactions is waiting for an I/O, the other transactions also cannot use the system resources and hence the entire arrangement is wasteful of resources. If some transaction T is very long, the other transaction will have to keep waiting till it is completed. Moreover, wherein hundreds of machines operate concurrently becomes unthinkable. Hence, in general, the serial scheduling concept is unacceptable in practice.

However, once the operations are interleaved, so that the above-cited problems are overcome, unless the interleaving sequence is well thought of, all the problems that we encountered in the beginning of this block become addressable. Hence, a methodology is to be adopted to find out which of the interleaved schedules give correct results and which do not.

A schedule *S* of *n* transactions is "serializable" if it is equivalent to some serial schedule of the some *n* transactions. Note that there are *n*! different serial schedules possible to be made out of *n* transaction. If one goes about interleaving them, the number of possible combinations becomes unmanageably high. To ease our operations, we form two disjoint groups of non-serial schedules- these non-serial schedules that are equivalent to one or more serial schedules, which we call "serializable schedules" and those that are not equivalent to any serial schedule and hence are not serializable once a non-serial schedule is serializable, it becomes equivalent to a serial schedule and by our previous definition of serial schedule will become a "correct" schedule. Now can one prove the equivalence of a non-serial schedule to a serial schedule?

The simplest and the most obvious method to conclude that two such schedules are equivalent are to find out their results. If they produce the same results, then they can be considered equivalent. i.e., if two schedules are "result equivalent", then they can be considered equivalent. However, such an oversimplification is full of problems. Two sequences may produce the same set of results of one or even a large number of initial values, but still may not be equivalent. Consider the following two sequences:

S_1	S_2
read_tr(X)	read_tr(X)
X=X+X	X=X*X
write_tr(X)	write_tr(X)

For a value X=2, both produce the same result. Can be conclude that they are equivalent? Though this may look like a simplistic example, with some imagination, one can always come out with more sophisticated examples wherein the "bugs" of treating them as equivalent are less obvious. However, the concept still holds -result equivalence cannot mean schedule equivalence. One more refined method of finding equivalence is available. It is called "conflict equivalence". Two schedules can be said to be conflict equivalent, if the order of any two conflicting operations in both the schedules is the same (note that the conflicting operations essentially belong to two different transactions and if they access the same data item, and at least one of them is a write_tr(X) operation). If two such conflicting operations appear in different orders in different schedules, then it is obvious that they produce two different databases in the end and hence they are not equivalent.

11.8.1 Testing for Conflict Serializability of a Schedule

We suggest an algorithm that tests a schedule for conflict serializability.

1. For each transaction T_i, participating in the schedule *S*, creates a node labeled T_1 in the precedence graph.
2. For each case where T_j executes a read_tr(X) after T_i executes write_tr(X), create an edge from T_i to T_j in the precedence graph.
3. For each case where T_j executes write_tr(X) after T_i executes a read_tr(X), create an edge from T_i to T_j in the graph.
4. For each case where T_j executes a write_tr(X) after T_i executes a write_tr(X), create an edge from T_i to T_j in the graph.
5. The schedule *S* is serializable if and only if there are no cycles in the graph.

If we apply these methods to write the precedence graphs for the four cases of Section 11.7, we get the following precedence graphs:

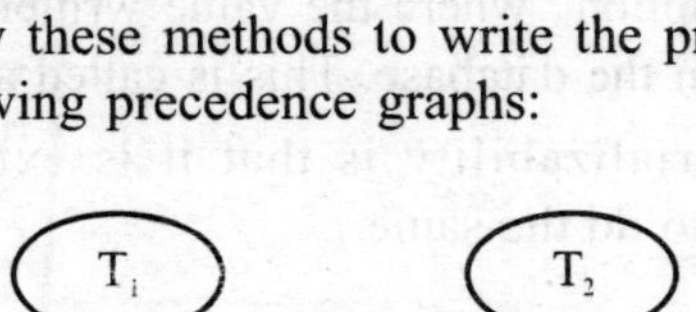

Schedule A

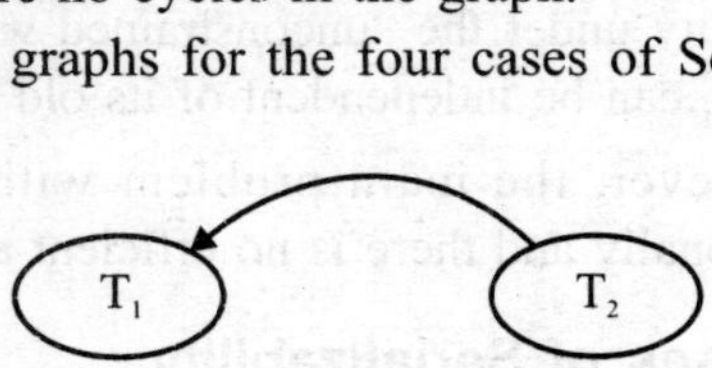

Schedule B

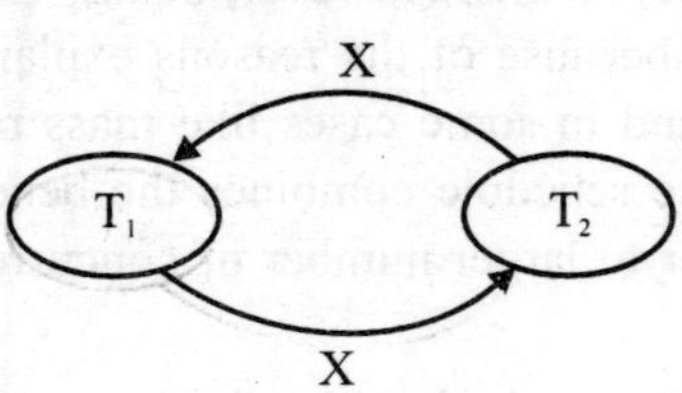

Schedule C

Schedule D

We may conclude that schedule D is equivalent to schedule A.

11.8.2 View Equivalence and View Serializability

Apart from the conflict equivalence of schedules and conflict serializability, another restrictive equivalence definition has been used with reasonable success in the context of serializability. This is called view serializability.

Two schedules S and S^1 are said to be "view equivalent" if the following conditions are satisfied.

(i) The same set of transactions participates in S and S^1 and S and S^1 include the same operations of those transactions.

(ii) For any operation $r_i(X)$ of T_i in S, if the value of X read by the operation has been written by an operation $w_j(X)$ of T_j (or if it is the original value of X before the schedule started) the same condition must hold for the value of X read by operation $r_i(X)$ of T_i in S^1.

(iii) If the operation $w_k(Y)$ of T_k is the last operation to write, the item Y in S, then $w_k(Y)$ of T_k must also be the last operation to write the item Y in S^1.

The concept being view equivalent is that as long as each read operation of the transaction reads the result of the same write operation in both the schedules, the write operations of each transaction must produce the same results. Hence, the read operations are said to see the same view of both the schedules. It can easily be verified when S or S^1 operate independently on a database with the same initial state, they produce the same end states. A schedule S is said to be view serializable, if it is view equivalent to a serial schedule.

It can also be verified that the definitions of conflict serializability and view serializability are similar, if a condition of " constrained write assumption" holds on all transactions of the schedules. This condition states that any write operation $w_i(X)$ in T_i is preceded by a $r_i(X)$ is T_i and that the value written by $w_i(X)$ in T_i depends only on the value of X read by $r_i(X)$. This assumes that computation of the new value of X is a function f(X) based on the old value of X read from the database. However, the definition of view serializability is less restrictive than that of conflict serializability under the "unconstrained write assumption" where the value written by the operation $w_i(X)$ in T_i can be independent of its old value from the database. This is called a "blind write".

However, the main problem with view serializability is that it is extremely complex computationally and there is no efficient algorithm to do the same.

11.8.3 Uses of Serializability

If one were to prove the serializability of a schedule S, it is equivalent to saying that S is correct. Hence, it guarantees that the schedule provides correct results. However, being serializable is not the same as being serial. A serial scheduling inefficient because of the reasons explained earlier, which leads to under utilization of the CPU, I/O devices and in some cases like mass reservation system, becomes untenable. On the other hand, a serializable schedule combines the benefits of concurrent execution (efficient system utilization, ability to cater to larger number of concurrent users) with the guarantee of correctness.

However, all is not well yet. The scheduling process is done by the operating system routines after taking into account various factors like system load, time of transaction submission, priority of the process with reference to other process and a large number of other factors. In addition, since a very large number of possible interleaving combinations are possible, it is extremely difficult to determine before hand the manner in which the transactions are interleaved. In other words, getting the various schedules it is difficult, let alone testing them for serializability.

Hence, instead of generating the schedules, checking them for serializability and then using them, most DBMS protocols use a more practical method–impose restrictions on the transactions themselves. These restrictions, when followed by every participating transaction, automatically ensure serializability in all schedules that are created by these participating schedules.

In addition, since transactions are being submitted at different times, it is difficult to determine when a schedule begins and when it ends. Hence serializability theory can be used to deal with the problem by considering only the committed projection C(C*S*) of the schedule. Hence, as an approximation, we can define a schedule *S* as serializable if it is committed C(C*S*) is equivalent to some serial schedule.

11.9 SUMMARY

The chapter began with the discussion of transactions and their role in data base updating. The transaction, which is a logical way of describing a basic database operation, is handy in analyzing various database problems. We noted that basically a transaction does two operations–a read_tr(X) and a write_tr(X), though other operations are added later on for various other purposes.

It was noted that in order to maintain system efficiency and also for other practical reasons, it is essential that concurrent operations are done on the database. This in turn leads to various problems–like the lost update problem, the temporary update problem the incorrect summary problem etc.

In addition, often a transaction cannot complete its scheduled operations successfully for a variety of reasons. In such cases, a recovery mechanism to unto the partial updating of transaction is needed.

To study these concepts systematically, the concept of system states was introduced. The idea of maintaining a system log to help in data recovery, the concept of commit point of transaction, when the modifications offered by a transaction actually takes effect and also the desirable ACID properties of the transactions was introduced.

Further, it was possible for us, using these concepts, to talk about a "schedule" of a set of transactions and also methods of analyzing the recoverability properties of the schedules by finding out whether the schedule was "serializable" or not. Different methods of testing the serializability and also their effect on recoverability or otherwise of the system were discussed.

REVIEW QUESTIONS

1. State two reasons why concurrent operations on databases are needed.
2. State any three data problems that can happen due to improper concurrency control.
3. Why is recovery needed in database systems?
4. Define a system log.

5. **What is a "commit point" of a transaction?**
6. **What are the four desirable of transactions-commonly called ACID properties?**
7. **What is a schedule?**
8. **What is a serializable schedule?**
9. **State how a precedence graph helps in deciding serializability?**
10. **What is roll back?**

CHAPTER 12

Concurrency Control Techniques

In this chapter, you will learn

12.0 INTRODUCTION

In this chapter, you are introduced to the concept of locks–A lock is just that–you can lock an item such that only you can access that item. These concepts become useful in read and write operations, so that a data that is currently being written into is not accessed by any other transaction until the writing process is complete. The transaction writing the data simply locks up the item and returns only after its operations are complete–possibly, after it has committed itself to the new value.

We discuss about a binary lock–which can either lock or unlock the item. There is also a system of shared/exclusive lock in which the write locked item can be shared by other transactions in the read mode only. Then there is also a concept of two-phase locking to ensure that serializability is maintained by way of locking.

However, the concept of locking may lead to the possibility of deadlocks–wherein two or more transactions may end up endlessly waiting for items locked by the other transactions. The detection and prevention of such dead locks are also dealt with.

You are also introduced to the concept of *Time Stamps*. Each transaction carries a value indicating when it came in to the system. This can help, in various operations of concurrency control, recoverability etc. By ordering the schedules in terms of their time stamps, it is possible to ensure serializability. We sèe the various algorithms that can do this ordering.

12.1 LOCKING TECHNIQUES FOR CONCURRENCY CONTROL

Many of the important techniques for concurrency control make use of the concept of the lock. A lock is a variable associated with a data item that describes the status of the item with respect to the possible operations that can be done on it. Normally every data item is associated with a unique lock. They are used as a method of synchronizing the access of database items by the transactions that are operating concurrently. Such controls, when implemented properly can overcome many of the problems of concurrent operations listed earlier. However, the locks themselves may create a few problems, which we shall be seeing in some detail in subsequent sections.

12.2 TYPES OF LOCKS AND THEIR USES

12.2.1 Binary Locks

A binary lock can have two states or values (1 or 0) one of them indicates that it is locked and the other says it is unlocked. For example, if we presume 1 indicates that the lock is on and 0 indicates it is open, then if the lock of item(X) is 1 then the read_tr(X) cannot access the time as long as the lock's value continues to be 1. We can refer to such a state as lock (X).

The concept works like this. The item X can be accessed only when it is free to be used by the transactions. If, say, its current value is being modified, then X cannot be (infact should not be) accessed, until the modification is complete. The simple mechanism is to lock access to X as long as the process of modification is on and unlock it for use by the other transactions only when the modifications are complete.

Therefore, we need two operations lockitem(X) which locks the item and unlockitem(X) which opens the lock. Any transaction that wants to makes use of the data item, first checks the lock status of X by the lockitem(X). If the item X is already locked, (lock status = 1) the transaction will have to wait. Once the status becomes = 0, the transaction accesses the item, and locks it (makes its status = 1). When the transaction has completed using the item, it issues an unlockitem (X) command, which again sets the status to 0, so that other transactions can access the item.

Notice that the binary lock essentially produces a 'mutually exclusive' type of situation for the data item, so that only one transaction can access it. These operations can be easily written as an algorithm as follows:

```
lockitem(X):
Start: if Lock(X)=0, /* item is unlocked*/
          then Lock(X)=1 /*lock it*/
          else
          {
                    wait(until Lock(X)=0) and
     the lock manager wakes up the transaction)}
          go to start
End;
```

The locking algorithm:

unlockitem(X):

Lock(X) ≠ 0; ("unlock the item")

{ If any transactions are waiting,

wakeup one of the waiting transactions }

The unlocking algorithm:

The only restrictions on the use of the binary locks are that they should be implemented as indivisible units (also called "critical sections" in operating systems terminology). That means no interleaving operations should be allowed, once a lock or unlock operation is started, until the operation is completed. Otherwise, if a transaction locks a unit and is interleaved with many other transactions, the locked unit may become unavailable for long times to come with catastrophic results.

To make use of the binary lock schemes, every transaction should follow certain protocols:

1. A transaction T must issue the operation lockitem(X), before issuing a read_tr(X) or write_tr(X).
2. A transaction T must issue the operation unlockitem(X) after all read_tr(X) and write_tr(X) operations are complete on X.
3. A transaction T will not issue a lockitem(X) operation if it already holds the lock on X (i.e., if it had issued the lockitem(X) in the immediate previous instance)
4. A transaction T will not issue an unlockitem(X) operation unless it holds the lock on X.

Between the lock(X) and unlock(X) operations, the value of X is held only by the transaction T and hence no other transaction can operate on X, thus many of the problems discussed earlier are prevented.

12.3 SHARED/EXCLUSIVE LOCKS

While the operation of the binary lock scheme appears satisfactory, it suffers from a serious drawback. Once a transaction holds a lock (has issued a lock operation), no other transaction can access the data item. However, in large concurrent systems, this can become a disadvantage. It is obvious that more than one transaction should not go on writing into X or while one transaction is writing into it, no other transaction should be reading it, no harm is done if several transactions are allowed to simultaneously read the item. This would save the time of all these transactions, without in anyway affecting the performance.

This concept gave rise to the idea of shared/exclusive locks. When only read operations are being performed, the data item can be shared by several transactions, only when a transaction wants to write into it that the lock should be exclusive. Hence, the shared/exclusive lock is also sometimes called multiple mode lock. A read lock is a shared lock (which can be used by several transactions), whereas a writelock is an exclusive lock. Therefore, we need to think of three operations, a readlock, a writelock and unlock. The algorithms can be as follows:

```
readlock(X):
Start:  if Lock(X) = "unlocked"
            Then {
                  Lock(X) ← "read locked",
                  No. of reads(X) ←1
                  }
        else if Lock(X) = "read locked"
                  then no. of reads(X) = no. of reads(X)0+1;
        else {wait until Lock(X) ← "unlocked" and the lock manager
                  wakes up the transaction)}
        go to start
End;
```

Readlock operation:

```
writelock(X)
    Start: if Lock(X) = "unlocked"
           Then Lock(X) ← "unlocked".
    else { wait until Lock(X) = "unlocked" and
           the lock manager wakes up the transaction}
    go to start
    End;
```

The writelock operation:

```
unlock(X)
    if lock(X) = "write locked"
           Then { Lock(X) ← "unlocked"
                  Wakeup one of the waiting transaction, if any
                  }
           else if Lock(X) = "read locked"
           then { no. of reads(X) ← no. of reads –1
                  if no. of reads(X)=0
                        then { Lock(X) = "unlocked"
                  wakeup one of the waiting transactions, if any
                  }
```

The unlock operation:

The algorithms are fairly straight forward, except that during the unlocking operation, if a number of read locks are there, then all of them are to be unlocked before the unit itself becomes unlocked.

To ensure smooth operation of the shared/exclusive locking system, the system must enforce the following rules:

1. A transaction T must issue the operation readlock(X) or writelock(X) before any read or write operations are performed.
2. A transaction T must issue the operation writelock(X) before any write_tr(X) operation is performed on it.
3. Transactions T must issue the operation unlock(X) after all read_tr(X) are completed in T.
4. A transaction T will not issue a readlock(X) operation if it already holds a readlock or writelock on X.
5. A transaction T will not issue a writelock(X) operation if it already holds a readlock or writelock on X.

12.4 CONVERSION LOCKS

In some cases, it is desirable to allow lock conversion by relaxing the conditions (4) and (5) of the shared/ exclusive lock mechanism i.e., if a transaction T already holds is, type of lock on an item X, it may be allowed to convert it to other types. For example, it is holding a readlock on X, it may be allowed to upgrade it to a writelock. All that the transaction does is to issue a writelock(X) operation. If T is the only transaction holding the readlock, it may be immediately allowed to upgrade itself to a writelock, otherwise it has to wait until the other readlocks (of other transactions) are released. Similarly, if it is holding a writelock(X), T may be allowed to downgrade it to readlock(X). The algorithms of the previous sections can be amended to accommodate the conversion locks and this has been left as on exercise to the students.

Before we close the section, it should be noted that use of binary locks does not by itself guarantee serializability. This is because of the fact that in certain combinations of situations, a key holding transaction may end up unlocking the unit too early. This can happen because of a variety of reasons, including a situation wherein a transaction feels it is no more needing a particular data unit and hence unlocks, it but may be indirectly writing into it at a later time (through some other unit). This would result in ineffective locking performance and the serializability is lost. To guarantee such serializability, the protocol of two phase locking is to be implemented, which we will see in the next section.

12.5 TWO-PHASE LOCKING

A transaction is said to be following a two-phase locking if the operation of the transaction can be divided into two distinct phases. In the first phase, all items that are needed by the transaction are acquired by locking them. In this phase, no item is unlocked even if its operations are over. In the second phase, the items are unlocked one after the other. The first phase can be thought of as a growing phase, wherein the store of locks held by the transaction keeps growing. In the second phase, called the shrinking phase, the number of locks held by the transaction keep shrinking.

```
readlock(Y)
read_tr(Y)        Phase I
writelock(X)
---------------------------------------------
unlock(Y)
read_tr(X)        Phase II
X=X+Y
write_tr(X)
unlock(X)
```

A two-phase locking example: The two-phase locking, though provides serializability has a disadvantage. Since the locks are not released immediately after the use of the item is over, but is retained till all the other needed locks are also acquired, the desired amount of interleaving may not be derived – worse, while a transaction T may be holding an item X, though it is not using it, just to satisfy the two-phase locking protocol, another transaction T_1 may be genuinely needing the item, but will be unable to get it till T releases it. This is the price that is to be paid for the guaranteed serializability provided by the two-phase locking system.

12.6 DEADLOCK AND STARVATION

A deadlock is a situation wherein each transaction T_1 which is in a set of two or more transactions is waiting for some item that is locked by some other transaction T^1 in the set i.e., taking the case of only two transactions T_1^1 and T_2^1 , T_1^1 is waiting for an item X which is with T_2^1 , and is also holding another item Y. T_1^1 will release Y when X becomes available from T_2^1 and T_1^1 can complete some operations. Meanwhile T_2^1 is waiting for Y held by T_1^1 and T_2^1 will release X only Y, held by T_1^1 is released and after T_2^1 has performed same operations on that. It can be easily seen that this is an infinite wait and the dead lock will never get resolved.

T_1^1	T_2^1
readlock(Y)	
read_tr(Y)	
	readlock(X)
	read_tr(X)
writelock(X)	
	writelock(Y)

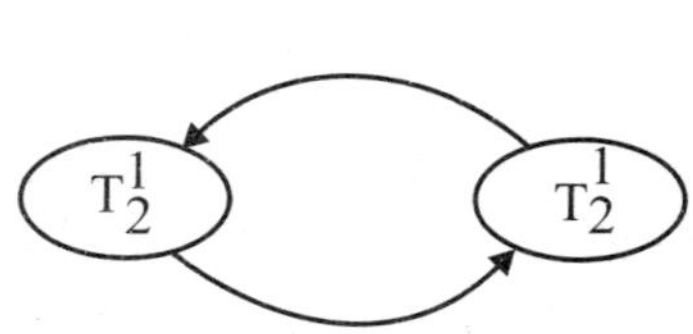

The status graph

A partial schedule leading to deadlock: While in the case of only two transactions, it is rather easy to notice the possibility of deadlock, though preventing it may be difficult. The case may become more complicated, when more then two transactions are in a deadlock and even identifying a deadlock may be difficult.

12.6.1 Deadlock Prevention Protocols

The simplest way of preventing deadlock is to look at the problem in detail. Deadlock occurs basically because of a transaction has locked several items, but could not get one more item and is not releasing other items held by it. The solution is to develop a protocol wherein a transaction will first get all the items that it needs and then only locks them i.e., if it cannot get any one/more of the items, it does not hold the other items also, so that these items can be useful to any other transaction that may need them. Their method, though prevents deadlocks, further limits the prospects of concurrency.

A better way to deal with deadlocks is to identify the deadlock when it occurs and then take some decision. The transaction involved in the deadlock may be blocked or aborted or the transaction can preempt and abort the other transaction involved. In a typical case, the concept of transaction time stamp TS(T) is used. Based on when the transaction was started, (given by the time stamp, larger the value of TS, younger is the transaction), two methods of deadlock recovery are devised.

1. Wait-die method: suppose a transaction T_i tries to lock an item X, but is unable to do so because X is locked by T_j with a conflicting lock. Then if $TS(T_i) < TS(T_j)$, (T_i is older then T_j) then T_i waits. Otherwise, (if T_i is younger than T_j) then T_i is aborted and restarted later with the same time stamp. The policy is that the older of the transactions will have already spent sufficient efforts and hence should not be aborted.
2. Wound-wait method: If $TS(T_i) < TS(T_j)$, (T_i is older then T_j), abort and restart T_j with the same time stamp later. On the other hand, if T_i is younger then T_i is allowed to wait.

It may be noted that in both cases, the younger transaction will be aborted. However, the actual method of aborting is different. Both these methods can be proved to be deadlock free, because no cycles of waiting as seen earlier are possible with these arrangements.

There is another class of protocols that do not require any time stamps. They include the 'no waiting algorithm' and the 'cautious waiting' algorithms. In the no-waiting algorithm, if a transaction cannot get a lock, it is aborted immediately (no waiting). It is restarted again at a later time. However, since there is no guarantee that the new situation. Is dead lock free, it may have to abort again. This may lead to a situation where a transaction may end up being aborted repeatedly.

To overcome this problem, the cautious waiting algorithm was proposed. Here, suppose the transaction T_i tries to lock an item X, but cannot get X since X is already locked by another transaction T_j. Then the solution is as follows: If T_j is not blocked (not waiting for it other locked item) then Ti is blocked and allowed to wait. Otherwise, T_i is aborted. This method not only reduces repeated aborting, but can also be proved to be deadlock free, since out of T_i and T_j, only one is blocked, after ensuring that the other is not blocked.

12.6.2 Deadlock Detection & Timeouts

The second method of dealing with deadlocks is to detect deadlocks as and when they happen. The basic problem with the earlier suggested protocols is that they assume that we know what happenings are in the system–which transaction is waiting for which item and so on. However, in a typical case of concurrent operations, the situation is fairly complex and it may not be possible to predict the behaviour of transaction.

In such cases, the easier method is to take on deadlocks as and when they happen and try to solve them. A simple way to detect a deadlock is to maintain a "wait for" graph. One node in the graph is created for each executing transaction. Whenever a transaction T_i is waiting to lock an item X that is currently held by T_j, an edge ($T_i \rightarrow T_j$) is created in their graph. When T_j releases X, this edge is dropped. It is easy to see that whenever there is a deadlock situation, there will be loops formed in the "wait-for" graph, so that suitable corrective action can be taken. Again, once a deadlock has been detected, the transaction to be aborted is to be chosen. This is called the "victim selection" and generally, newer transactions are selected for victimization.

Another easy method of dealing with deadlocks is the use of timeouts. Whenever a transaction is made to wait for periods longer than a predefined period, the system assumes that a deadlock has occurred and aborts the transaction. This method is simple and with low overheads, but may end up removing the transaction, even when there is no deadlock.

12.6.3 Starvation

The other side effect of locking in starvation, which happens when a transaction cannot proceed for indefinitely long periods, though the other transactions in the system, are continuing normally. This may happen if the waiting schemes for locked items are unfair i.e., if some transactions may never be able to get the items, since one or the other of the high priority transactions may continuously be using them. Then the low priority transaction will be forced to "starve" for want of resources.

The solution to starvation problems lies in choosing proper priority algorithms – like first-come-first serve. If this is not possible, then the priority of a transaction may be increased every time it is made to wait/aborted, so that eventually it becomes a high priority transaction and gets the required services.

12.7 CONCURRENCY CONTROL BASED ON TIME STAMP ORDERING

12.7.1 The Concept of Time Stamps

A time stamp is a unique identifier created by the DBMS, attached to each transaction, which indicates a value that is measure of when the transaction came into the system. Roughly, a time stamp can be thought of as the starting time of the transaction, denoted by TS (T).

They are generated by a counter that is initially zero and is incremented each time its value is assigned to the transaction. The counter is also given a maximum value and if the reading goes beyond that value, the counter is reset to zero, indicating, most often, that the transaction has lived its life span inside the system and needs to be taken out. A better way of creating such time stamps is to make use of the system time/date facility or even the internal clock of the system.

12.7.2 An Algorithm for Ordering the Time Stamp

The basic concept is to order the transactions based on their time stamps. A schedule made of such transactions is then serializable. This concept is called the time stamp ordering (To). The algorithm should ensure that whenever a data item is accessed by conflicting operations in the schedule, the data is available to them in the serializability order. To achieve this, the algorithm uses two time stamp values.

1. **read_Ts (X):** This indicates the largest time stamp among the transactions that have successfully read the item X. Note that the largest time stamp actually refers to the youngest of the transactions in the set (that has read X).
2. **write_Ts(X):** This indicates the largest time stamp among all the transactions that have successfully written the item X. Note that the largest time stamp actually refers to the youngest transaction that has written X.

The above two values are often referred to as "read time stamp" and "write time stamp" of the item X.

12.7.3 The Concept of Basic Time Stamp Ordering

Whenever a transaction tries to read or write an item X, the algorithm compares the time stamp of T with the read time stamp or the write stamp of the item X, as the case may be. This is done to ensure that T does not violate the order of time stamps. The violation can come in the following ways:

1. Transaction T is trying to write X
   (a) If read_Ts(X) > Ts(T) or if write_Ts(X) > Ts(T) then abort and roll back T and reject the operation. In plain words, if a transaction younger than T has already read or written X, the time stamp ordering is violated and hence T is to be aborted and all the values written by T so far need to be rolled back, which may also involve cascaded rolling back.
   (b) If read_Ts(X) < TS(T) or if write_Ts(X) < Ts(T), then execute the write_tr(X) operation and set write TS(X) to TS(T) i.e., allow the operation and the write time stamp of X to that of T, since T is the latest transaction to have accessed X.
2. Transaction T is trying to read X
   (a) If write_Ts(X) > TS(T) , then abort and roll back T and reject the operation. This is because a younger transaction has written into X.
   (b) If write_Ts(X) < = TS(T), execute read_tr(X) and set read_Ts(X) to the larger of the two values, namely TS(T) and current read_Ts(X).

This algorithm ensures proper ordering and also avoids deadlocks by penalizing the older transaction when it is trying to overhaul the operation done by an younger transaction. Of course, the aborted transaction will be reintroduced later with a "new" time stamp. However, in the absence of any other monitoring protocol, the algorithm may create starvation in the case of some transactions.

12.7.4 Strict Time Stamp Ordering

This variation of the time stamp ordering algorithm ensures that the schedules are "strict" (so that recoverability is enhanced) and serializable. In this case, any transaction T that tries to read or write such that write_TS(X) < TS(T) is made to wait until the transaction T' that originally wrote into (hence whose time stamp matches with the writetime time stamp of X, i.e., TS(T') = write_TS(X)) is committed or aborted. This algorithm also does not cause any dead lock, since T waits for T' only if TS(T) > TS(T').

12.8 MULTIVERSION CONCURRENCY CONTROL TECHNIQUES

The main reason why some of the transactions have to be aborted is that they try to access data items that have been updated (by transactions that are younger than it is). One way of overcoming this problem is to maintain several versions of the data items, so that if a transaction tries to access an updated data item, instead of aborting it, it may be allowed to work on the older version of data. This concept is called the multiversion method of concurrency control.

Whenever a transaction writes a data item, the new value of the item is made available, as also the older version. Normally the transactions are given access to the newer version, but in case of conflicts, the policy is to allow the 'older' transaction to have access to the 'older' version of the item.

The obvious drawback of this technique is that more storage is required to maintain the different versions. However, in many cases, this may not be a major drawback, since most database applications continue to retain the older versions anyway, for the purposes of recovery or for historical purposes.

12.8.1 Multiversion Technique based on Time Stamp Ordering

In this method, several version of the data item X, which we call X_1, X_2, .. X_k are maintained. For each version X_i two time stamps are appended

(i) **read_Ts(X_i):** the read timestamp of X_i indicates the largest of all time stamps of transactions that have read X_i. (This, in plain language means the youngest of the transactions, which has read it).

(ii) **write_Ts(X_i):** The write time stamp of X_i indicates the time stamp of the transaction time stamp of the transaction that wrote X_i.

Whenever a transaction T writes into X, a new version X_{K+1} is created, with both write. TS(X_{K+1}) and read_Ts(X_{k+1}) being set to TS(T). Whenever a transaction T reads into X, the value of read_Ts(X_i) is set to the larger of the two values namely read_Ts(X_i) and TS(T).

To ensure serializability, the following rules are adopted.

(i) If T issues a write_tr(X) operation and X_i has the highest write_Ts(X_i) which is less than or equal to TS(T), and has a read_Ts(X_i) > TS(T), then abort and roll back T, else create a new version of X, say X_k with read_Ts(X_k) = write_Ts(X_k) = TS(T).

In plain words, if the highest possible write time stamp among all versions is less than or equal to that of T, and if it has been read by a transaction younger than T, then, we have no option but to abort T and roll back all it's effects otherwise a new version of X is created with it's read and write time stamps initiated to that of T.

(ii) If a transaction T issues a read_tr(X) operation, find the version X_i with the highest write_Ts(X_i) that is also less than or equal to TS(T) then return the value of X_i to T and set the value of read_Ts(X_i) to the value that is larger amongst TS(T) and current read_Ts(X_i).

This only means, try to find the highest version of X_i that T is eligible to read, and return its value of X to T. Since T has now read the value find out whether it is the youngest transaction to read X by comparing it's timestamp with the current read_Ts stamp of X. If X is younger (if time stamp is higher), store it as the youngest time stamp to visit X, else retain the earlier value.

12.8.2 Multiversion Two-Phase Locking Certify Locks

Note that the motivation behind the two-phase locking systems has been discussed previously. In the standard locking mechanism, writelock is an exclusive lock—i.e., only one transaction can use a write locked data item. However, no harm is done, if the item write locked by a transaction is read by one/more other transactions. On the other hand, it enhances the "interleavability" of operation. That is, more transactions can be interleaved. This concept is extended to the multiversion locking system by using what are known as "multiple-mode" locking schemes. In this, there are three locking modes for the item: read, write and certify i.e., a unit can be locked for read(X), write(X) or certify(X), as also it can remain unlocked. To see how the scheme works, we first see how the normal read, write system works by means of a lock compatibility table.

Lock compatibility Table

	Read	Write
Read	Yes	No
Write	No	No

The explanation is as follows:

If there is an entry "yes" in a particular cell, if a transaction T holds the type of lock specified in the column header and if another transaction T' requests for the type of lock specified in row header, the T' can obtain the lock, because the lock modes are compatible. For example, there is a yes in the first cell. Its column header is read. So if a transaction T holds the read lock, and another transaction T' requests for the readlock, it can be granted. On the other hand, if T holds a writelock and another T' requests for a readlock it will not be granted, because the action now has shifted to the first row, second column element. In the modified (multimode) locking system, the concept is extended by adding one more row and column to the tables.

	Read	Write	Certify
Read	Yes	Yes	No
Write	Yes	No	No
Certify	No	No	No

The multimode locking system works on the following lines. When one of the transactions has obtained a writelock for a data item, the other transactions may still be provided with the read locks for the item. To ensure this, two versions of the X are maintained. X(old) is a version, which has been written and committed by a previous transaction. When a transaction T wants a writelock to be provided to it, a new version X(new) is created and handed over to T for writing. While T continues to hold the lock for X(new) other transactions can continue to use X(old) under readlock.

Once T is ready to commit it should get exclusive "certify" locks on all items it wants to commit by writing. Note that "write lock" is no more an exclusive lock under our new scheme of things, since while one transaction is holding a write lock on X, one/more other transactions may be holding the readlocks of the same X. To provide certify lock, the system waits until all other read locks are cleared on the item. Note that this process has to repeat on all items that T wants to commit.

Once all these items are under the certify lock of the transaction, it can commit to its values. From now on, the X(new) become X(old) and X(new) values will be created only if another T wants a writelock on X. This scheme avoids cascading rollbacks. However, since a transaction will have to get exclusive certify rights on all items, before it can commit, a delay in the commit operation is inevitable. This may also leads to complexities like dead locks and starvation.

12.9 SUMMARY

This chapter introduced you to two very important concepts of concurrency control—namely the locking techniques and time stamp technique. In the locking technique, the data item, currently needed by a transaction, is kept locked until it completes with its use, possibility until the transaction commits or aborts. This would ensure that the other transactions do not either access or update the data erroneously. This can be implemented very easily by introducing a binary bit. 1 indicating it is locked and 0 indicates it is available. Any item that needs a locked item will have to simply wait. Obviously, this introduces time delays. Some delays can be reduced by noting that a write locked data item can be simultaneously readlocked by other transactions. This concept leads to the use of shared locks. It was also shown that locking can be used to ensure serializability. However, when different transactions keep different items locked with them, the situations of deadlock and starvation may crop in. Various methods of identifying the deadlocks and breaking them (mostly by penalizing one of the participating transactions were discussed.

We also looked into the concept of time stamps–wherein the transaction bears a stamp, which indicates when it came into the system. This can be used in order to ensure serializability–by ordering the transactions based on time stamps—we saw several such algorithms. The time stamps can also be used in association with the system log to ensure roll back operations continue satisfactorily.

REVIEW QUESTIONS

1. What are the two possible states of a binary lock?
2. Why is shared/exclusive locking scheme required?
3. What is two phase locking?
4. What is the major advantage of two phase locking?
5. What is a deadlock?
6. Why is the younger transaction aborted in deadlock breaking?
7. What is a wait for graph? What is its use?
8. What is starvation?
9. What is a timestamp?
10. What is multiversion concurrency control?

CHAPTER 13

Database Recovery Techniques

In this chapter, you will learn

13.0 INTRODUCTION

In this chapter, you are introduced to some of the database recovery techniques. You are introduced to the concept of caching of disk blocks and the mode of operation of these cached elements to aid the recovery process. The concept of "in place updating" (wherein this updated on the original disk location) as compared t^ shadowing (where a new location is used will be discussed).

The actual recovery process depends on whether the system uses the write ahead logging or not. In addition, the updated data may written back to the disk even before the system commits (which is called a "steal" approach or may wait until commit operation takes place (which is a "no steal" approach). Further, you are introduced to the concept of check pointing, which does a lot to improve the efficiency of the roll back operation. Based on these concepts, we write simple algorithms that do the roll back operation for single user and multi-user systems.

Finally, we look into the preliminaries of database ,ecurity and access control. The types of privileges that the DBA can provide at the discretionar, level and the concept of level-wise security mechanism are discussed.

13.1 CONCEPT OF RECOVERY

Recovery most often means bringing the database back to the most recent consistent state, in the case of transaction failures. This obviously demands that status information about the previous consistent states is made available in the form a "log" (which has been discussed in one of the previous sections in some detail).

A typical algorithm for recovery should proceed on the following lines:

1. If the database has been physically damaged or there are catastrophic crashes like disk crash etc., the database has to be recovered from the archives. In many cases, a reconstruction process is to be adopted using various other sources of information.
2. In situations where the database is not damaged but has lost consistency because of transaction failures etc., the method is to retrace the steps from the state of the crash (which has created inconsistency) until the previously encountered state of consistency is reached. The method normally involves undoing certain operation, restoring previous values using the log etc.

In general, two broad categories of these retracing operations can be identified. As we have seen previously, most often, the transactions do not update the database as and when they complete the operation. So, if a transaction fails or the system crashes before the commit operation, those values need not be retraced. So no "undo" operation is needed.

However, if one is still interested in getting the results out of the transactions, then a "Redo" operation will have to be taken up. Hence, this type of retracing is often called the "No-Undo/Redo algorithm". The whole concept works only when the system is working on a "deferred update" mode.

However, this may not be the case always. In certain situations, where the system is working on the "immediate update" mode, the transactions keep updating the database without bothering about the commit operation. In such cases however, the updating will be normally onto the disk also. Hence, if a system fails when the immediate updating are being made, then it becomes necessary to undo the operations using the disk entries. This will help us to reach the previous consistent state. From there onwards, the transactions will have to be redone. Hence, this method of recovery is often termed as the Undo/Redo algorithm.

13.1.1 The Role of the Operating System in Recovery

In most cases, the operating system functions play a critical role in the process of recovery. Most often, the system maintains a copy of some parts of the DBMS (called pages) in a fast memory called the cache. Whenever data is to be updated, the system first checks whether the required record is available in cache. If so, the corresponding record in the cache is updated. Since the cache size is normally limited, it cannot hold the entire DBMS, but holds only a few pages. When a data, located in a page that is not currently with the cache is to be updated, the page is to be brought to cache. To do this, some page of the cache will have to be written back to the disk to make room for this new page.

When a new page is brought to the cache, each record in it is associated with a bit, called the "dirty bit". This indicates whether the bit has been modified or not. Initially its value is 0 and when and if it is modified by a transaction, the bit is made 1. Note that when the page is written back to the disk, only those records whose dirty bits are 1 are to be updated. (This of course implies "inplace Writing" i.e., the page is sent back to it's original space in the disk, where the "not updated data" is still in place. Otherwise, the entire page needs to be rewritten at a new location on the disk).

In some cases, a "shading" concept is used, wherein the updated page is written else where in the disk, so that both the previous and updated versions are available on the disk.

13.2 WRITE AHEAD LOGGING

When in place updating is being used, it is necessary to maintain a log for recovery purposes. Normally before the updated value is written on to the disk, the earlier value (called Before Image Value (BFIM)) is to noted down elsewhere in the disk for recovery purposes. This process of recording entries is called the "write–ahead logging" (write ahead of logging). It is to be noted that the type of logging also depends on the type of recovery. If No-Undo/Redo type of recovery is being used, then only those values, which could not be written back before the crash, need to be logged. But in a Undo/Redo types, the values before the image was created as well as those that were computed, but could not be written back need to be logged.

Two other update mechanisms need brief mention. The cache pages, updated by the transaction, cannot be written back to the disk, by the DBMS manager, until and unless the transaction commits. If the system strictly follows this approach, then it is called a "no steal" approach. However, in some cases, the protocol allows the writing of the updated buffer back to the disk, even before the transaction commits. This may be done, for example, when some other transaction is in need of the results. This is called the "steal" approach.

Secondly, if all pages are updated once the transaction commits, then it is a "force approach", otherwise it is called a "no force" approach.

Most protocols make use of steal/no force strategies, so that there is no urgency of writing back to the buffer once the transaction commits.

However, just the before image (BIM) and after image (AIM) values may not be sufficient for successful recovery. A number of lists, including the list of active transaction (those that have started operating, but have not committed yet), committed transactions as also aborted transactions need to be maintained, to avoid a brute force method of recovery.

13.3 ROLE OF CHECK POINTS IN RECOVERY

A "Check point", as the name suggests, indicates that everything is fine up to the point. In a log, when a checkpoint is encountered, it indicates that all values up to that have been written back to the DBMS on the disk. Any further crash/system failure will have to take care of the data appearing beyond this point only. Put the other way, all transactions that have their commit entries in the log before this point need no rolling back.

The recovery manager of the DBMS will decide at what intervals, checkpoints need to be inserted (in turn, at what intervals data is to be written back to the disk). It can be either after specific periods of time (say M minutes) or specific number of transaction (t transactions) etc., when the protocol decides to check point, it does the following:

(a) Suspend all transaction executions temporarily.

(b) Force writes all memory buffers to the disk.

(c) Insert a check point in the log and force write the log to the disk.

(d) Resume the execution of transactions.

The force writing need not only refer to the modified data items, but can include the various lists and other auxiliary information indicated previously.

However, the force writing of all the data pages may take some time and it would be wasteful to halt all transactions until then. A better way is to make use of the "Fuzzy check pointing" where in the check point is inserted and while the buffers are being written back (beginning from the previous check point) the transactions are allowed to restart. This way the I/O time is saved. Until all data up to the new check point is written back, the previous check point is held valid for recovery purposes.

13.4 RECOVERY TECHNIQUES BASED ON DEFERRED UPDATE

This is a very simple method of recovery. Theoretically, no transaction can write back into the database, until it has committed. Until then, it can only write into a buffer. Thus in case of any crash, the buffer needs to be reconstructed, but the DBMS need not be recovered.

However, in practice, most transactions are very long and it is dangerous to hold all their updates in the buffer, since the buffers can run out of space and may need a page replacement. To avoid such situations, where in a page is removed inadvertently, a simple two pronged protocol is used.

1. A transaction cannot change the DBMS values on the disk until it commits.
2. A transaction does not reach commit stage until all it's update values are written on to the log and log itself in force written on to the disk.

Notice that in case of failures, recovery is by the No-UNDO/REDO techniques, since all data will be in the log if a transaction fails after committing.

13.5 AN ALGORITHM FOR RECOVERY USING THE DEFERRED UPDATE IN A SINGLE USER ENVIRONMENT

In a single user environment, the algorithm is a straight application of the REDO procedure i.e., it uses two lists of transactions: The committed transactions since the last check point and the currently active transactions when the crash occurs, apply the REDO to all write_tr operations of the committed transactions from the log. In addition, let the active transactions run again.

The assumption is that the REDO operations are "idem potent" i.e., the operations produce the same results irrespective of the number of times they are redone provided, they start from the same initial state. This is essential to ensure that the recovery operation does not produce a result that is different from the case where no crash was there to begin with.

(Through this may look like a trivial constraint, students may verify themselves that not all DBMS applications satisfy this condition).

In addition, since there was only one transaction active (because it was a single user system) and it had not updated the buffer yet, all that remains to be done is to restart this transaction.

13.6 DEFERRED UPDATE WITH CONCURRENT EXECUTION

Most of the DBMS applications, we have insisted repeatedly, are multi-user in nature and the best way to run them is by concurrent execution. Hence, protocols for recovery from a crash in such cases are of prime importance.

To simplify the matters, we presume that we are in talking of strict and serializable schedules i.e., there is strict two phase locking and they remain effective until the transactions commit themselves. In such a scenario, an algorithm for recovery could be as follows:

Use two lists: The list of committed transactions T since the last check point and the list of active checkpoints T^1 REDO all the write operations of committed transactions in the order in which they were written into the log. The active transactions are simply cancelled and resubmitted.

Note that once we put the strict serializability conditions, the recovery process does not vary too much from the single user system.

Note that in the actual process, a given item X may be updated a number of times, either by the same transaction or by different transactions at different times. What is important to the user is it's final value. However, the above algorithm simply updates the value whenever it's value was updated in the log. This can be made more efficient by the following manner. Instead of starting from the check point and proceeding towards the time of the crash, traverse the log from the time of the crash backwards. Whenever a value is updated, for the first time, update it and maintain the information that it's value has been updated. Any further updating of the same can be ignored.

This method though guarantees correct recovery has some drawbacks. Since the items remain locked with the transactions until the transaction commits, the concurrent execution efficiency comes down. In addition, lot of buffer space is wasted to hold the values, until the transactions commit. The number of such values can be large, when the long transactions are working in concurrent mode, they delay the commit operation of one another.

13.7 RECOVERY TECHNIQUES ON IMMEDIATE UPDATE

In these techniques, whenever a write_tr(X) is given, the data is written on to the database, without bothering about the commit operation of the transaction. However, as a rule, the update operate is accompanied by writing on to the log(on the disk), using a write ahead logging protocol.

This helps in undoing the update operations whenever a transaction fails. This rolling back can be done by using the data on the log. Further, if the transaction is made to commit only after writing on to the log, there is no need for a redo of these operations after the transaction has failed, because the values are available in the log. This concept is called the UNDO/NO-REDO recovery algorithm. On the other hand, if some transaction commits before writing all it's values, then a general UNDO/REDO type of recovery algorithm is necessary.

13.7.1 A Typical UNDO/REDO Algorithm for an Immediate Update Single User Environment

Here, at the time of failure, the changes envisaged by the transaction may have already been recorded in the database. These must be undone. A typical procedure for recovery should follow the following lines:

(a) The system maintains two lists: The list of committed transactions since the last checkpoint and the list of active transactions (only one active transaction, infact, because it is a single user system).

(b) In case of failure, undo all the write_tr operations of the active transaction, by using the information on the log, using the UNDO procedure.

(c) For undoing a write_tr(X) operation, examine the corresponding log entry write_tr(T,X, oldvalue, newvalue) and set the value of X to oldvalue. The sequence of undoing must be in the reverse order, in which operations were written on to the log.

(d) REDO the write_tr operations of the committed transaction from the log in the order in which they were written in the log, using the REDO procedure.

13.7.2 The UNDO/REDO Recovery based on Immediate Update with Concurrent Execution

In the concurrent execution scenario, the process becomes slightly complex. In the following algorithm, we presume that the log includes checkpoints and the concurrency protocol uses strict schedules i.e., the schedule does not allow a transaction to read or write an item until the transaction that wrote the item previously has committed. Hence, the danger of transaction failures is minimum. However, deadlocks can force abort and UNDO operations. The simplistic procedure is as follows:

(a) Use two lists maintained by the system: The committed transactions list(since the last check point) and the list of active transactions.

(b) Undo all write_tr(X) operations of the active transactions, which have not yet committed, using the UNDO procedure. The undoing operation must be in the reverse order of writing process in the log.

(c) Redo all write_tr(X) operations of the committed transactions from the log in the order in which they were written into the log.

Normally, the process of redoing the write_tr(X) operations begins at the end of the log and proceeds in the reverse order, so that when a X is written into more than once in the log, only the latest entry is recorded, as discussed in a previous section.

13.8 SHADOW PAGING

It is not always necessary that the original database be updated by overwriting the previous values. As discussed in an earlier section, we can make multiple versions of the data items, whenever a new update is made. The concept of shadow paging illustrates this:

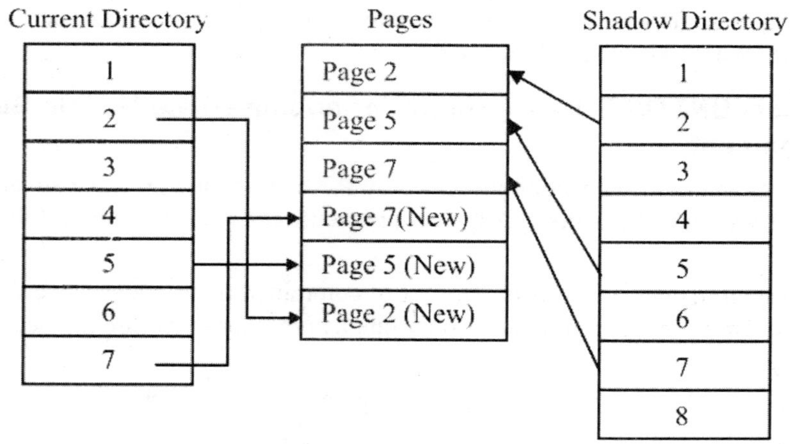

In a typical case, the database is divided into pages and only those pages that need updating are brought to the main memory (or cache, as the case may be). A shadow directory holds pointers to these pages. Whenever an update is done, a new block of the page is created (indicated by the suffice(new) in the figure) and the updated values are included there. Note that (i) the new pages are created in the order of updating and not in the serial order of the pages. A current directory holds pointers to these new pages. For all practical purposes, these are the "valid pages" and they are written back to the database at regular intervals.

Now, if any rollback is to be done, the only operation to be done is to discard the current directory and treat the shadow directory as the valid directory.

One difficulty is that the new, updated pages are kept at unrelated spaces and hence the concept of a "continuous" database is lost. More importantly, what happens when the "new" pages are discarded as a part of UNDO strategy? These blocks form "garbage" in the system. (The same thing happens when a transaction commits the new pages become valid pages, while the old pages become garbage). A mechanism to systematically identify all these pages and reclaim them becomes essential.

13.9 BACKUP AND RECOVERY IN THE CASE OF CATASTROPHIC FAILURES

Not all the methods discussed so far presume one condition–i.e., the system failure are catastrophic–i.e., the log and the shadow directory etc. stored on the disk are immune from failure and are available for the UNDO/REDO operation. However, what happens when the disk also crashes?

To over come such effects, normally the database is backed up in permanent media like tapes and is stored elsewhere. In the case of a crash, the latest backup copy needs to be copied back and the system should start working from there onwards.

However, even this may become a laborious process. Therefore, often the logs are also copied and kept as backup. Note that the size of the logs can be much smaller than the actual size of the database. Hence, between two scheduled database backups, several log backups can be taken and stored separately.

In case of failures, the backup restores the situation, as it was, when the last backup was taken. The logs taken since then can be used to reflect the changes done up to the time last log was backup (not up to the time log was taken). From then on, ofcourse, the transactions will have to operate again.

13.10 SOME ASPECTS OF DATABASE SECURITY AND AUTHORIZATION

It is common knowledge that the databases should be held secure, against damages, unauthorized accesses and updating. A DBMS typically includes a "database security and authorization subsystem" that is responsible for the security of the database against unauthorized accesses and attacks. Traditionally, two types of security mechanisms are in use.

(i) **Discretionary security mechanisms:** Here each user (or a group of users) is granted privileges and authorities to access certain records, pages or files and denied access to others. The discretion normally lies with the database administer (DBA).

(ii) **Mandatory security mechanisms:** These are standard security mechanisms that are used to enforce multilevel security by classifying the data into different levels and allowing the users (or a group of users), access to certain levels only based on the security policies of the organization. Here the rules apply uniformly across the board and the discretionary powers are limited.

While all these discussions assume that a user is allowed access to the system, but not to all parts of the database, at another level, effects should be made to prevent unauthorized access of the system by outsiders. This comes under the purview of the security systems.

Another type of security enforced in the "statistical database security" often large databases are used to provide statistical information's about various aspects like, say income levels, qualifications, health conditions etc. These are derived by collecting a large number of individual data. A person who is doing the statistical analysis may be allowed access to the "statistical data" which is an aggregated data, but he should not be allowed access to individual data i.e., he may know, for example, the average income level of a region, but cannot verify the income level of a particular individual. This problem is more often encountered in government and quasi-government organizations and is studied under the concept of "statistical database security".

It may be noted that in all these cases, the role of the DBA becomes critical. He normally logs into the system under a DBA account or a superuser account, which provides full capabilities to manage the Database, ordinarily not available to the other uses. Under the superuser account, he can manage the following aspects regarding security.

(i) Account creation: He can create new accounts and passwords to users or user groups.

(ii) Privilege granting: He can pass on privileges like ability to access certain files or certain records to the users.

(iii) Privilege revocation: The DBA can revoke certain or all privileges granted to one/several users.

(iv) Security level assignment: The security level of a particular user account can be assigned, so that based on the policies, the users become eligible/not eligible for accessing certain levels of information.

Another aspect of having individual accounts is the concept of "database audit". It is similar to the system log that has been created and used for recovery purposes. If we can include in the log entries details regarding the user's name and account number who has created/used the transactions which are writing the log details, one can have record of the accesses and other usage made by the user. This concept becomes useful in follow-up actions, including legal examinations, especially in sensitive and high security installations.

Another concept is the creation of "views". While the database record may have large number of fields, a particular user may be authorized to have information only about certain fields. In such cases, whenever he requests for the data item, a "view" is created for him of the data item, which includes only those fields, which he is authorized to have access to. He may not even know that there are many other fields in the records.

The concept of views becomes very important when large databases, which cater to the needs of various types of users are being maintained. Every user can have and operate upon his view of the database, without being bogged down by the details. It also makes the security maintenance operations convenient.

13.11 SUMMARY

We started with the concept on need of recovery techniques. We saw how the operating uses cache memory and how this concept can be used to recover the databases. The two concepts of inplace updating and shadowing and how the rollback is to be done in each case was discussed.

Definitions and details of steal/nonsteal approach, force/nonforce approach etc. were given. We also saw the mechanism of introducing check points, how they help in the recovery process and the various trade offs. Simple algorithms for the actual recovery operation were described.

The last section described the need for database security, the various methods of providing it by access control methods and the role of the DBA were discussed.

REVIEW QUESTIONS

1. What is deferred update?
2. What is a cache?
3. What is a "dirty bit" in the concept of cache?
4. What is inplace updating?
5. Define steal approach of updating.
6. What is a check point?
7. What is a shadow page?
8. What is the method of recovery in the case of a catastrophic crash?
9. What is multilevel security mechanism?
10. What is a superuser account?

CHAPTER 14

Distributed Database

In this chapter, you will learn

14.0 INTRODUCTION

Distributed databases system is a compilation of data with different parts under the control of separate DBMSs running on different computers. These computers are associated together and communicate with one another through various communication techniques. DBMS can handle both local and global transactions.

The main advantages of Distributed Data Base Management System are:

1. Distributed database management system allows each site to store and maintain its own database, causing the immediate and efficient access to data.
2. It allows accessing the data stored at remote sites. At the same time users can retain the control to its own site to access the local data.
3. If one site is not working due to any reason (Example, Communication link goes down) the system will not be down because other sites of the network can possibly continue functioning. Moreover, when data are replicated at two or more sites, required data may still be available from a site, which is still operable.
4. New sites can be added to the system anytime with no or little efforts.
5. If a user needs to access the data from multiple sites then the desired query can be sub-divided into sub-queries and the parts evaluated in parallel.

Although, Distributed Data Base Management System is the need of the day, it results into a complex structure and since the data is available to the users throughout a network makes security inherently more complex for distributed databases than with its centralized counterparts.

14.0.1 Transaction Processing in DDBMS

Transaction in a distributed database management system access records by issuing read and write operations. Each distributed database management system consists of a Transaction Manager (TM), a Data Manager (DM) and a Scheduler. Transactions communicate with TMs; TMs talks to Schedulers regarding each row and write of the transaction; Schedulers communicate among themselves and also with DMs; and the DMs manage the data.

Consider the Figure 14.1, which explains the transaction processing in DDBMS.

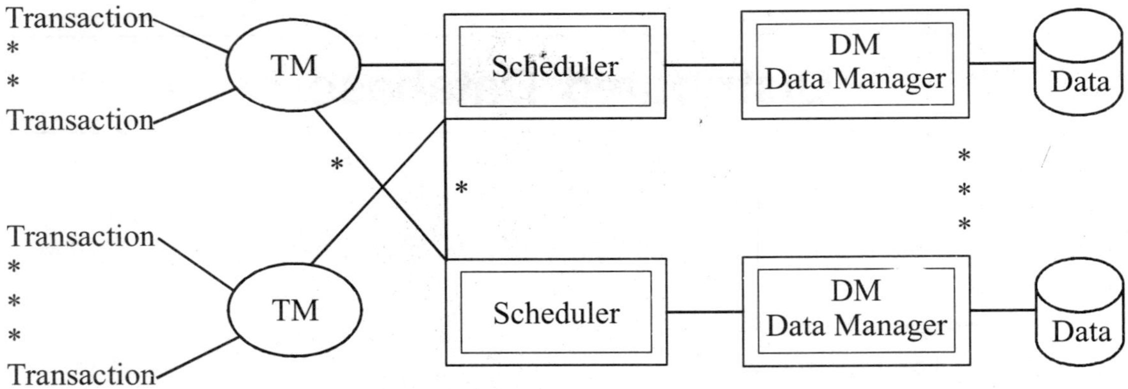

Figure 14.1: *Transaction processing in DDBMS*

14.1 DATA FRAGMENTATION

Data fragmentation is a method in which different relations of a relational database system can be subdivided and distributed among different network sites. Suppose we have a relation S and it is fragmented, it means it is divided into subsets (Fragments) $S_1, S_2, \ldots S_n$.

The union of these fragments re-constructs the original relation S.

There are two types of Data fragmentation:

1. Horizontal Fragmentation
2. Vertical Fragmentation

In horizontal fragmentation tuples are divided into subsets (fragments) whereas in vertical fragmentation attributes are divided into subsets.

14.1.1 Horizontal Fragmentation

As we defined previously, in horizontal fragmentation tuples of a relation are divided into number of subsets. For example, consider a relation EMP, as shown in Figure 14.2. This relation can be subdivided into '*n*' different fragments, each of which contains tuples belonging to a particular *DEPTNO*. If above relation have three Departments 10, 20, and 30 then there may be three different fragments:

EMP NO	ENAME	JOB	MGR	HIREDATE	SAL	COMM	DEPTNO
7369	SMITH	CLERK	7902	17-DEC-80	800		20
7499	ALLEN	SALESMAN	7698	20-FEB-81	1600	300	30
7521	WARD	SALESMAN	7698	22-FEB-81	1250	500	30
7566	JONES	MANAGER	7839	02-APR-81	2975		20
7654	MARTIN	SALESMAN	7698	28-SEP-81	1250	1400	30

Contd...

7698	BLAKE	MANAGER	7839	01-MAY-81	2850		30
7782	CLARK	MANAGER	7839	09-JUN-81	2450		10
7788	SCOTT	ANALYST	7566	19-APR-87	3000		20
7839	KING	PRESIDENT		17-NOV-81	5000		10
7844	TURNER	SALESMAN	7698	08-SEP-81	1500	0	30
7876	ADAMS	CLERK	7788	23-MAY-87	1100		20
7900	JAMES	CLERK	7785	03-DEC-81	950		30
7902	FORD	ANALYST	7566	03-DEC-81	3000		20
7934	MILLER	CLERK	7782	23-JAN-82	1300		10

Figure 14.2: *Relation - EMP*

$$EMP10 = \sigma_{deptno=\text{“10”}}(EMP)$$
$$EMP20 = \sigma_{deptno=\text{“20”}}(EMP)$$
$$EMP30 = \sigma_{deptno=\text{“30”}}(EMP)$$

These three fragments shown in Figures 14.3, 14.4 and 14.5, can now be stored on different networks.

EMP NO	ENAME	JOB	MGR	HIREDATE	SAL	COMM	DEPTNO
7782	CLARK	MANAGER	7839	09-JUN-81	2450		10
7839	KING	PRESIDENT		17-NOV-81	5000		10
7934	MILLER	ERK	7782	23-JAN-82	1300		

Figure 14.3: *Relation EMP10*

EMP NO	ENAME	JOB	MGR	HIREDATE	SAL	COMM	DEPTNO
7369	SMITH	CLERK	7902	17-DEC-80	800		20
7566	JONES	MANAGER	7839	02-APR-81	2975		20
7788	SCOTT	ANALYST	7566	19-APR-87	3000		20
7876	ADAMS	CLERK	7788	23-MAY-87	1100		20
7902	FORD	ANALYST	7566	03-DEC-81	3000		20

Figure 14.4: *Relation EMP20*

EMP NO	ENAME	JOB	MGR	HIREDATE	SAL	COMM	DEPTNO
7499	ALLEN	SALESMAN	7698	20-FEB-81	1600	300	30
7521	WARD	SALESMAN	7698	22-FEB-81	1250	500	30
7654	MARTIN	SALESMAN	7698	28-SEP-81	1250	1400	30
7698	BLAKE	MANAGER	7839	01-MAY-81	2850		30
7844	TURNER	SALESMAN	7698	08-SEP-81	1500	0	30
7900	JAMES	CLERK	–7698	03-DEC-81	950		30

Figure 14.5: *Relation EMP30*

The reconstruction of relation EMP can be obtained by taking the union of all fragmentations, that is:

EMP = EMP1 ∪ EMP2

14.1.2 Vertical Fragmentation

Vertical fragmentation is very much similar to horizontal fragmentation. In horizontal fragmentation tuples of a relation are divided into numbers of subsets whereas in vertical fragmentation attributes are divided into number of subsets.

Vertical fragmentation is accomplished by adding a special attribute called tuple-id. A tuple-id is a logical address for every tuple. Since each tuple in any relation must have a unique address, which is achieved by adding tuple-id attribute.

EMPNO	ENAME	JOB	MGR	HIREDATE	SAL	COMM	DEPTNO	TUPLE-ID
7369	SMITH	CLERK	7902	17-DEC-80	800		20	1
7499	ALLEN	SALESMAN	7698	20-FEB-81	1600	300	30	2
7521	WARD	SALESMAN	7698	22-FEB-81	1250	500	30	3
7566	JONES	MANAGER	7839	02-APR-81	2975		20	4
7654	MARTIN	SALESMAN	7698	28-SEP-81	1250	1400	30	5
7698	BLAKE	MANAGER	7839	01-MAY-81	2850		30	6
7782	CLARK	MANAGER	7839	09-JUN-81	2450		10	7
7788	SCOTT	ANALYST	7566	19-APR-87	3000		20	8
7839	KING	PRESIDENT		17-NOV-81	5000		10	9
7844	TURNER	SALESMAN	7698	08-SEP-81	1500		30	10
7876	ADAMS	CLERK	7788	23-MAY-87	1100		20	11
7900	JAMES	CLERK	7698	03-DEC-81	950	0	30	12
7902	FORD	ANALYST	7566	03-DEC-81	3000		20	13
7934	MILLER	CLERK	7782	23-JAN-82	1350		10	14

Figure 14.6: *EMP relation*

Suppose we want to make two fragments of this relation EMP, EMP1 and EMP2.

Then each fragment can be defined as:

$$EMP1 = \pi_{Empno, Ename, Job, tuple\text{-}id}(EMP)$$

$$EMP2 = \pi_{Sal, Deptno, tuple\text{-}id}(EMP)$$

which is shown in Figures 14.7 and 14.8.

EMPNO	ENAME	JOB	TUPLE-ID
7369	SMITH	CLERK	1
7499	ALLEN	SALESMAN	2
7521	WARD	SALESMAN	3
7566	JONES	MANAGER	4
7654	MARTIN	SALESMAN	5
7698	BLAKE	MANAGER	6
7782	CLARK	MANAGER	7
7788	SCOTT	ANALYST	8
7839	KING	PRESIDENT	9
7844	TURNER	SALESMAN	10
7876	ADAMS	CLERK	11
7900	JAMES	CLERK	12
7902	FORD	ANALYST	13
7934	MILLER	CLERK	14

Figure 14.7: *EMP1 relation*

SAL	DEPTNO	TUPLE-ID
800	20	1
1600	30	2
1250	30	3
2975	20	4
1250	30	5
2850	30	6
2450	10	7
3000	20	8
5000	10	9
1500	30	10
1100	20	11
950	30	12
3000	20	13
1350	10	14

Figure 14.8: *EMP2 relation*

To reconstruct the original EMP relation from the fragments, we join different individual fragments, as shown below:

EMP=EMP1 X EMP2

14.2 CONCURRENCY CONTROL IN DISTRIBUTED DATABASE

In a distributed DBMS, the main database is subdivided into fragments and stored on different sites. Once a transaction is submitted at one site, the transaction manager at that site breaks the main transaction into a collection of sub transactions. These sub transactions are then executed at different site, where relevant data is stored in the shape of fragments. The transaction manager co-ordinates with different sub transaction activities in order to get the end result.

In case of distributed DBMS we need to pay additional concentration for concurrency control and recovery. We shall at the moment discuss how lock and unlock are implemented in a distributed environment, which is called *"lock management"*. Lock management can be distributed across different sites in many ways, as discussed below:

Primary site technique: In this case a single site is in charge of handling lock and unlocks requests for all objects. In this method a single site, primary site, is designated to be the coordinator site for all database items. All locks are kept on that site and all requests for locking and unlocking are sent there. This method is an extension of centralized locking approach. This technique is not complex, but this technique has some disadvantages. One is that all locking requests are sent to a single site, which can make a site overloaded. Secondly, in case of primary site failure will paralyze the whole system since all locking information's are kept on primary site.

Primary site with backup: In this method we preserve a copy of primary site, which is known as *"backup site"*. In this case all locking information's are maintained at both sites. So in case if primary site fails then backup site acts as a primary site and another backup site is chosen and all locking information's are then copied on that new chosen backup site. It slows down the process of acquiring locks because all locks requests and granting of locks are recorded at both, primary and backup, sites before a response is sent to the requesting transaction. The problem of the primary and backup site becoming overloaded with requests and slowing down the system remains un-dimished.

Fully distributed: In this case requests to lock and unlock are stored at site and these locks are handled by lock manger at that site where the copy is stored. The primary site technique is not practical because if primary site fails, which controls all locking, then whole system is paralyze. In second method primary site technique with backup overcomes this problem as it maintains a copy of primary site. But in this case reading an object requires communication with two sites (primary and backup site).

This problem is avoided in this fully distributed method. In this methods, locking is done at the site where the copy to be read resides. However, while writing, locks must be set at all sites where copies are modified in the fully distributed schemes, whereas locks needs only be set at one site in other two schemes.

So we can conclude that fully distributed system is more attractive scheme if reads are more frequent than writes.

Query Processing in Distributed Database

In distributed database, we may need to access the data from multiple sites. This data is to be transferred from one site to another site, which was not the case of centralized DBMS, because in centralized system the entire data is stored only at one location. By the cost of data transfer we mean the cost of transferring the data or the complete data file from one site to another site and then displaying the output on the desired site. If the amount of data transfer is less then it will improve the performance of query processing. To appreciate that how the data should be transferred from one site to another with minimum transfer cost, consider an illustration, given below.

In EMP relation, total number of records is 14(by default) and the size of each record is approximately 100 Bytes. The memory for some of the fields, which may be required in the query, is given below.

ename 20B, deptno 4B

The size of EMP relation will be 100*14 = 1400 Bytes.

Similarly, in DEPT relation there are 4 records and the size of each record is 50B. The size of the fields is

deptno 4B, dname 15B

So the size of DEPT relation will be 4*50=200 Bytes.

Now suppose that we want to execute a query to display the name of the employees along with their department names. The relational algebra expression for this will be

$$\pi_{\text{ename,dname}}(\sigma_{\text{emp.deptno = dept.deptno}}(\text{EMP X DEPT}))$$

If all the employees have the departments and in each department there is at least one employee then the result of the above query will return 14 records. Suppose the size of the resultant record is 40Bytes. So the total size of resultant will be 40*14 = 560 Bytes.

If these two relations, EMP and DEPT are at different sites, say sitel and site2 respectively and result is to be displayed at third site, say site3 then following three possibilities occur:

(i) Sending the data of EMP relation (sitel) and DEPT relation (site2) to the site3, where both the relations will take part in execution of the query and then resultant data will be displayed on this site. In this case, the total cost of data transfer will be cost of sending data from sitel and site2 to site 3 and that will be 1400 + 200 = 1600 Bytes.

(ii) Sending the data of EMP relation sitel to site2, execute the query at site2 and then finally send the resultant to site3. In this case the total cost will be the cost of data transfer of EMP relation to site2 plus the cost of sending the resultant from site2 to site3. So this will be 1400 + 560 = 1960 Bytes.

(iii) Lastly in sending the data of DEPT relation site2 to sitel and then after executing the query on sitel, sending the result to site3, the total cost will be 200 + 560 = 760 Bytes.

The optimal choice depends upon the sizes of the relations and results. It is very much clear from the above three cases that strategy 3 is having the minimum overhead for sending the resultant to its desired location.

In another example, suppose the result is to be displayed at site2 itself. Now there are two possibilities.

Transfer the data from sitel to site2 and then execute query to display the desired result at the same site. The cost will be 1400 Bytes.

Transfer the data from site2 to sitel, execute the query there and then send the output to the site2. The cost will be 200 + 560 = 760 Bytes.

In this case second approach gives the better optimization. A more complex strategy, which works better sometimes is by using the semi-join operation, is given below.

Data transfer using the semi-join: In the above example, we send the whole relation from one site to another site to get the desired output. On the other hand, in semi-join approach we send the reduced number of records from one site to another site. For the same query, in place of sending the whole DEPT relation site2 to sitel, we just send the data of joining column (deptno) to sitel. At sitel this column is joined to the deptno column of EMP relation and then the joining column (deptno) and the required columns (ename) are sent back to the site2. There again joining takes place to take the required attributes from DEPT relation and finally the result is displayed at the same site site2. In this case the total cost of data transfer will be:

Cost of sending deptno of DEPT relation to sitel + cost of sending deptno and ename from sitel to site2

$$= 4*4 + (4 + 20)*14 = 352 \text{ Bytes}$$

Using semi-join operations,,we transferred just 352 Bytes, which was 760 Bytes in previous case. The semi-join operation is denoted by A × Bcl = c2 where A and B are the relations from which result is to be extracted and cl and c2 are the domain compatible attributes example, deptno attribute in EMP and DEPT relations.

CHAPTER **15**

Introduction to Data Warehousing and Data Mining

In this chapter, you will learn

- 15.0 Introduction
- 15.1 Concepts of Data Warehousing
  - 15.1.1 Data warehousing terminology and definitions
  - 15.1.2 Characteristics of data warehouses
  - 15.1.3 Data Modeling for data ware houses
  - 15.1.4 How to build a data warehouse
  - 15.1.5 Typical functionality of data warehouses
- 15.2 Data Mining
  - 15.2.1 The foundations of data mining
  - 15.2.2 An overview of data mining technology
  - 15.2.3 Profitable applications of data mining
- 15.3 Summary

15.0 INTRODUCTION

A data warehouse is a "subject-oriented, integrated, time-variant, nonvolatile collection of data in support of management's decision-making process..."

There is no doubt that corporate data has grown in both volume and complexity during the last 15 years. In the 1980's, it was not uncommon for businesses to work with data in megabytes and gigabytes. Today, that is the size of one PC hard drive. Contemporary corporate systems manage data in measures of terabytes and petabytes. This trend towards increased information storage is clearly not reversing. In addition, increasing processing power (advances in hardware) and sophistication of analytical tools and techniques have resulted in the development of data warehouses. These data warehouses provide storage, functionality, and responsiveness to queries beyond the capabilities of transaction-oriented databases. Accompanying this ever-increasing power has come a great demand to improve the data access performance of databases. Traditional databases balance the requirement of data access with the need to ensure integrity of data.

In modern organizations, users of data are often completely removed from the data sources. Many people only need read-access to data, but still need a very rapid access to a larger volume of data than can conveniently be downloaded to the desktop. Often such data comes from multiple databases. Because many of the analyses performed are recurrent and predictable, software vendors and systems support staff have begun to design systems to support these functions.

At present, there is a great need to provide decision-makers from middle management to top-level officials with information at the correct level of detail to support decision-making. Business environments are more competitive and dynamic than ever. Nearly all organizations are implementing some form of total quality management (TQM), engaged in downsizing or 'right-sizing' activity and are vigorously attempting to 're-invent' themselves with their customers. Business that will prosper will have access to corporate knowledge repositories to make sound business decisions. The number of individuals within an organization with a "need to know" is growing. Data warehousing, on-line analytical processing (OLAP) and data mining are the emerging database technologies provide this functionality.

The market for such support has been growing rapidly since the mid-1990s. As managers and middle level users become increasingly aware of the growing sophistication of analytic capabilities of these database systems, they looked for increasingly for more sophisticated support for their key organizational decisions, which are to be taken during their daily activities.

15.1 CONCEPTS OF DATA WAREHOUSING

A data warehouse is a computer system designed to give business decision makers instant access to information. Because data warehouses have been developed in numerous organizations to meet particular needs, there is no single, canonical definition of the term data warehouse. We already know that the database is defined as a collection of related data and a database system as a database and database software together. A data warehouse is also a collection of information as well as a supporting system. However, a clear distinction exists. Traditional databases are transactional oriented, normally these databases are relational, object-oriented, network, or hierarchical. Data warehouses have the distinguishing characteristic that they are mainly intended for decision support applications. They are optimized for data retrieval, not for routine transaction processing. Moreover, data warehouses are quite distinct from traditional databases in their structure, functioning, performance, and purpose. Data warehouse users use special software that allows them to create and access information when they need it.

15.1.1 Data Warehousing Terminology and Definitions

Data warehousing is characterized as "a subject-oriented, integrated, nonvolatile, time-variant collection of data in support of management's decisions". Data warehouses provide access to data for complex analysis, knowledge discovery, and decision-making.

Data warehouses support high-performance demands on an organization's data and information. Different types of applications like on-line analytical processing (OLAP), decision support system (DSS), and data mining applications, are supported.

OLAP (on-line analytical processing) is a term used to describe the analysis of complex data from the data warehouse. This is the general activity of querying and presenting text and number data from data warehouses. In the hands of skilled knowledge workers, OLAP tools use distributed computing capabilities for analyses that require more storage capacity and processing power than can be economically and efficiently located on an individual desktop computer. OLAP databases are also known as multidimensional databases or MDDBs.

Decision-Support Systems (DSS) also known as Executive Information System (EIS) support an organization's leading decision makers, like managers and top level officials, with higher-level data for complex and important decisions. Another technology data mining is used for knowledge discovery, the process of searching data for unanticipated new knowledge.

Traditional databases support on-line transaction processing (OLTP), which includes insertions, updates, and deletions, along with supporting information query requirements. Traditional relational databases are optimized to process queries that may touch a small part of the database and transactions that deal with insertions or updates of a few tuples (rows of a table) per relation to process. Thus, they cannot be optimized for OLAP, DSS, or data mining applications. By contrast, data warehouses are designed precisely to support efficient extraction, processing, and presentation for analytic and decision-making purposes. In comparison to traditional databases, data warehouses generally contain very large amounts of data from multiple sources that may include databases from different data models and sometimes files acquired from independent systems and platforms.

15.1.2 Characteristics of Data Warehouses

If we want to discuss data warehouses and to distinguish them from transactional databases calls for an appropriate data model. The multidimensional data model is a better fit for OLAP and decision-support technologies. In contrast to multidatabases, which provide access to disjoint and usually heterogeneous databases, a data warehouse is frequently a store of integrated data from multiple sources, processed for storage in a multidimensional model. Unlike most transactional databases, data warehouses typically support time-series and trend analysis, both of these require more historical data than are generally maintained in any other transactional databases. Compared with traditional transactional databases, data warehouses are nonvolatile in nature. That means that information in the data warehouses changes far less often and may be regarded as non-real-time with periodic updating. In transactional systems, transactions are the unit and are the agent of change to the database; but in case of, data warehouse information is much more coarse gained and are refreshed according to a careful choice of refresh policy, usually incremental. Warehouse updates are handled by the warehouse's acquisition component that provides all required preprocessing.

We can also describe data warehousing more generally as "a collection of decision support technologies, aimed at enabling the knowledge worker (executive, manager, analyst, and other officials), to make better and faster decisions, which are part of their work". The following figure gives an overall view of the conceptual structure of a data warehouse. It shows the entire data warehousing process. This process includes possible cleaning and reformatting of data before its warehousing. At the back end of the process, OLAP, data mining, and DSS may generate new relevant information such as rules; this information is shown in the figure going back into the warehouse. Figure 15.1 also shows that data sources may include files. Earlier we used to store data in data files rather than databases.

Data warehouses have the following distinctive characteristics. These characteristics are originally coined by Codd.

- Multidimensional conceptual view
- Generic dimensionality
- Unlimited dimensions and aggregation levels
- Unrestricted cross-dimensional operations
- Dynamic sparse matrix handling
- Support for multi-user
- Accessibility support

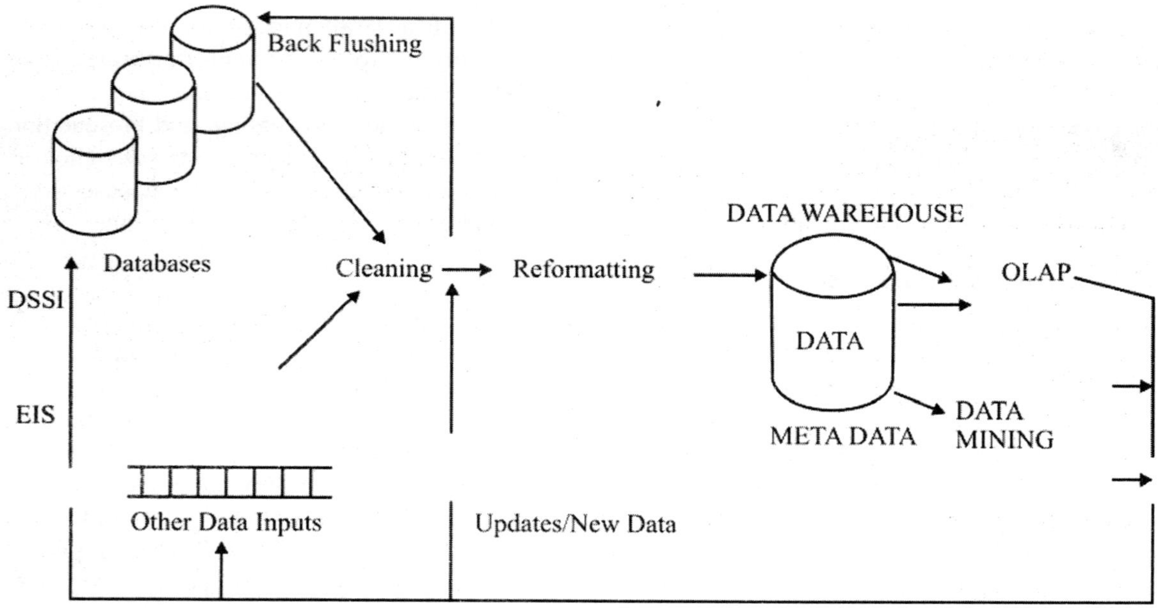

Figure 15.1: *The overall process of data warehousing*

- Transparent
- Supports client-server architecture
- Also supports flexible reporting of data

Because of the reason that the data warehouses encompass large volumes of data, data warehouses are generally an order of magnitude, sometimes two orders of magnitude, larger than the source databases. The large volume of data, likely to be in terabytes or petabytes is an issue that has been dealt with through data marts, enterprise-wide data warehouses, virtual data warehouses, central data warehouses, and distributed data warehouses.

- **Data marts** generally are targeted to a subset of the organization, such as a department, and are more tightly focused. It is designed to serve a particular community of knowledge workers. The emphasis of a data mart is on meeting the specific demands of a particular group of knowledge users in terms of analysis, content, presentation, and ease-of-use.
- **Enterprise-wide data warehouses:** These are huge projects requiring lot of investment of time and resources. Many benefits are possible with these types of warehouses.
- **Virtual data warehouses:** These provide views of operational databases that are materialized for efficient access. This approach can also put the largest unplanned query load on operational systems. This approach provides the ultimate in flexibility as well as the minimum amount of redundant data that must be loaded and maintained. This approach can also put the largest unplanned query load on operational systems. Virtual data warehouses often provide a starting point for organizations to learn what end-users are really looking for.

- **Central data warehouses:** Central data warehouses are what most people think of when they first are introduced to the concept of data warehouse. The central data warehouse is a single physical database that contains all of the data for a specific functional area, department, division, or enterprise. Central data warehouses are often selected where there is a common need for informational data and there are large numbers of end-users already connected to a central computer or network. A central data warehouse may contain data for any specific period. Usually, central data warehouses contain data from multiple operational systems. Central data warehouses are real. The data stored in the data warehouse is accessible from one place and must be loaded and maintained on a regular basis. Normally, data warehouses are built around advanced RDBMS or some form of multi-dimensional informational database server.
- **Distributed data warehouses:** Distributed data warehouses are just what their name implies. They are data warehouses in which the certain components of the data warehouse are distributed across a number of different physical databases. Increasingly, large organizations are pushing decision-making down to lower and lower levels of the organization and in turn pushing the data needed for decision making down (or out) to the LAN or local computer serving the local decision-maker. Distributed Data Warehouses usually involve the most redundant data and, as a consequence, most complex loading and updating processes.

15.1.3 Data Modeling for Data Warehouses

Multidimensional models take advantage of inherent relationships in data to populate data in multidimensional matrices called data cubes. These data cubes may be called hypercube if they have more than three dimensions. For data that lend themselves to dimensional formatting, query performance in multidimensional matrices can be much better than in the relational data model. Three examples of dimensions in a corporate data warehouse would be the corporation's fiscal periods, products, and regions.

A standard spreadsheet, what we have seen is a good example for two-dimensional matrix. One example would be a spreadsheet of regional sales by product sold for a particular time. Products sold could be shown as rows, with sales revenues obtained for each region comprising the columns. Adding a time dimension, such as an organization's fiscal quarters, would produce a three-dimensional matrix, which could be represented using a data cube.

In case of three-dimensional data cube that organizes product sales data by fiscal quarters and sales regions. Each cell could contain data for a specific product sold specific fiscal quarter, and specific region. By including additional dimensions, a data hypercube could be produced, although more than three dimensions difficult to be visualized at all or difficult to present graphically. The data can be queried directly in any combination of dimensions, bypassing complex database queries. Tools exist for viewing data according to the user's choice of dimensions. Changing form one-dimensional hierarchy (orientation) to another is easily accomplished in a data cube by a technique called pivoting; this technique is also called rotation. In this technique the data cube can be thought of as rotating to show a different orientation of the axes, the user needs. For example, you might pivot the data cube to show regional sales revenues as rows the fiscal quarter revenue totals as columns, and the company's products in the third dimension. Hence, this technique is equivalent to having a regional sales table for each product separately, where each table shows quarterly sales for that product region by region.

Multidimensional models readily provide two hierarchical views called roll-up display and drill-down display. Roll-up display moves up the hierarchy, grouping into larger units along a dimension (e.g., summing weekly data by quarter or by year). A drill-down display provides the opposite capability, furnishing a finer-grained view, perhaps disaggregating country sales by region and then regional sales by sub region and also breaking up products by different styles.

The multidimensional storage model involves two types of tables: dimension tables and fact tables. A dimension table consists of tuples of attributes of the dimension. A fact table can be thought of as having tuples, one per a recorded fact. This fact contains some measured or observed variable(s) and identifies them with pointers to dimension tables. The fact table contains the data and the dimensions identify each tuple in that data stored. Two common multidimensional schemas, associated with multidimensional storage model are the star schema and the snowflake schema. The star schema consists of a fact table with a single table for each dimension. The snowflake schema is a variation on the star schema in which the dimensional tables from a star schema are organized into a hierarchy by normalizing them. Some of the installations are normalizing data warehouses up to the third normal form so that they can access the data warehouse to the finest level of detail, depending on the information required.

Data warehouse storage also makes use of indexing techniques to support high performance data access. A technique called bitmap indexing constructs a bit vector for each value in a domain (column) being indexed. It works very well for domains of low-cardinality. There is a 1 bit placed in the jth position in the vector of the jth row contains the value being indexed. For example, imagine an inventory of 50,000 cars with a bitmap index on car size. If there are two car sizes–economy, and compact, then there will be two-bit vectors, each containing 50,000 bits. Bitmap indexing can provide considerable input/output and storage space advantages in low-cardinality domains. With bit vectors a bitmap index can provide dramatic improvements in comparison, aggregation, and join performance. In a star schema, dimensional data can be indexed to tuples in the fact in the fact table by join indexing. Join indexes are traditional indexes to maintain relationships between primary key and foreign key values. They relate the values of a dimension of a star schema to rows in the fact table. For example, consider a sales fact table that has city and fiscal quarter as dimensions. If there is a join index maintains the tuple IDs of tuples containing that city. Join indexes may involve multiple dimensions.

Data warehouse storage can facilitate access to summary data by taking further advantage of the nonvolatility of data warehouses and a degree of predictability of the analyses that will be performed using them. Two approaches have been used for this purpose:

(1) Smaller tables which includes summary data such as quarterly sales or revenue by product line, and

(2) Encoding of level (e.g., daily sales, weekly sales, quarterly, and annual) into existing tables.

By comparison, the overhead of creating and maintaining such type of aggregations would likely be excessive in a volatile, transaction-oriented database.

15.1.4 How to Build a Data Warehouse

In constructing a data warehouse, builders of the data warehouse should take a broad view of the anticipated use of the warehouse for various data needs. There is no way to anticipate all possible queries or analyses during the design phase. However, the design should specifically support ad-hoc querying, that is, accessing data with any meaningful combination of values for the attributes in the dimension or fact tables. For example, a marketing-intensive consumer-products company would require different ways of organizing the data warehouse than would a nonprofit organization like charity focused on fund raising. An appropriate schema will be chosen that reflects anticipated usage.

Acquisition of data for the warehouse involves the following steps:

- The extract step is the first step of getting data into the data warehouse environment. Extracting means reading and understanding the source data, and copying the parts that are needed. The data must be extracted from multiple, heterogeneous sources, for example, databases or other data feeds such as those containing financial market data or environmental data.
- Data must be formatted for consistency within the warehouse. Names, meanings, and domains of data from unrelated sources must be reconciled. For instance, subsidiary companies of a large corporation may have different fiscal calendars with quarters ending on different dates, making it difficult to aggregate financial data by quarter. Various credit cards may report their transactions differently, making it difficult to compute all credit sales. These format inconsistencies must be resolved.
- The data must be cleaned to ensure validity. Data cleaning is an involved and complex process that has been identified as the largest labor-demanding component of data warehouse construction. For input data, cleaning must occur before the data are loaded into the warehouse. There is nothing about cleaning data that is specific to data warehousing and that could not be applied to a host database. Cleaning the data by correcting misspellings, resolving domain conflicts, dealing with missing data elements, and parsing into standard formats. However, since input data must be examined and formatted consistently, data warehouse builders should take this opportunity to check for validity and quality. Recognizing erroneous and incomplete data is difficult to automate, and cleaning that requires automatic error correction can be even tougher. Some aspects, such as domain checking, ear easily coded into data cleaning routines, but automatic recognition of other data problems can be more challenging. After such problems have been taken care of, similar data from different sources must be coordinated for loading into the warehouse. As data managers in the organization discover that their data are being cleaned for input into the warehouse, they will likely want to upgrade their data with the cleaned data. The process of returning cleaned data to the source is called back flushing.
- The data must be fitted into the data model of the warehouse. Data from the various sources must be installed in the data model of the warehouse. Data may have to be converted from relational, object-oriented, or legacy databases (network and/or hierarchical) to a multidimensional model.
- The data must be loaded or populated into the warehouse. The large volume of data in the warehouse makes loading the data a significant task. Monitoring tools for loads as well as methods to recover from incomplete or incorrect loads are required. With the huge volume of data in the warehouse, incremental updating is usually the only feasible approach.

As we have discussed earlier, databases must strike a balance between efficiency in transaction processing and supporting query requirements (ad-hoc user requests), but a data warehouse is typically optimized for access from a decision maker's needs. Data storage in a data warehouse reflects this specialization of what is required and involves the following processes:

- Storing the data according to the data model of the warehouse
- Creating and maintaining required data structures for this purpose
- Creating and maintaining appropriate data access paths
- Providing for time-variant data as new data are added in future
- Supporting the updating of warehouse data
- Refreshing the data periodically
- Purging data.

Although adequate time can be devoted initially for constructing the warehouse, the large volume of data in the warehouse generally makes it impossible to simply reload the warehouse in its entirely later on. Alternatives include selective (partial) refreshing of data and separate warehouse versions. When the warehouse uses an incremental data refreshing mechanism, data may need to be periodically purged; for example, a warehouse that maintains data on the previous twenty business quarters may periodically purge its data each year.

Data warehouses must be designed with full consideration of the environment in which they will reside. Important design considerations of data warehouses will include the following:

- Usage projections of data warehouse
- The fit of the data model
- Characteristics of available sources of data
- Design involved in the metadata component
- Modular component design
- Design for manageability and change
- Considerations of distributed and parallel architecture.

We are going to discuss each of these design considerations in turn. Warehouse design is initially driven by usage projections; that is, by expectations about who will be the users of the warehouse and in what way they use. Choice of a data model to support this usage is a key initial decision. Usage projections and the characteristics of the warehouse's data sources are both taken into accounts. Modular design is a practical necessity to allow the warehouse to evolve with the organization and its information environment. In addition, a well-built data warehouse must be designed for maintainability, enabling the warehouse managers to effectively plan for and manage change while providing optimal support to users. You know the term metadata, metadata was defined as the description of a database including its schema definition. Also called data dictionary. This metadata repository is a key data warehouse component. The metadata repository includes both technical and business metadata. The first, technical metadata, covers details of acquisition processing, storage structures, data descriptions, warehouse operations and maintenance, and access support functionality. The second, business metadata, includes the relevant business rules required and organizational details involved supporting the warehouse.

The architecture of the organization's distributed computing environment is a major determining characteristic for the design of the warehouse. There are two basic distributed data warehouse architectures, they are

- The distributed warehouse and
- The federated warehouse.

For a distributed warehouse, all the issues of distributed databases are relevant, for example, partitioning, communications, replication, and consistency concerns. A distributed architecture can provide benefits particularly important to warehouse performance, such as improved load balancing, scalability of performance, and higher availability. A single replicated metadata repository would reside at each of the distribution site.

The plan behind the federated warehouse is like that of the federated database: a decentralized confederation of autonomous data warehouses, each with its own metadata repository. Given the magnitude of the challenge inherent to data warehouses, it is likely that such federations will consist of smaller-scale components, such as data marts. Large organizations may choose to federate data marts rather than build huge data warehouses.

15.1.5 Typical Functionality of Data Warehouses

Data warehouses exist to facilitate complex, data-intensive, and frequent ad-hoc queries. Accordingly, data warehouses must provide far greater and more efficient query support than the same is demanded of transactional databases. The data warehouse access component supports enhanced spreadsheet functionality, efficient query processing, structured queries, ad-hoc queries, data mining, and materialized views. In particular, enhanced, spreadsheet functionality includes support for state-of-the-art spreadsheet applications (e.g., MS Excel) as well as for OLAP applications programs. These offer preprogrammed functionality's such as the following:

- Roll-up: Here Data is summarized with increasing generalization (e.g., weekly to quarterly to annually).
- Drill-down: Here increasing levels of detail are revealed (the complement of roll-up).
- Pivot: Cross tabulation (also referred as rotation) is performed.
- Slice and dice: performing projection operations on the dimensions.
- Sorting: Data is sorted by specified value.
- Selection: Data is available by value or range as per requirement.
- Derived attributes: Attributes are computed by operations on stored and derived values.

Because of the reason that the data warehouses are free from the restrictions of the transactional environment there is an increased efficiency in query processing. Among the tools and techniques used are query transformation, index intersection and union, special ROLAP (relational OLAP) and MOLAP (multidimensional OLAP) functions, SQL extensions, advanced join methods, and intelligent scanning.

Improved performance has also been obtained with parallel processing. Parallel server architectures include symmetric multiprocessor (SMP), cluster, and massively parallel processing (MPP), and combinations of these.

Knowledge workers and decision-makers, executives and managers use tools ranging from parametric queries to ad-hoc queries to data mining. Thus, the access component of the data warehouse must provide support of structured queries (both parametric ad-hoc). These together make up a managed query environment. Data mining itself uses techniques from statistical analysis and artificial intelligence. Statistical analysis can be performed by advanced spreadsheets, by sophisticated statistical analysis software, or by custom-written programs. Techniques such as lagging, moving averages, and regression analysis are also commonly employed. Artificial intelligence techniques, which may include genetic algorithms and neural networks, are used for classification and are employed to discover knowledge from the data warehouse that may be unexpected or difficult to specify in queries.

Data warehousing and database views: Some people have considered data warehouses to be an extension of database views. Materialized views as one way of meeting requirements for improved access to data. Materialized views have been explored for their performance enhancement. Views, however, provide only a subset of the functions and capabilities of data warehouses. Views and data warehouses are alike in that they both read-only extracts from databases and subject-orientation. However, data warehouses are different from views in the following ways:

- Data warehouses exist as persistent storage instead of being materialized on demand.
- Data warehouses are not usually relational, but rather they are multidimensional.
- Views of a relational database are relational called virtual tables.
- Data warehouses can be indexed to optimize performance. Views cannot be indexed independent from of the underlying databases.
- Data warehouses characteristically provide specific support of functionality; views cannot.
- Data warehouses provide large amounts of integrated and often temporal data, generally more than is contained in one database, whereas views are an extract of a database.

15.2 DATA MINING

Data mining, the extraction of hidden predictive information from large databases, is a powerful new technology with great potential to help companies focus on the most important information in their data warehouses. Data mining tools predict future trends and behaviors, allowing businesses to make proactive, knowledge-driven decisions. The automated, prospective analyses offered by data mining move beyond the analyses of past events provided by retrospective tools typical of decision support systems. Data mining tools can answer business questions that traditionally were too time consuming to resolve. They scour databases for hidden patterns, finding predictive information that experts may miss because it lies outside their expectations.

Over the last three and a half decades, many organizations have generated a large amount of machine-readable data in the form of files and databases. These data were collected due to traditional database operations. To process this data, we have the database technology available to us that supports query languages like SQL (Structured Query Language). The problem with SQL is that it is a structured language that assumes the user is aware of the database schema. The description of the database is called the database schema, which is specified during the database design and is not expected to change frequently. SQL supports operations of relational algebra that allow a user to select from tables (rows and columns of data) or join related information from tables based on common fields.

Most companies already collect and refine massive quantities of data. Data mining techniques can be implemented rapidly on existing software and hardware platforms to enhance the value of existing information resources, and can be integrated with new products and systems as they are brought on-line. When implemented on high performance client/server or parallel processing computers, data mining tools can analyze massive databases to deliver answers to questions such as, "Which clients are most likely to respond to my next promotional mailing, and why?"

In the previous section we looked into the data warehousing technology affords types of functionality, that of consolidation, aggregation, and summarization of data. It lets us view the same information along multiple dimensions.

In this section, we will focus our attention on yet another very popular area of interest known as data mining. As the term connects, data mining refers to the mining or discovery of new information in terms of patterns or rules from vast amounts of data. To be practically useful, data mining must be carried out efficiently on large files and databases.

15.2.1 The Foundations of Data Mining

Data mining techniques are the result of a long process of research and product development. This evolution began when business data was first stored on computers, continued with improvements in data access, and more recently, generated technologies that allow users to navigate through their data in real time. Data mining takes this evolutionary process beyond retrospective data access and navigation to prospective and proactive information delivery. Data mining is ready for application in the business community because it is supported by three technologies that are now sufficiently mature:

- Massive data collection
- Powerful multiprocessor computers
- Data mining algorithms.

Commercial databases are growing at unprecedented rates. A recent survey of data warehouse projects found that 24% of respondents are beyond the 50-gigabyte level, while 54% expect to be there by near future. In some industries, such as retail, these numbers can be much larger. The accompanying need for improved computational engines can now be met in a cost-effective manner with parallel multiprocessor computer technology. Data mining algorithms embody techniques that have existed for at least 15 years, but have only recently been implemented as mature, reliable, understandable tools that consistently outperform older statistical methods.

In the evolution from business data to business information, each new step has built upon the previous one. For example, dynamic data access is critical for drill-through in data navigation applications, and the ability to store large databases is critical to data mining.

The core components of data mining technology have been under development for decades, in research areas such as statistics, artificial intelligence, and machine learning. Today, the maturity of these techniques, coupled with high-performance relational database engines and broad data integration efforts, make these technologies practical for current data warehouse environments.

15.2.2 An Overview of Data Mining Technology

Data mining and data warehousing: The goal of a data warehouse is to support decision making with data. Data mining can be used in conjunction with a data warehouse to help with certain types of decisions. Data mining consists of finding interesting trends or patterns in large datasets, in order to guide decisions about future activities. Data mining can be applied to operational databases with individual transactions. To make data mining more efficient, the data warehouse should have an aggregated or summarized collection of data. Data mining helps in extracting meaningful new patterns that cannot be found necessarily by merely querying or processing data or metadata in the data warehouse. Data mining applications should therefore be strongly considered early, during the design of a data warehouse. In addition, data mining tools should be designed to facilitate their use in conjunction with data warehouses. In fact, for very large databases running into terabytes of data, successful use of database mining applications will depend first on the construction of a data warehouse.

Data mining as part of the knowledge discovery process: Knowledge Discovery in Databases, frequently abbreviated as KDD, typically encompasses more than data mining. The knowledge discovery process or short KDD process, can roughly be comprises of six different phases; data selection, data cleaning, enrichment, data transformation or encoding, data mining, and the reporting and display of the discovered information. The raw data first undergoes a data selection step, in which we identify the target dataset and relevant attributes. In the data-cleaning phase, we remove the noise, transform field values to common units, generate new fields through combination of existing fields, and bring the data into the relational schema that is used as input to the data mining activity. Data enrichment and transformation or encoding phase is carried out on such data. In the data-mining step, the actual patterns required are extracted. In the last phase the reports are generated and displayed.

All the above six phases can be easily explained with the help of an example. Consider a transaction database maintained by a speciality consumer goods retailer. Suppose the client data includes customer name, zip code, phone number, date of purchase, item-code, price, quantity, and total amount. A variety of new knowledge can be discovered by KDD processing on this client database. During data selection, data about specific items or categories of items, or from stores in a specific region or area of the country, may be selected. The data cleaning process then may correct invalid zip codes or eliminate records with incorrect phone prefixes. Enrichment typically enhances the data with additional sources of information. For example, given the client names and phone numbers, the store may be able to produce other data about age, income, and credit rating and append them to each record. Data transformation and encoding may be done to reduce the amount of data. For instance, item codes may be grouped in terms of product categories into audio, video, supplies, electronic gadgets, camera, accessories, and so on. Zip codes may be aggregated into geographic regions, incomes may be divided into number of ranges, and so on. If data mining were based on an existing warehouse for this retail store chain, we would expect that the cleaning have already been applied. It is only after such preprocessing that data mining techniques are used to mine different rules and patterns. For example, the result of mining may be to discover:

- **Association rules:** *Example*—for this is whenever a customer buys video equipment, he or she also buys another electronic gadget along with it. Whenever customer buys bread, he also buys jam bottle.
- **Sequential patterns:** *Example*—in this case is, suppose a customer buys a camera, and within a month he or she buys photographic supplies, and within two months an accessory item. A customer who buys more than twice in the other periods may be likely to buy at least once during festival period.
- **Classifications trees:** *Example*—customers may be classified by frequency of visits, by types of financing used to buy, by amount of purchase, or by affinity for types of items to be purchased, and some revealing statistics may be generated for such classes.

We can see that many possibilities exist for discovering new knowledge about buying patterns, relating factors such as age, income-group, place of residence, to what and how much the customers purchase. This information can then be utilized to plan additional store locations based on demographics, to run store promotions, to combine items in advertisements, or to plan seasonal marketing strategies. As this retail-store example discussed earlier shows, data mining must be preceded by significant data preparation before it can yield useful information that can directly influence business decisions. The business decisions can be implemented.

The results obtained from data mining may be reported in a variety of formats, such as listings, graphical outputs, summary tables, or information visualizations.

Data mining goals and knowledge discovery: If we look at, the goals of data mining fall into the following classes: prediction, identification, classification, and optimization.

- **Prediction:** Data mining can show how certain attributes within the data will behave in the future. Examples of predictive data mining include the analysis of buying transactions to predict what consumers will buy under certain discounts, how much sales volume a store would generate in a given period, and whether deleting a product line would yield more profits, and weather adding a new product would yield more profits. In such applications, business logic is used will be coupled with data mining.
- **Identification:** Data patterns can be used to identify the existence of an item, an event, or an activity. For example, intruders trying to break a system may be identified by the programs executed, files accessed, and CPU time per session. Existence of a gene may be identified by certain sequences of nucleotide symbols in the DNA sequence, in case of biological applications. The area known as authentication is a form of identification. It tells whether a user is indeed a specific user or one from an authorized class; it involves a comparison of parameters or images or signals against a database, which contains all of these.
- **Classification:** Data mining can partition the data so that different classes or categories can be identified based on combinations of parameters. For example, customers in a supermarket can be categorized into discount-seeking shoppers, shoppers in hurry, loyal and regular shoppers, and infrequent shoppers. This classification may be used in different analysis of customer buying transactions as a post-mining activity. Sometimes classification based on common domain knowledge is used as an input decomposes the mining problem and makes it simpler. For instance, different types of foods like, health foods, party foods, or school lunch foods are distinct categories in the supermarket business. It makes sense to analyze relationships within and across categories as separate problems. Such type of categorization may be used to encode the data appropriately before subjecting it to further data mining.
- **Optimization:** One final and foremost goal of data mining may be to optimize the use of limited resources such as time, space, money, or materials and to maximize output variables such as sales or profits under a given set of constraints.

Types of knowledge discovered during data mining: The term "knowledge" is very broadly interpreted as involving some degree of intelligence. Knowledge is often classified as inductive and deductive. Data mining addresses inductive knowledge. Knowledge can be represented in many forms: in an unstructured sense, it can be represented by rules, or prepositional logic. In a structured form, it may be represented in decision trees, semantic networks, neural networks, or hierarchies of classes or frames. The knowledge discovered during data mining can be described in five ways, as follows:

(1) Association rules: These rules correlate the presence of a set of items with another range of values for another set of variables.

Examples:

(a) When a customer buys a pen, he is likely to buy an inkbottle.

(b) When a female retail shopper buys a handbag, she is likely to buy shoes.

(2) Classification hierarchies: Here the goal is to work from an existing set of events or transactions to create a hierarchy of classes.

Examples:

(a) A population may be divided into six ranges of credit worthiness based on a history of previous credit transactions.

(b) A model may be developed for the factors that determine the desirability of location for a particular store to be opened on a 1–10 scale.

(c) Mutual funds may be classified based on performance data using characteristics such as their growth, income, and stability in the market.

(3) Sequential patterns: A sequence of actions or events is sought.

Example:

If a patient underwent cardiac bypass surgery for blocked arteries and an aneurysm and later developed high blood urea within a year of surgery, he or she is likely to suffer from kidney failure near future. Detection of sequential patterns is equivalent to detecting association among events with certain temporal relationships.

(4) Patterns within time series: Similarities can be detected within positions of the time series. These are the examples follow with the stock market price data as a time series:

(a) Stocks of a utility company X power and a financial company Y, securities show the same pattern during 1996 in terms of closing stock price.

Examples:

(b) Two Products show the same selling patterns in summer season but a different one in winter season.

(5) Categorization and segmentation: A given population of events or items can be partitioned or segmented into sets of "similar" elements.

Examples:

(a) An entire population of treatment data on a particular disease may be divided into groups based on the similarity of side effects produced.

(b) The web accesses made by a collection of users against a set of documents (say, in a digital library) may be analyzed in terms of the keywords of documents to reveal clusters or categories of users.

For most of the applications in data mining, the desired knowledge is a combination of the above types.

The most commonly used techniques in data mining are give below:

- **Artificial neural networks:** Non-linear predictive models that learn through training and resemble biological neural networks in structure.
- **Decision trees:** Tree-shaped structures that represent sets of decisions. These decisions generate rules for the classification of a dataset. Specific decision tree methods include Classification and Regression Trees (CART) and Chi Square Automatic Interaction Detection (CHAID) .
- **Genetic algorithms:** Optimization techniques that use process such as genetic combination, mutation, and natural selection in a design based on the concepts of evolution.
- **Nearest neighbor method:** A technique that classifies each record in a dataset based on a combination of the classes of the k record(s) most similar to it in a historical dataset (where $k^{3}1$). Sometimes called the k-nearest neighbor technique.
- **Rule induction:** The extraction of useful if—then rules from data based on statistical significance.

Many of these technologies have been in use for more than a decade in specialized analysis tools that work with relatively small volumes of data. These capabilities are now evolving to integrate directly with industry-standard data warehouse and OLAP platforms.

15.2.3 Profitable Applications of Data Mining

A wide range of companies have deployed successful applications of data mining. While early adopters of this technology have tended to be in information-intensive industries such as financial services and direct mail marketing, the technology is applicable to any company looking to leverage a large data warehouse to better manage their customer relationships.

Two critical factors for success with data mining are: a large, well-integrated data warehouse and a well-defined understanding of the business process within which data mining are to be applied (such as customer prospecting, retention, campaign management, and so on).

Some Successful Application Areas

A credit card company can leverage its vast warehouse of customer transaction data to identify customers most likely to be interested in a new credit product. Using a small test mailing, the attributes of customers with an affinity for the product can be identified. Recent projects have indicated more than a 20-fold decrease in costs for targeted mailing campaigns over conventional approaches.

A pharmaceutical company can analyze its recent sales force activity and their results to improve targeting of high-value physicians and determine which marketing activities will have the greatest impact in the next few months. The data needs to include competitor market activity as well as information about the local health care systems. The results can be distributed to the sales force via a wide-area network that enables the representatives to review the recommendations from the perspective of the key attributes in the decision process. The ongoing, dynamic analysis of the data warehouse allows best practices from throughout the organization to be applied in specific sales situations.

A large consumer package goods company can apply data mining to improve its sales process to retailers. Data from consumer panels, shipments, and competitor activity can be applied to understand the reasons for brand and store switching. Through this analysis, the manufacturer can select promotional strategies that best reach their target customer segments.

A diversified transportation company with a large direct sales force can apply data mining to identify the best prospects for its services. Using data mining to analyze its own customer experience, this company can build a unique segmentation identifying the attributes of high-value prospects. Applying this segmentation to a general business database such as those provided by Dun & Bradstreet can yield a prioritized list of prospects by region.

Each of these examples has a clear common ground. They leverage the knowledge about customers implicit in a data warehouse to reduce costs and improve the value of customer relationships. These organizations can now focus their efforts on the most important (profitable) customers and prospects, and design targeted marketing strategies to best reach them.

15.3 SUMMARY

In this chapter, we discussed two very important branches of database technology, which are going to play a significant role in the years to come. They are data warehousing and data mining.

Data warehousing can be seen as a process that requires a variety of activities to precede it. We introduced key concepts related to data warehousing. Data warehouses organize around subjects, as opposed to legacy application systems, which organize around processes. The data within the warehouse is integrated in that the final product is a fusion of various legacy system information's into a cohesive set of information. In the warehouse, it is critical to use consistent naming conventions, variable measurement standards, encoding structures and data attribution characteristics. In this sense, the warehouse is expected to accomplish a feat that no operational system alone can accomplish. We also discussed the characteristics of data warehouses, building a data warehouse and typical functionality of data warehouses.

Data mining may be thought as an activity that draws knowledge from an existing data warehouse. Data mining, the extraction of hidden predictive information from large databases, is a powerful new technology with great potential to help companies focus on the most important information in their data warehouses. Data mining tools predict future trends and behaviors, allowing businesses to make proactive, knowledge-driven decisions. The automated, prospective analyses offered by data mining move beyond the analyses of past events provided by retrospective tools typical of decision support systems. Data mining tools can answer business questions that traditionally were too time consuming to resolve. They scour databases for hidden patterns, finding predictive information that experts may miss because it lies outside their expectations. The six phases associated with data mining was also discussed.

CHAPTER 16

Internet Databases

16.0 INTRODUCTION

In the previous chapter we discussed about the emerging database technologies data warehousing and data mining. In this chapter we will be discussing about Internet databases. Files on the World Wide Web are identified through universal resource locators (URLs). A Web browser takes a URL, goes to the site containing the file, and asks the Web server at that site for the file. It then displays the file appropriately, taking into account the type of the file and the formatting instructions that it contains. HTML is a simple markup language used to describe a document, audio, video and even Java programs can be included in HTML documents. A Web server can access the data in a DBMS to construct a page requested by a Web browser.

A Web browser, which is a program usually, executing at a different site, request will be satisfied by a Web server, by executing a program. For example, Web server may have to access data in a DBMS. There are two ways which are possible for a Web server to execute a program. It can create a new process and communicate with it using the CGI protocol, or it can create a new thread for a Java Servlet. JavaBeans and Java Server Pages are Java based technologies that assist in creating and managing programs designed to be invoked by a Web server.

XML is an emerging document description standard that allows us to describe the content and structure of a document in addition to giving display directives. It is based upon HTML and SGML, which is a powerful document description standard that is widely used.

A search engine is a searchable database of Internet files collected by a computer program (called a wanderer, crawler, robot, worm, and spider). Indexing is created from the collected files, e.g., title, full text, size, URL, etc. There are no selection criteria for the collection of files, though evaluation can be applied to ranking schemes that return the results of a query.

16.1 THE WORLD WIDE WEB

The World Wide Web (WWW, or Web) is a distributed information systems based on hypertext. Documents stored under the web can be of several types. One of the most common types of documents is hypertext documents. These hypertext documents are formatted according to Hyper Text Markup Language (HTML). The HTML is based on (Standard Generalized Markup Language (SGML)). HTML documents contain text, font specifications and other formatting instructions. Links to other documents can be associated. Images can also be referenced with appropriate image formatting instructions. Formatted text with images is visually much more appealing than only a plain text. Thus the user will see formatted text along with images on the web system.

The Web makes it possible to access a file anywhere on the Internet. A file is identified by a universal resource locator (URL). These are nothing but pointers to documents. The following is an example of an URL.

http://www.riktesh.com/lecturenotes/dbbook/advanceddbtopics.html

This URL identifies a file called advanceddbtopics.html, stored in the directory /lecturenotes/ dbbook, this file is a document formatted using Hyper Text Makeup Language (HTML) and contains several links to other files (identified through their URLs).

More clearly the first part of the URL indicates how the document is to be accessed: "http" indicates that the document is to be accessed using the Hyper Text Transfer Protocol, which is a protocol used to transfer HTML documents. The second part gives the unique name of a machine on the Internet. The rest of the URL is the path name of the file on the machine.

The formatting commands are interpreted by a Web browser such as Microsoft's Internet Explorer or Netscape Navigator to display the document in an attractive manner, and the user can then navigate to other related documents by choosing links. A collection of such documents is called a Web site and is managed using a program called a Web server, which accepts URLs and returns the corresponding documents. Many organizations today maintain a Web site. The World Wide Web, or Web, is the collection of web sites that are accessible over the Internet.

An HTML link contains a URL, which identifies the site containing the linked file. When a user clicks on a link, the Web browser connects to the Web server at the destination Web site using a connection control called HTTP and submits the link's URL. When the browser receives a file from a Web server, it checks the file type by examining the extension of the file name. It displays the file according to the file's type and if necessary calls an application program to handle the file. For example, a file ending in **.txt** denotes an unformatted text file, which the Web browser displays by interpreting the individual ASCII characters in the file. More sophisticated document structures can be encoded in HTML, which has become a standard way of structuring Web pages for display. As another example, a file ending in **.doc** denotes a Microsoft Word document and the Web browser displays the file by invoking Microsoft Word.

Thus, the URLs provide a globally unique name for each document that can be accessed from a Web system. Since URLs are in the human readable from, a human or a user can use them directly to access a desired document, instead of navigating down a path from a predefined location. Since they allow the use of an Internet machine name, they are global in scope, and people can use them to create links across machines.

16.2 INTRODUCTION TO HTML

HTML is a simple language used to describe a document. It is also called a **markup Language** because HTML works by augmenting regular text with 'marks' that hold special meaning for a Web browser handling the document. Commands in the language are called tags and they consist (usually)

of a start tag and an end tag of the form <TAG> and </TAG>, respectively. For example, look at the HTML fragment shown in the figure below. It describes a Web page that shows a list of books on database management systems. The document is enclosed by the tags <HTML> and </HTML>, marking it as an HTML document. The remainder of the document-enclosed in <BODY> ... </BODY>— contains information about three books. Data about each book is represented as an unordered list (UL) whose entries are marked with the LI tag. HTML defines the set of valid tags as well as the meaning of the tags. For example, HTML specifies that the tag <TITLE> is a valid tag that denotes the title of the document. As another example, the tag <UL> always denotes an unordered list.

```
<HTML>
<HEAD>Some important books on DBMS</HEAD>
<BODY>
DBMS:
<UL>
   <LI>Author: Raghu Ramakrishnan</LI>
   <LI>Title:Database management Systems</LI>
   <LI> Published in 2000</LI>
   <LI> Published by McGraw Hill</LI>
   <LI> Softcover</LI>
</UL>
<UL>
   <LI>Author: Elmasri Navathe</LI>
   <LI>Title: Fundamentals of Database Systems</LI>
   <LI> Published in 2000</LI>
<LI> Published by Addison Wesley</LI>
<LI> Softcover</LI>
</UL>
<UL>
   <LI>Author: Silberschatz, Korth and Sudarshan</LI>
   <LI>Title:Database System Concepts</LI>
   <LI> Published in 2000</LI>
   <LI> Published by McGraw Hill</LI>
   <LI> Softcover</LI>
</UL>
</BODY>
</HTML>
```

Audio, video, and even programs, which are written in Java, a highly portable language can be included in HTML documents. When a user retrieves such a document using a suitable browser, images in the document are displayed, audio and video clips are played, and embedded programs are executed at the user's machine; the result is a rich multimedia presentation. The ease with which HTML documents can be created there are now visual editors that automatically generate HTML and accessed using Internet browsers has fueled the explosive growth of the Web.

16.3 DATABASES AND THE WORLD WIDE WEB

Many Internet users today have home pages on the Web, such pages often contain information about user's and world lives. Many companies are using the Web for day-to-day transactions. Interfacing the databases to the World Wide Web is very important. The Web is the cornerstone of electronic commerce, abbreviated as E-commerce. Many organizations offer products through their web sites, and customers can place orders by visiting a Web site. For such applications a URL must identify more than just a file, however rich the contents of the file; a URL must provide an entry point to services available on the Web site. It is common for a URL to include a form that users can fill in to describe what they want. If the requested URL identifies a form, the Web server returns the form to the browser, which displays the form to the user. After the user fills in the form, the form is returned to the Web server, and the information filled by the user can be used as parameters to a program executing at the same site as the Web server.

The use of a Web browser to invoke a program at a remote site leads us to the role of databases on the Web: The invoked program can generate a request to a database system. This capability allows to us to easily place a database on a computer network, and make services that rely upon database access available over the Web. This leads to a new and rapidly growing source of concurrent requests to a DBMS, and with thousands of concurrent users routinely accessing popular Web sites, new levels of scalability and robustness must be required.

The diversity of information available on the Web, its distributed nature, and the new uses that it is being put to lead to challenges for DBMSs that go beyond simply improved performance in traditional functionality. For instance, we require support for queries that are run periodically or continuously and that access data from several distributed sources. As an example, a user may want to be notified whenever a new item meeting some criteria is offered for sale at one of several Web sites, which he uses. Given many such user profiles, how can we efficiently monitor such type of users and notify them promptly as the items they are interested in become available in the market. As another instance of a new class of problems is, the emergence of the XML (Extended Markup Language) standard for describing data leads to challenges in managing and querying XML data.

16.4 ARCHITECTURE

The architecture of these types of databases requires, executing a program at the Web server's site, the server creates a new process and communicates with this process using the common gateway interface (CGI) protocol. The results of the program can be used to create an HTML document that is returned to the requestor. Pages that are computed in this manner at the time they are requested are called dynamic pages; pages that exist and are simply delivered to the Web browser are called static pages. Obtaining both dynamic and static web pages are part of this activity.

As an example, consider the sample page shown in the following figure. This Web page contains a form where a user can fill in the name of an author. If the user presses the 'send it' button, the

Perl script 'lookdbms_books.cgi' mentioned in Figure is executed as a separate process. The CGI protocol defines how the communication between the form and the script is performed.

```
<HTML>
<HEAD>
<TITLE>
The DBMS Book store</TITLE>
</HEAD>
<BODY>
<FORM action="lookdbms_books.cgi" method=post>
    Type an author name:
    <INPUT type="text" name="authorName" size=35 maxlength=50>
    <INPUT type="submit" value="Sent it">
    <INPUT type="reset" value="Clear form">
</FORM>
</BODY>
</HTML>
```

Figure 16.1 given below illustrates the processes created when the CGI protocol is invoked.

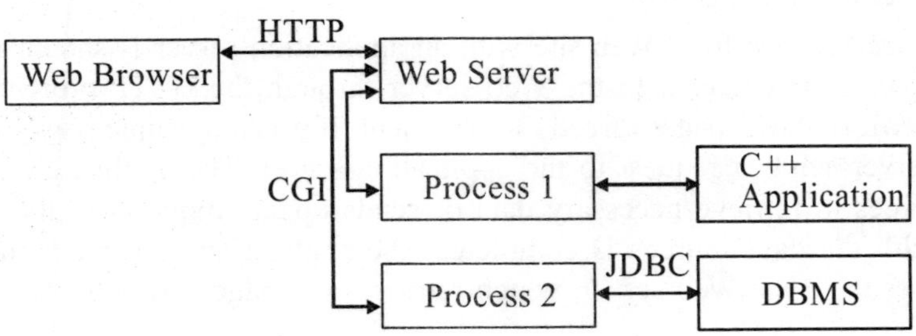

Figure 16.1: *Process Structure with CGI scripts*

16.5 APPLICATION SERVERS AND SERVER-SIDE JAVA

In the previous section, we discussed how the CGI protocol could be used to dynamically assemble Web pages whose content is computed on demand in the from of dynamic pages. However, since each page request results in the creation of a new process this solution does not scale well to a large number of simultaneous requests are made. This performance problem led to the development of specialized programs called application servers. An application server has prewritten threads or processes and thus avoids the startup cost of creating a new process for each request made. Application servers have evolved into flexible middle tier packages that provide many different functions in addition to eliminating the process-creation overhead:

- **Integration of heterogeneous data sources:** Most companies have data in many different database systems, from legacy systems like file oriented, network, hierarchical, relational, to modern object-relational systems. Electronic commerce applications require integrated access to all these type of data sources.

- **Transactions involving several data sources:** In electronic commerce applications, a user transaction might involve updates at several data sources. An application server can ensure transactional semantics across data sources by providing atomicity, isolation, and durability. The transaction boundary is the point at which the application server provides transactional semantics. If the transaction boundary is at the application server, very simple client programs are possible to take care of these transactions.
- **Security:** Security is most important because of the users of a Web application usually include the general population, database access is performed using a general-purpose user identifier that is known to the application server. While communication between the server and the application at the server side is usually not a security risk, communication between the client (Web browser) and the Web server could be a security threat or hazard. Encryption is usually performed at the Web server end, where a secure protocol, in most of the cases the Secure Sockets Layer (SSL) protocol, is used to communicate with the client.
- **Session management:** Often users would engage in business processes that take several steps to complete. Users expect the system to maintain continuity during a session, and several session identifiers such as cookies, URL extensions, and hidden fields in HTML forms can be used to identify a session. Application servers provide functionality to detect when a session starts and when it ends and to keep track of the sessions of individual users. This is called session management.

A possible Architecture for a Web site with an application server is shown in Figure 16.2. The client (a Web browser) interacts with the Web server through the HTTP protocol. The Web server delivers static HTML or XML pages directly to the client. If it is a dynamic page, in order to assemble them, the Web server sends a request to the application server. The application server contacts one or more data sources to retrieve necessary data or sends update requests to the data sources. After the interaction with the data sources is completed, the application server assembles the Web page and informs the result to the Web server, which retrieves the page and delivers it to the client.

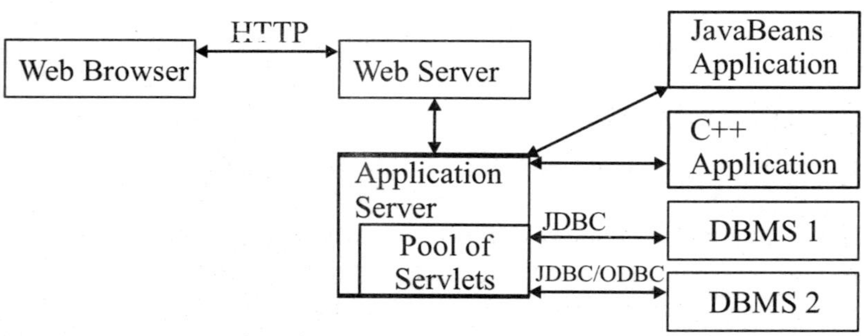

Figure 16.2: *Process structure in the Application Server Architecture*

The execution of business logic at the Web server's site, or server-side processing, has become a standard model for implementing more complicated business processes on the Internet. There are many different technologies for server-side processing. The Java Servlet API and Java Server Pages

(JSP) are important among them. Servlets are small programs that execute on the server side of a web connection. Just as applets dynamically extend functionality of a Web browser, Servlets dynamically extend the functionality of a Web server.

The **Java Servlet API** allows Web developers to extend the functionality of a Web server by writing small Java programs called Servlets that interact with the Web server through a well-defined API. A Servlet consists of mostly business logic and routines to format relatively small datasets into HTML. Java Servlets are executed in their own threads. Servlets can continue to execute even after the client request that led to their invocation is completed and can thus maintain persistent information between requests. The Web server or application server can manage a pool of Servlet threads, as shown in the above figure, and can therefore avoid the overhead of process creation for each request. Since Servlets are written in Java, they are portable between Web servers and thus allow platform-independent development of server-side applications.

Server-side applications can also be written using JavaBeans. JavaBeans are nothing but reusable software components written in Java that perform well-defined tasks and can be conveniently packaged and distributed (together with any Java Classes, graphics, and other files they need) in the form of JAR files. JavaBeans can be assembled to create larger applications and can be easily manipulated using visual tools.

Java Server Pages (JSP) is one more platform-independent alternative for generating dynamic content on the server side. These are Java application components that are downloaded, on demand, to the part of the system that needs them. While Servlets are very flexible and powerful, slight modifications, for example, in the appearance of the output page, require the developer to change the Servlet and the recompile the changes. JSP is designed to separate application logic from the appearance of the Web page, while at the same time simplifying and increasing the speed of the development process. JSP separates content from presentation by using special HTML tags inside a Web page to generate dynamic content. The Web server interprets these tags and replaces them with dynamic content before returning the page to the browser.

Together, JSP technology and Servlets provide an attractive alternative to the other types of dynamic Web scripting/programming that offers platform independence, enhanced performance, ease of administration, extensibility into the enterprise and most importantly, ease of use.

16.6 BEYOND HTML-XML

We already introduced the HTML in the previous paragraphs. While HTML is adequate to represent the structure of documents for display purposes the features available in the language are not sufficient to represent the structure of the data within a document for more general applications than a simple display. The HTML is inadequate for the exchange of complex documents.

Extensible Markup Language (XML) is a markup language that was developed to remedy the shortcomings of HTML. In contrast to having a fixed set of tags whose meaning is fixed by the language (as in HTML), XML allows the user to define new collections of tags that can be used to structure any type of data or document the user wishes to transmit. XML is an important bridge between the document-oriented view of data implicit in HTML and the schema-oriented view of data that is central to a DBMS. XML has the potential to make database systems more tightly integrated into Web applications than ever before.

XML emerged from the confluence of other two technologies, SGML and HTML. The Standard Generalized Markup Language (SGML) is a metalanguage that allows the definition of data and document interchange languages such as HTML. The SGML is complex and requires sophisticated programs to make use of its full potential. XML was developed to have much of the power of SGML while remaining relatively simple. Nonetheless, XML, like SGML, allows the definition of new document markup languages. Although XML does not prevent a user from designing tags that encode the display of the data in a Web browser, there is a style language for XML called Extensible Style Language (XSL). XSL is a standard way of describing how an XML document that adheres to a certain vocabulary of tags should be displayed.

An XML document contains (or is made of) the following building blocks:

- Elements
- Attributes
- Entity references
- Comments
- Document type declarations (DTDs).

Elements, also called tags, are the primary building blocks of an XML document. The start of the content of an element ELM is marked with <ELM>, which is called the start tag, and the end of the content end is marked with </ELM>, called the end tag. Elements must be properly nested. Start tags that appear inside the content of other tags must have a corresponding end tag.

An element can have descriptive attributes that provide additional information about the element. The values of attributes are set inside the start tag of an element. All attribute values must be enclosed in quotes.

Entities are shortcuts for portions of common text or the content of external files and the usage of an entity in the XML document is called an entity reference. Wherever an entity reference appears in the document, it is textually replaced by its content. Entity references start with a '&' and end with a ';'.

We can insert comments anywhere in an XML document. Comments start with <! - and end with -> . Comments can contain arbitrary text except the string —.

In XML, we can define our own markup language. A DTD is a set of rules that allows us to specify our own set of elements, attributes and entities. Thus, a DTD is basically a grammar that indicates what tags are allowed, in what order they can appear, and how they can be nested.

16.7 XML-QL: QUERYING XML DATA

Given that data is encoded in a way that reflects structure in XML documents, we have the opportunity to use a high level language that exploits this structure so conveniently retrieve data from within such documents. Such a language would bring XML data management much closer to database management than the text-oriented paradigm of HTML documents. Such a language would also allow us to easily translate XML data between different DTDs, as is required for integrating data from multiple data sources.

The one specific query language for XML called XML-QL that has strong similarities to several query languages that have been developed in the database community. Many relational and object-relational database system vendors are currently looking into support for XML in their database engines. Several vendors of object-oriented database management systems already offer database engines that can store XML data whose contents can be accessed through graphical user interfaces, server-side Java extensions, or by means of XML-QL queries.

16.8 SEARCH ENGINES

A search engine is a searchable database of Internet files collected by a computer program (called a wanderer, crawler, robot, worm, and spider). Indexing is created from the collected files, e.g., title, full text, size, URL, etc. There are no selection criteria for the collection of files, though evaluation can be applied to ranking schemes that return the results of a query.

The World Wide Web, also known as WWW and the Web, comprises a vast collection of documents stored in computers all over the world. These specialized computers are linked to form part of a worldwide communication system called the Internet. When you conduct a search, you direct your computer's browser to go to Web sites where documents are stored and retrieve the requested information for display on your screen. The Internet is the communication system by which the information travels.

A search engine might well be called a search engine service or a search service. As such, it consists of three components:

- **Spider:** Program that traverses the Web from link to link, identifying and reading pages.
- **Index:** Database containing a copy of each Web page gathered by the spider.
- **Search and retrieval mechanism:** Technology that enables users to query the index and that returns results in a schematic order.

16.8.1 Search Tools and Methods

A search tool is a computer program that performs searches. It employs a computer program to access Web sites and retrieve information. Each search tool is owned by a single entity, such as person, company or organization, which operates it from a master computer. When you use a search tool, your request travels to the tool's Web site. There, it conducts a search of its database and directs the response back to your computer. A search method is the way a search tool requests and retrieves information from its Web site.

A search begins at a selected search tool's Web site, reached by means of its address or URL. Each tool's Web site comprises a store of information called a database. This database has links to other databases at other Web sites, and the other Web sites have links to still other Web sites and so on. Thus, each search tool has extended search capabilities by means of a worldwide system of links.

Types of Search Tools

There are essentially four types of search tools, each of which has its own search method. The following describe these search tools:

1. A **directory search tool** searches for information by subject matter. It is a hierarchical search that starts with a general subject heading and follows with a succession of increasingly more specific sub-headings. The search method it employs is known as a subject search.

Tips: Choose a subject search when you want general information on a subject or topic. Often, you can find links in the references provided that would lead to specific information you want.

Advantage: It is easy to use. In addition, information placed in its database is reviewed and indexed first by skilled persons to ensure its value.

Disadvantage: Because directory reviews and indexing is so time consuming, the number of reviews is limited. Thus, directory databases are comparatively small and their updating frequency is relatively low. In addition, descriptive information about each site is limited and general.

Examples: Encyclopedia Britannica, LookSmart, Yahoo

2. A **search engine tool** searches for information through use of keywords and responds with a list of references or hits. The search method it employs is known as a keyword search.

   Tip: Choose a keyword search to obtain specific information, since its extensive database is likely to contain the information sought.

   Advantage: Its information content or database is substantially larger and more current than that of a directory search tool.

   Disadvantage: Not very exacting in the way it indexes and retrieves information in its database, which makes finding relevant documents more difficult.

   Examples: AltaVista, Google, Excite, Hotpot, Info seek, Northern Light

3. A **directory with search engine** uses both the subject and keyword search methods interactively as described above. In the directory search part, the search follows the directory path through increasingly more specific subject matter. At each stop along the path, a search engine option is provided to enable the searcher to convert to a keyword search. The subject and keyword search is thus said to be coordinated. The further down the path the keyword search is made, the narrower is the search field and the fewer and more relevant the hits.

   Tip: Use when you are uncertain whether a subject or keyword search will provide the best results.

   Advantage: Ability to narrow the search field to obtain better results.

   Disadvantage: This search method may not succeed for difficult searches.

4. A **multi-engine search tool** (sometimes called a meta-search) utilizes a number of search engines in parallel. The search is conducted via keywords employing commonly used operators or plain language. It then lists the hits either by search engine employed or by integrating the results into a single listing. The search method it employs is known as a meta search.

   Tip: Use to speed up the search process and to avoid redundant hits.

   Advantage: Tolerant of imprecise search questions and provides fewer hits of likely greater relevance.

   Disadvantage: Not as effective as a search engine for difficult searches.

   Examples: Dogpile, Mamma, Metacrawler, SavvySearch.

A Little About Some Search Engines

Just a word about some of the recommended search engines…in the Internet world.

About Google

- This engine is relatively new but is getting a lot of good reviews
- Google uses a complicated mathematical analysis, calculated on more than a billion hyperlinks on the web, to return high-quality search results so you do not have to sift through junk. This analysis allows Google to estimate the quality, or importance, of every web page it returns
- Important pages mean nothing to you if they don't match your query, so Google uses sophisticated text-matching techniques to find pages that are both important and relevant to your search
- In a survey by PC World Google was the clear winner as it produced relevant returns in every category tested interface is very easy to use.

About Yahoo!

- Although it is probably the oldest, best-known and most visited search site, most do not realize that is it NOT a search engine!
- Yahoo! is primarily a web directory; it is based upon user submissions, not a true search engine
- It uses Google as its search engine
- Covers in excess of 1 million sites organized into 14 main categories
- Pioneered the trend among search companies to become one-stop information "portals"
- According to a PC World rating of search sites, the portal features of Yahoo! distract you from getting information quickly.

About AltaVista

- The largest search engine on the web, covers in excess of 150 million web pages in its database
- Started by Digital Equipment Corporation (DEC) in 1995, acquired by Compaq Computer later
- Displays 10 hits per screen ranked by relevance to your keywords; brief site description included
- Also available is "Discovery" which adds a convenient button to the desktop taskbar to enable you to search the web from whatever application you are using
- Uses "Ask Jeeves" technology for standard searches, "traditional" keywords with boolean operators for advanced searches
- But in a survey by PC World performed the worst of the pure search engines rated often pointed to home pages rather than to pages that provided the answer sought.

About InfoSeek

- Its database contains ~50 million Web pages
- Reputedly one of the most accurate search engines based upon a CNet review in 1998

- Returned more relevant documents than any other engine tested
- 7 out of 10 hits listed were on target
- Provided the fewest broken links (about 3 out of 100 hits listed)
- Provided virtually no duplicates
- Has established a relationship with Disney's GO Network to deliver handpicked content in the form
- "Best of the Net" recommendations feature
- Also available is "InfoSeek Desktop" which adds a convenient button to the desktop taskbar to enable you to search the web from whatever application you are using.

The following is the general procedure, For those just starting to learn the search process.

- Connect to the Internet via your browser [e.g., Netscape or MS Explorer]
- In the browser's location box, type the address [i.e., URL] of your search tool choice. Press Enter. The Home Page of the search tool appears on your screen.
- Type your query in the address box at the top of the screen. Press Enter.
- Your search request travels via phone lines and the electronic backbone of the Internet to the search tool's Web site. There, your query terms are matched against the index terms in the site's database. The matching references are returned to your computer by the reverse process and displayed on your screen.
- The references returned are called "hits" and are ranked according to how well they match your query.

Now, conduct the searches to become familiar with each of the four types search tools described above:

16.9 SUMMARY

In this chapter we discussed about the Internet databases. The World Wide Web (WWW, or Web) is a distributed information systems based on hypertext. The Web makes it possible to access a file anywhere on the Internet. A file is identified by a universal resource locator (URL). These are nothing but pointers to documents. HTML is a simple language used to describe a document. It is also called a **markup Language** because HTML works by augmenting regular text with 'marks' that hold special meaning for a Web browser handling the document.

Many Internet users today have home pages on the Web, such pages often contain information about user's and world lives. The use of a Web browser to invoke a program at a remote site leads us to the role of databases on the Web. The execution of business logic at the Web server's site, or server-side processing, has become a standard model for implementing more complicated business processes on the Internet. There are many different technologies for server-side processing. The Java Servlet API and Java Server Pages (JSP) are important among them.

Extensible Markup Language (XML) is a markup language that was developed to remedy the shortcomings of HTML.

A search engine is a searchable database of Internet files collected by a computer program (called a wanderer, crawler, robot, worm, and spider).

CHAPTER 17

Emerging Database Technologies

17.0 INTRODUCTION

In the previous chapter, we discussed about Internet databases. In this chapter, we will discuss about the emerging technologies in databases.

Relational database systems support a small, fixed collection of data types, which has proven adequate for traditional application domains such as administrative data processing. in many application domains, however, much more complex kinds of data must be handled. Keeping this option, ANSI and ISO SQL standardization committees have for some time been adding features to the SQL specification to support object-oriented data management. The current version of SQL in progress including these extensions is often referred to as "SQL3".

Mobile databases in one more emerging technology in the database area. Recent advances in wireless technology have led to mobile computing, a new dimension in data communication and data processing. In addition, availability of portable computers and wireless communications has created a new breed of nomadic database users. The mobile computing environment will provide database applications with useful aspects of wireless technology.

The price of main memory is now low enough that we can buy enough main memory to hold the entire database for many applications. This leads to the concept of main memory databases.

In an object-relational DBMS, users can define abstract data types (ADTs) with appropriate methods, which is an improvement over an RDBMS. Nonetheless, supporting just ADTs falls short of what is required to deal with very large collections of multimedia objects, including audio, images, free text, text marked up in HTML or variants, sequence data, and videos. We need database systems that store data such as image, video and audio data. Multimedia databases are growing in importance.

Geographic information systems (GIS) are used to collect, model, store, and analyze information describing physical properties of the geographical world.

Currently available DBMSs provide little support for queries over ordered collections of records, or sequences, and over temporal data. Such queries can be easily expressed and often efficiently executed by systems that support query languages designed for sequences. Temporal and Sequence databases is another emerging technology in databases.

Information visualization is also one among the emerging technologies in database. As computers become faster and main memory becomes cheaper, it becomes increasingly feasible to create visual presentations of data, rather than just text-based reports. Data visualization makes it easier for users to understand the information in large complex datasets. The need for visualization is especially important in the context of decision support.

The biological sciences encompass an enormous variety of information's. This wealth of information that has been generated, classified, and stored for centuries has only recently become a major application of database technology. Genetic has emerged as an ideal field for the application of information technology. We call this as genome data management.

Digital Libraries are an important and active research area. Conceptually, a digital library is an analog of a traditional library-at large collection of information sources in various media—coupled with the advantages of digital technologies.

17.1 SQL3 OBJECT MODEL

ANSI and ISO SQL standardization committees have for some time been adding features to the SQL specification to support object-oriented data management. The current version of SQL in progress including these extensions is often referred to as "SQL3". SQL3 object facilities primarily involve extensions to SQL's type facilities; however, extensions to SQL table facilities can also be considered relevant. Additional facilities include control structures to make SQL a computationally complete language for creating, managing, and querying persistent object-like data structures. The added facilities are intended to be upward compatible with the current SQL92 standard. This and other sections of the Features Matrix describing SQL3 concentrate primarily on the SQL3 extensions relevant to object modeling. However, numerous other enhancements have been made in SQL as well. In addition, it should be noted that SQL3 continues to undergo development, and thus the description of SQL3 in this Features Matrix does not necessarily represent the final, approved language specifications.

The parts of SQL3 that provide the primary basis for supporting object-oriented structures are:

- user-defined types (ADTs, named row types, and distinct types)
- type constructors for row types and reference types
- type constructors for collection types (sets, lists, and multisets)
- user-defined functions and procedures
- support for large objects (BLOBs and CLOBs)

One of the basic ideas behind the object facilities is that, in addition to the normal built-in types defined by SQL, user-defined types may also be defined. These types may be used in the same way as built-in types. For example, columns in relational tables may be defined as taking values of user-defined types, as well as built-in types. A user-defined abstract data type (ADT) definition encapsulates attributes and operations in a single entity. In SQL3, an abstract data type (ADT) is defined by specifying a set of declarations of the stored attributes that represent the value of the ADT, the operations that define the equality and ordering relationships of the ADT, and the operations that define the behavior (and any virtual attributes) of the ADT. Operations are implemented by procedures called routines. ADTs can also be defined as subtypes of other ADTs. A subtype inherits the structure and behavior of its supertypes (multiple inheritance is supported). Instances of ADTs can be persistently stored in the database only by storing them in columns of tables.

A row type is a sequence of field name/data type pairs resembling a table definition. Two rows are type-equivalent if both have the same number of fields and every pair of fields in the same position have compatible types. The row type provides a data type that can represent the types of rows in tables, so that complete rows can be stored in variables, passed as arguments to routines, and returned as return values from function invocations. This facility also allows columns in tables to contain row values. A named row type is a row type with a name assigned to it. A named row type is effectively a user-defined data type with a non-encapsulated internal structure (consisting of its fields). A named row type can be used to specify the types of rows in table definitions. A named row type can also be used to define a reference type. A value of the reference type defined for a specific row type is a unique value, which identifies a specific instance of the row type within some (top level) database table. A reference type value can be stored in one table and used as a direct reference ("pointer") to a specific row in another table, just as an object identifier in other object models allows one object to directly reference another object. The same reference type value can be stored in multiple rows, thus allowing the referenced row to be "shared" by those rows.

Collection types for sets, lists, and multisets have also been defined. Using these types, columns of tables can contain sets, lists, or multisets, in addition to individual values.

Tables have also been enhanced with a subtable facility. A table can be declared as a subtable of one or more supertables (it is then a direct subtable of these supertables), using an UNDER clause associated with the table definition. When a subtable is defined, the subtable inherits every column from its supertables, and may also define columns of its own. The subtable facility is completely independent from the ADT subtype facility.

It is also possible to define user-defined functions and procedures in SQL3.

The BLOB (Binary Large Object) and CLOB (Character Large Object) types have been defined to support very large objects. Instances of these types are stored directly in the database (rather than being maintained in external files).

17.2 MOBILE DATABASES

Recent advances in wireless technology have led to mobile computing, a new dimension in data communication and data processing. In addition, availability of portable computers and wireless communications has created a new breed of nomadic database users. The mobile computing environment will provide database applications with useful aspects of wireless technology. The mobile computing platform allows users to establish communication with other users and to manage their work while they are using mobile. At one level these users are simply accessing a database through a network, which is similar to distributed DBMSs. At another level the network as well as data and user characteristics now have several novel properties, which affect basic assumptions in many components of a DBMS, including the query engine, transaction manager, and recovery manager. This feature is especially useful to geographically dispersed organizations. Typical examples might be weather reporting services, taxi dispatchers, and traffic police, this is also very useful in financial market reporting and information brokering applications.

In case of mobile databases:

- Users are connected through a wireless link whose bandwidth is ten times less than Ethernet and 100 times less than ATM networks. Communication costs are therefore significantly higher in proportion to I/O and CPU costs.
- User's locations are constantly changing, and mobile computers have a limited battery life. Therefore, the true communication costs reflect connection time and battery usage in addition to bytes transferred, and changes constantly depending on location. Data is frequently replicated to minimize the cost of accessing it from different locations.
- As a user moves around, data could be accessed from multiple database servers within a single transaction. The likelihood of losing connections is also much greater than in a traditional network. Centralized transaction management may therefore be impractical, especially if some data is resident at the mobile computers.

17.2.1 Mobile Computing Architecture

Mobile computing architecture is a distributed architecture where a number of computers generally referred to as **Fixed Hosts (FS)** and **Base Stations (BS)** are interconnected through a high-speed wired network. Fixed hosts are general-purpose computers that are not equipped to manage mobile units but can be configured to do so. Base stations are equipped with wireless interfaces and can communicate with mobile units to support data access.

Mobile Units (MU) (or hosts) and base stations communicate through wireless channels having bandwidths significantly lower than those of a wired network. Mobile units are battery powered portable computers that move freely in a geographic mobility domain, an area that is restricted by the limited bandwidth of wireless communication channels. To manage the mobility of units, the entire geographic mobility domain is divided into smaller domains called cells. The mobile computing discipline requires that the movement of mobile units be restricted within the geographic mobility domain, while having information access contiguity during movement guarantees that the movement of a mobile unit across cell boundaries will have no effect on the data retrieval process.

Mobile computing platform can be described under client server architecture. That means we may sometimes refer to a mobile unit as a client or sometimes as a user, and the base stations as servers. Each cell is managed by a base station, which contains transmitters and receivers for responding to the information processing needs of clients located in the cell. Clients and servers communicate through wireless channels.

17.2.2 Types of Data used in Mobile Computing Applications

Applications, which run on mobile units (or hosts), have different data requirements. Users of these types of applications either engage in office activities or personal communications, or they may simply receive updates on frequently changing information around the world.

Mobile applications can be categorized into the following two ways:

- Vertical applications
- Horizontal applications.

In vertical applications users access data within a specific cell, which is already defined and access is denied to users outside of that cell. For example, users can obtain information on the location of near by hotels, or doctors or emergency centers within a cell or parking availability data at an airport cell.

In horizontal applications, users cooperate on accomplishing a task, and they can handle data distributed throughout the system. The horizontal application market is massive.

Data to be used in the above applications may be classified into three categories.

1. **Private data:** A single user owns this type of data and manages it. No other user may access this data.
2. **Public data:** This data can be used by anyone who can have permission to read it. Only one source updates this type of data. Examples include stock prices or weather bulletins.
3. **Shared data:** This data is accessed both in read and write modes by groups of users. Examples are inventory data for products in a company, which can be updated to maintain the current status of inventory.

Public data is primarily required and managed by vertical applications, while shared data is used by horizontal applications.

17.3 MAIN MEMORY DATABASES

We know that the price of main memory is now low enough that we can buy enough main memory to hold the entire database for many applications; with 64-bit addressing, modern CPUs also have very large address spaces. Some commercial systems now have several gigabytes of main memory. This shift prompts a re-examination of some basic DBMS design decisions, since disk accesses no longer dominate processing time for a memory resident database:

- Main memory does not survive system crashes, and so we still have to implement logging and recovery to ensure transaction atomicity and durability. Log records must be written to stable storage at commit time, and this process could become a bottleneck. To minimize this problem, rather than commit each transaction as it completes, we can collect completed transactions as it completes, and commit them in batches; this is called group commit. Recovery algorithms can also be optimized since pages rarely have to be written out to make room for other pages.
- The implementation of main-memory operations has to be optimized carefully since disk accesses are no longer the limiting factor for performance.
- A new criterion must be considered while optimizing queries, namely the amount of space required executing a plan. It is important to minimize the space overhead because exceeding available physical memory would lead to swapping pages to disk (through the operating system's virtual memory mechanisms), greatly slowing down execution.
- Page-oriented data structures become less important (since pages are no longer the unit of data retrieval), and clustering is not important (since the cost of accessing any region of main memory is uniform.)

Overall main-memory databases differ from disk databases in that data is resident in shared main-memory. Such databases are important for real-time applications such as telecommunications and control applications. The design of the database has to provide support for versioning and user controlled concurrency control, to support real-time transactions. Processes must be allowed direct access to data, to avoid delays in a server process. Memory corruption becomes a possibility due to such open access, and hence error detection is a priority. Similarly, process failures must be detected and recovered from, so that the system is not brought to a halt by an errant process. The fact that data is memory resident can be utilized to significantly improve performance over disk databases, where accesses have to go through a buffer manager, and where dirty pages may have to be written to disk at any time to make space for new pages.

17.4 MULTIMEDIA DATABASES

In an object-relational DBMS, users can define abstract data types (ADTs) with appropriate methods, which is an improvement over an RDBMS. Nonetheless, supporting just ADTs falls short of what is required to deal with very large collections of multimedia objects, including audio, images, free text, text marked up in HTML or variants, sequence data, and videos. Industrial applications such as collaborative development of engineering designs also require multimedia database management, and are being addressed by several vendors. Currently the following types of multimedia data are available on the systems.

- **Text:** may be formatted or unformatted. Standards like SGML, or variations such as HTML are being used for ease of parsing structured documents.
- **Graphics:** Drawings are the examples for this type of data.
- **Images:** Includes photographs, still images, drawings etc. these are encoded in standard formats such as bitmap, JPEG, and MPEG.
- **Animations:** Temporal sequences of image or graphic data.
- **Video:** A set of temporally sequenced photographic data for presentation at special rates - for example 24 frames per second, 30 frames per second.
- **Structured audio:** A sequence of audio components comprising of note, tone, duration etc.
- **Audio:** sample data generated from recordings in a string of bits in digitized form. Analog recordings are typically converted into digital form before storage.
- **Composite or mixed multimedia data:** A combination of the above data. For example, audio and video can be mixed.

Multimedia data may be stored, delivered, and utilized in many different ways. Applications may be categorized based on their data management characteristics. The following are some of the applications and challenges in this area:

- **Content-based retrieval:** Users must be able to specify selection conditions based on the contents of multimedia objects. For example, users may search for images using queries such as: "Find all images that are similar to this image" and "Find all images that contain atleast three circles." As images are inserted into the database, the DBMS must analyze them and automatically extract features that will help answer such content-based queries. This information can then be used to search for images that satisfy a given query. As another example, users would like to search for documents of interest using information retrieval techniques and keyword searches. Vendors are moving towards incorporating such techniques into DBMS products.

- **Managing repositories of large objects:** Traditionally, DBMSs have concentrated on tables that contain a large number of tuples, each of which is relatively small. Once multimedia objects such as images sound clips, and videos are stored in a database, individual objects of very large size have to be handled efficiently. For example, compression techniques must be carefully integrated into the DBMS environment. As another example, distributed DBMSs must develop techniques to efficiently retrieve such objects. Some more examples include repositories of satellite images, engineering drawings and design, space photographs, and radiology scanned pictures.
- **Video-on-demand:** Many companies want to provide video-on-demand services that enable users to dial into a server and request a particular video. The video must then be delivered to the user's computer in real time, reliably and inexpensively. Ideally, users must be able to perform familiar VCR functions such as fast-forward and reverse. From a database perspective, the server has to contend with specialized real-time constraints; video delivery rates must be synchronized at the server and at the client, taking into account the characteristics of the communication network.
- **Collaborative work using multimedia information:** In this type of application the engineers may execute a complex design task by merging drawings, generating new documentation and etc. doctors collaborating among themselves analyzing multimedia patient data and information in real time as it is generated in case of a telemedicine application.

All of the above application areas present major challenges for the design of multimedia database systems.

17.4.1 Multimedia Database Applications

Large-scale applications of multimedia databases can be expected in the years to come. Some important applications are,

Documents and records management: A large number of manufacturing industries, business firms, banks, insurance companies, hospitals wants to keep very detailed records and a variety of documents. The data may include engineering design, manufacturing data, accounts and customer's data, insurance claim records, detailed medical records of patients, and other publishing material. All these type of data involves maintaining multimedia data.

Marketing and advertising: Multimedia databases may be used for marketing various products manufactured, through advertisement. This is possible via Internet.

Entertainment and travel: Multimedia information can be used to provide virtual tours and art galleries. The file industry has already used the power of multimedia data to provide special effects. Various types of animations are created.

Education and training: Teaching materials for all types of students, professionals can be designed from multimedia sources. Digital libraries, provides vast repositories of educational material, can be used by students and researchers.

Knowledge dissemination: The phenomenal growth in electronic books, catalogs, manuals, encyclopedias and repositories of information on many topics. All these modes help for knowledge dissemination.

17.5 GEOGRAPHIC INFORMATION SYSTEMS

Geographic information systems (GIS) are used to collect, model, store, and analyze information describing physical properties of the geographical world. Geographic Information Systems (GIS) contain spatial information about villages, cities, states, countries, streets, roads, highways, lakes, rivers, hills, and other geographical features, and support applications to combine such spatial information with non-spatial data. It also contains nonspatial data, such as census counts, economic data, and sales or marketing information. Spatial data is stored in either raster or vector formats. In addition, there is often a temporal dimension, as when we measure rainfall at several locations over time. An important issue with spatial data sets is how to integrate data from multiple sources, since each source may record data using a different coordinate system to identify locations.

Now let us consider how spatial data in a GIS is analyzed. Spatial information is most naturally thought of as being overlaid on maps. Typical queries include "What cities lies between X and Y" and "What is the shortest route from city X to Y". These kinds of queries can be addressed using the techniques available. An emerging application is in-vehicle navigation aids. With Global positioning Systems (GPS) technology, a car's location can be pinpointed, and by accessing a database of local maps, a driver can receive directions from his or her current location to a desired destination; this application also involves mobile database access!

In addition to this, many applications involve interpolating measurements at certain locations across an entire region to obtain a model, and combining overlapping models. For example, if we have measured rainfall at certain locations, we can use the TIN approach to triangulate the region with the locations at which we have measurements being the vertices of the triangles. Then, we use some form of interpolation to estimate the rainfall at points within triangles. Interpolation, triangulation, map overlays, visualizations of spatial data, and many other domain-specific operations are supported in GIS products.

17.6 TEMPORAL AND SEQUENCE DATABASES

Currently available DBMSs provide little support for queries over ordered collections of records, or sequences, and over temporal data. Typical sequence queries include "Find the weekly moving average of the BSE index" and "Find the first five consecutively increasing temperature readings" (from a trace of temperature observations). Such queries can be easily expressed and often efficiently executed by systems that support query languages designed for sequences. Some commercial SQL systems now support such SQL extensions.

The first example given is also a temporal query. However, temporal queries involve more than just record ordering. For example, consider the following query: "Find the longest interval in which the same person managed two different departments." If the period during which a given person managed a department is indicated by two fields from and to, we have to reason about a collection of intervals, rather than a sequence of records. Further, temporal queries require the DBMS to be aware of the anomalies associated with calendars (such as leap years). Temporal extensions are likely to be incorporated in future versions of the SQL standard.

A distinct and important class of sequence data consists of DNA sequences, which are being generated at a rapid pace by the biological community. These are in fact closer to sequences of characters in text than to time sequences as in the above examples. The field of biological information management and analysis has become very popular in recent years, and is called bioinformatics.

Biological data, such as DNA sequence data, is characterized by complex structure and numerous relationships among data elements, many overlapping and incomplete or erroneous data fragments (because experimentally collected data from several groups, often working on related problems, is stored in the databases), a need to frequently change the database schema itself as new kinds of relationships in the data are discovered, and the need to maintain several versions of data for archival and reference.

17.7 INFORMATION VISUALIZATION

As computers become faster and faster and main memory becomes very cheap, it becomes increasingly feasible to create visual presentations of data, rather than just text-based reports, which we used to generate earlier. Data visualization makes it easier for users to understand the information in large complex datasets. The challenge here is to make it easy for users to develop visual presentation of their data and to interactively query such presentations. Although a number of data visualization tools are available, efficient visualization of large datasets presents many challenges.

The need for visualization is especially important in the context of decision support; when confronted with large quantities of high-dimensional data and various kinds of data summaries produced by using analysis tools such as SQL, OLAP, and data mining algorithms, the information can be overwhelming. Visualization of the data, together with the generated summaries, can be a powerful way to sift through this information and spot interesting trends or patterns. The human eye, after all, is very good at finding patterns. A good framework for data mining must combine analytic tools to process data, and bring out latent anomalies or trends, with a visualization environment in which a user can notice these patterns and interactively drill down to the original data for further analysis.

17.8 GENOME DATA MANAGEMENT

17.8.1 Biological Sciences and Genetics

The biological sciences encompass an enormous variety of information. Environmental science gives us a view of how species live and interact in a world filled with natural phenomena. Biology and ecology involves study of particular species. Anatomy focuses on the overall structure of an organism, documenting the physical aspects of individual bodies. Traditional medicine and physiology break the organism into systems and tissues and strive to collect information on the workings of these systems and the organism as a whole. Histology and cell biology delve into the tissue and cellular levels and provide knowledge about the inner structure and function of the cell. This wealth of information that has been generated, classified, and stored for centuries has only recently become a major application of database technology. This is called genome data management.

Genetic has emerged as an ideal field for the application of information technology. In a broad sense, it can be thought of as the construction of models based on information about genes-which can be defined as basic units of heredity and populations and the seeking out of relationships in that information. The study of genetics can be divided into three branches:

(1) Mendelian genetics,

(2) Molecular genetics, and

(3) Population genetics.

Mendelian genetics is the study of the transmission of traits between generations. Molecular genetics is the study of the chemical structure and function of genes at the molecular level. Population genetics is the study of how genetic information varies across populations of organisms.

Molecular genetics provides a more detailed look at genetic information by allowing researches to examine the composition, structure, and function of genes. The origins of molecular genetics can be traced to two important discoveries.

The first discovery occurred was in 1869 when Friedrich Miescher discovered nuclein and its primary component, deoxyribonucleic acid (DNA). In subsequent research DNA and a related compound, ribonucleic acid (RNA), were found to be composed of nucleotides (a sugar, a phosphate, and a base, which combined to form nucleic acid) linked into long polymers via the sugar and phosphate.

The second discovery was the demonstration in 1944 by Oswald Avery that DNA was indeed the molecular substance carrying genetic information. Genes were thus shown to be composed of chains of nucleic acids arranged linearly on chromosomes and to serve three primary functions:

(1) Replicating genetic information between generations,

(2) Providing blueprints for the creation of polypeptides, and

(3) Accumulating changes—thereby allowing evolution to occur.

17.8.2 The Genome Database (GDB)

This Genome database is created in the year 1989. This database is a catalog of human gene mapping data. There is a process that associates a piece of information with a particular location on the human genome. The GDB system is built around SYBASE RDBMs. SYBASE is a commercial relational database management system, and its data are modeled using standard Entity-Relationship methods. GDB distributes a Database Access Toolkit, to improve data integrity and to simplify the programming for application writers.

17.9 DIGITAL LIBRARIES

Digital libraries are an important and active research area. Conceptually, a digital library is an analog of a traditional library-at large collection of information sources in various media—coupled with the advantages of digital technologies. However, digital libraries differ from their traditional counterparts in significant ways: storage is digital, remote access is quick and easy, and materials are copied from a master version. Furthermore, keeping extra copies on hand is easy and is not hampered by budget and storage restrictions, which are major problems in traditional libraries. Thus, digital technologies overcome many of the physical and economic limitations of traditional libraries.

The introduction to the April 1995 Communications of the ACM special issue on digital libraries describes them as the "opportunity . . . to fulfill the age-old dream of every human being: gaining ready access to humanity's store of information". We defined a database quite broadly as a "collection of related data." Unlike the related data in a database, a digital library encompasses a multitude of sources, many unrelated. Logically, databases can be components of digital libraries.

The magnitude of these data collections as well as their diversity and multiple formats provide challenges for research in this area. The future progression of the development of digital libraries is likely to move from the present technology of retrieval of information via the Internet, through Net searches of indexed information in repositories, to a time of information correlation and analysis by intelligent networks. Various techniques for collecting information, storing it, and organizing it to support informational requirements learned in the decades of design and implementation of databases will provide the baseline for development of approaches appropriate for digital libraries. Search, retrieval, and processing of the many forms of digital information will make use of the lessons learnt from database operations carried out already on those forms of information.

17.10 SUMMARY

Relational databases have been in use for over two and a half decades. A large portion of the applications of the relational databases have been in the commercial world, supporting such tasks as transaction processing for insurance sectors, banks, stock exchanges, reservations for a variety of business, inventory and payroll for almost all companies. In this unit we discussed the emerging database technologies, which have become increasingly important in the recent years. SQL3 data model, mobile databases, multimedia databases, main memory databases, geographic information systems, temporal and sequence databases, information visualization, genome data management and digital libraries are among the new technology trends.